Chama Stories

"True Confessions of a Ten Year Old
Pentecostal Preacher's Kid."

Rolando Benavidez

authorHOUSE®

AuthorHouse™
1663 Liberty Drive, Suite 200
Bloomington, IN 47403
www.authorhouse.com
Phone: 1-800-839-8640

First published by AuthorHouse 04/09/2009

ISBN: 978-1-4389-4465-4 (hc)
ISBN: 978-1-4208-3692-9 (sc)

Printed in the United States of America
Bloomington, Indiana

This book is printed on acid-free paper.

For
Racquel & Kenny
RJ & Tanya
&
Bonnie

'Recollection is the only paradise
from which we cannot be turned out'

Jean Paul Richter

Chama Stories

Finky,
The Outhouse,
The Miracle,
&
My Angel

F inky Malacara was three years older than me and was the self-appointed authority on girls, fishing, fighting, homemade weapons, sports, Jesus, and, well, everything. He was also expert at cussing, telling dirty jokes (although at the time I didn't *completely* understand *all* of them, but I took his word that they were "really dirty") and teaching us younger guys all the "important things in life," like how to "give the finger," and other *things* that got me into plenty of trouble.

I was "educated" by Finky once a year every summer when my family would go to Chama, New Mexico, for the annual Central Latin American Assemblies of God Summer Camp Meeting. My father, Macedonio Santos Sr., was the elected Superintendent of the six-state Pentecostal Conference, so we had to go one week before it started to make sure everything was in place and ready for the thousand or so faithful who would be arriving from Colorado, New Mexico, Utah, Idaho, Wyoming, Nebraska and from other parts of the United States and even as far away as Mexico, Central and South America, to come celebrate a full weeks' worth of Pentecostal fire, great music, a ton of incredible food and everything else in between. And we stayed the week after it ended to make sure everything was put away and secure for the coming year.

I loved this yearly pilgrimage to the Northern New Mexico mountains. It was the highlight of my year. Nothing else even came close. It seemed like my family's entire year was planned around this "happening." My dad and older brother Max would pack three weeks' worth of clothes and supplies for five kids and two adults into our old, white, wooden trailer. They would cover it with a canvas tarp, tie it down so nothing would fly away, hitch it up to our old Plymouth, pack us all in, my mom would pray for 'traveling mercy,' and we would take off. On the way we would stop and drop off my half-mutt, half-beagle Tippy with my *Tia* Tulles in Santa Fe. My dad didn't like to see him tied up in the campground; that's why we had to leave him behind. I hated leaving him, but I agreed with my dad, Tippy wasn't used to being tied up and I knew he would be miserable.

By the time we got to Camel Rock outside of Espanola, my sadness at having to leave Tippy began to disappear, and I began in earnest to look for all the familiar landmarks heading into Chama. When we passed Echo Canyon, I knew we were very close and my pulse would begin to quicken. When we passed the Trout Lakes' turn-off and headed down the mountain into the small village of Cebolla, I would take in a real deep breath and fill my nostrils and lungs with that incredibly crisp mountain air that was thick with the aroma of freshly cut wood from the sawmills and fireplaces burning in the small houses along the road. As we sped past Tierra Amarilla and over the Brazos River Bridge, my heart would race just thinking that in a few minutes I would actually be hearing the water as it gushed over the rocks in the Chama River. When Rabbit's Peak came into view I knew we had arrived, and a few seconds after that I would be running out of the car to go stand and just feast my eyes *and* ears on that most gorgeous of God's waterways, the Chama River, or as my dad called it, "The Jordan River of the Western Hemisphere."

I didn't fully understand the heavy spiritual significance of all that was going on in the big "Tabernacle" on top of the hill where the adults would gather for their daily business meetings and their nightly encounters with the Holy Ghost. But I did understand what was going on in my small world of exploring, water snake hunting, bear and deer sightings, worm digging, trout fishing, army playing, cow chip throwing, bottle collecting for Brother Chavez, Nutty-Buddy and delicious, greasy hamburger-eating from the *comedor,* riding on the water truck, getting nickels and dimes from Brother Boni's ears, daily almost drowning in the river and generally just having the time of my life. It was also the only time of year that I got new clothes. Except for underwear. My mother never thought it was necessary to buy me new underwear. She would just sew my big brother Max's *old* underwear, and then I would wear them until they became shreds. Then when I wore those out, and my brother hadn't given me any for awhile, she would make me wear my sister Sarai's panties. Not the silky, lacy ones (thank God!), just the plain cotton ones. But still...they were *panties*. I used to have nightmares of Finky finding out that I wore my sister's panties. But my mother did that with most everything. I'm pretty sure that it was because we never had much money that she had a difficult time throwing *anything* away. She made things *last*. I can't remember drying with a towel that had any terrycloth left on it. I was the fifth and last child in the family, so by the time the towels got down to me they were so thin I could *see* through them. If my dad got blessed with a "Pentecostal handshake" and he went and bought a quart of orange juice, she would make it into *four* quarts. It wasn't too pulpy, but it *did* have the taste of orange juice. So even if we didn't have a lot, my mother always made it *seem* like we had a lot. She was the best. I loved her. In *spite* of the panties.

My mother also didn't like to go to Chama very much. Even though she had actually been born in the village of Chama, she dreaded being without running water and other modern amenities for three weeks. I thought it was pretty neat to chop wood, get water from a well, and use an outhouse. She would rather be back in Albuquerque with her gas stove, her faucet with running water and a toilet that actually flushed. My poor mom. She was the pillar of the family, but those three weeks really did wear her out. She also hated for me to hang out with Finky.

"'*Mi 'jito*, why do you even have to be around that boy?" she would ask.

"I *don't* have to be around him, but he always finds *me*," I said. And it was the truth. Finky *always* seemed to find me.

"Well, try to stay away from him," she said. "He's a bad influence. I wish Brother Malacara would do something about him." She brought me real close to her face. "And don't let him teach you anything, you understand?" She looked straight into my eyes, our noses almost touching.

I knew she was still remembering the summer of 1956 when Finky had taught me to "give the finger." My father had been invited to give a weeklong revival in San Bernadino, California, and it had been going great until I taught the Pastor's two sons how to "give the finger." Finky had told me that people would laugh when I gave them the finger, and I *still* didn't know what it *really* meant, but it seemed to have the *opposite* effect. Well, I showed my two new little friends how to put their fingers just right, then we sat on the curb and were "giving the finger" to all the cars that passed by until one of the cars stopped and a man got out and started yelling and running towards us. We got up and ran in the church and hid in the baptistry. I remembered my mom saying the church was a "safe haven for all who are in trouble." Well, we were in trouble, and it *did* protect us from the man in the car, but it didn't protect us from our parents, who found us and gave us a good beating.

"Where did you learn to do that?" the pastor asked, as he grabbed his two boys from the baptistry.

"From him!" they cried, pointing at me.

"And where did you learn that?" my dad said, holding the back of my shirt with one hand and beating me with the other.

"Finky!" I yelled, trying to get out of the way of the blows. "Finky taught me!"

"Well, don't you ever do that again! Do you hear me?"

I heard him, but I couldn't answer, because I was crying too much.

And you think I would've learned, but as soon as we got back to Albuquerque, I showed one of my brother's friends what I had learned at the camp meeting. At the time, I was sitting on a brick fence and my brother was in front of me with some of his other friends and his friend Bobby was standing in back of me with a bow and arrow that he was showing everybody. I twisted around and held up my finger to Bobby.

"Hey, what are you doing?" Bobby asked, kind of irritated.

"Nothin'," I said, still holding my finger up.

"Well, you better point that thing somewhere else," he said.

"It's just a finger," I said, holding my hand higher.

"You better point it somewhere else or I'll shoot," Bobby said. He put an arrow in the string, drew it back and pointed it at me.

"Mario!" my brother yelled, "Put your hand down! I'm going to tell mom what you're doing."

"What," I said, "it's only a little finger."

I turned around to hold up my finger to Bobby when I heard a 'twang' and the next thing I knew, something hit my back hard, and I fell off the fence screaming because of the pain. The tip of the arrow had actually *stuck* in my back and I couldn't believe that Bobby had actually *shot* me with an arrow!

Max ran over to me and took the arrow out and started running after Bobby, who was already halfway up the street, and I started running home screaming and wondering if I was going to die and what was Tippy going to do without me.

My mother came out of the house when she heard me screaming. It was something that happened often, but she still hadn't gotten used to it. She took me inside and checked my back and assured me that I was not going to die. Max came in and told her what had happened and that he had chased Bobby and caught him and broken his bow and hit him with it. I turned and looked at my brother through my tears and for the first time was very happy and proud to be wearing his old worn-out and patched-up shorts. Of course, *that* day, wouldn't you know, I had worn out *his* old underwear and was wearing my sister's panties.

As she cleaned and bandaged the small puncture in my back, my mom proceeded to lecture me for a long time on not doing the things "that Malacara boy" taught me and made me promise not to "give the finger" again. And that's why she didn't want me hanging out with Finky, because I always came back from camp meeting with something "new" that I had learned.

But this was the summer camp meeting of 1959, I was ten years old and I was feeling pretty good because things had been going smoothly. My two older sisters, Rachel and Anna, had gotten married a few years earlier, so my sister Sarai and me finally had our own beds in the small cabin. My dad seemed happy with the way the church business and services were going, the fishing was great as was the special music and the deliciously greasy food, and my mom was happy because I had managed, for the most part, to avoid Finky, and we were already four days into the meeting and I still hadn't gotten into any *major* trouble.

So far about the only exciting thing that had happened was Max dragging me back to the cabin after I'd almost drowned again. Five male Bible School students had been busted skinny-dipping with some of the local girls at two o'clock in the morning by Brother Chinche and his ever-present military flashlight and posse. Virgie Medina's two older brothers, Jose and Joey, were, as was their habit every summer, getting drunk every night at Foster's Saloon in town, then they would come back just in time for the altar call and be surrounded by all the Bible School students (including the ones busted for skinny-dipping) who would cry loudly for their salvation, then Jose and Joey would also cry and get saved *again*. But so far, for *me*...no trouble. No Camp Security bringing me to my mother after another Finky-inspired disaster. Nothing. It had been pretty peaceful.

Well, that was about to change. Even though I was only ten years old, I had come to be very wary when things were *too* peaceful. Little did I know, but the things that would happen at *this* summer's camp meeting would change me forever.

That Saturday afternoon at about one o'clock, six hours before the evening service, me and my friend Chato were playing army in back of the campground. Chato was two years younger than me and he had these thick, black-framed glasses that were held on to his head with a big rubberband. But he never let wearing glasses keep him from playing army or football or running in the river, or anything! And even though his mother was afraid for him to be with me so much, (she had heard how I was always almost drowning) he was usually by my side from the morning until we went to our separate cabins at night. He was a preacher's kid too.

Well, we found a log to sit on, laid our wooden "guns" across our laps and were putting cardboard patches from empty popcicle boxes over the holes on the bottom of our shoes when we saw Finky and JoJo Baltazar running up to us. JoJo was Finky's enforcer, and he made sure we laughed at everything Finky said. He was also meaner than Finky and took great pleasure in administering beatings whenever the occasion presented itself. Which was pretty often. JoJo didn't need much of an excuse to jump on us. I think JoJo was mean because his real long face, huge forehead, and bulging eyes made him look just like a grasshopper. Plus, he had a lot of pimples. I used to think that every time he looked in the mirror he got even madder. Occasionally, I would get the idea to tell JoJo to switch last names with Finky because Malacara meant "bad face," but, wisely, I avoided a *serious* beating by never mentioning it.

Sometimes, in my real *weak* moments, I would start to feel sorry for JoJo because of how he looked, until he jumped on me and sat on my chest laughing and slapping me until I started to cry, and then I would just hate him and be very happy that he looked like a grasshopper with an acne problem.

Finky, on the other hand, had a real round face, like a ball. He also had small, mean eyes. And he was very white, like a pink white. As a matter of fact, he was the first white Spanish person I had ever seen. I asked my mother how come he was so white. We used to call white people "English" back then.

"Mom, how come Finky looks like an English?"

My mother looked up from the wood-burning stove where

9

she had just turned a tortilla. "Que?" she asked, wrinkling her brow.

"Finky-- how come I can almost see through his skin?" I tore a piece of fresh tortilla and let it melt in my mouth. My mom used to make the fattest, softest tortillas around. Everybody in the camp would come to our cabin and want to taste them.

"Mario, when are you going to learn to wash your hands before you eat? Look at those hands. They're filthy! *Cochino,* get away from the food!"

"*Cochino*" was one of my mom's favorite words for me. It literally meant "pig." Her other favorite word for me was "*malcriado,*" which meant "badly raised," which was kind of a strange word for her to use on me because <u>she</u> was raising me.

"Well, how come he looks English?"

"*Mi 'jito,* I don't have time for this. Please go outside and play! Your dad's coming home and I have to have this food ready and then we have to get ready to go to church. And that means you too. So don't go too far, and stay away from that Finky boy!"

I grabbed the rest of the tortilla and ran out of the cabin, but before I got out of the screened-in porch, my brother Max grabbed me and picked me up and carried me out.

"Gimme some of that," he said, tearing half the tortilla for himself. Max was five years older than me, and had developed a very nasty habit of always taking my food when my parents weren't looking. Even at the table.

After he had the tortilla he put me down. "It's because God's punishing them," Max said, with his mouth full of tortilla.

"What?"

"Finky. God's punishing all the English with no color."

We both sat by the outside fire pit, finishing the tortilla and wondering if we should risk the wrath of Cidelia (my mom) by stealing another one.

11

"Really?" I asked, savoring that last bite of tortilla, and not sure if Max was telling me the truth.

"That's right," he said. He lay back in the tall grass. "He gave them the money and He gave us the color. Have you ever seen an English without any money?"

I had, but very few and far between. I wondered what he was getting at. What did Finky being white have anything to do with money?

"As a matter of fact," Max said, sitting back up and looking at me, "Have you ever seen any of your English friends wear their big brother's old shorts or their sister's panties?"

"Hey," I whispered, nervously looking around, "You promised you'd never say anything!"

"Don't worry, your secret's safe with me." He laughed and put a long grass stem in his mouth. "Listen, God let them have most of the money, see, but He took away their color and made them kind of dull and boring. Except for the girls. English girls ain't boring." Actually, there wasn't a female of any race, color, creed, nationality, religion, height, width, length, longitudinal, latitudinal, extra-terrestrial or other *species* that Max found boring.

He paused and quit chewing his grass stem long enough to see if I was getting what he was saying. I wasn't sure if I was.

"And then God saw that we didn't have very much money, so He gave us some beautiful color *and* He made us great kissers. Girls love us brown boys, kid. Latin lovers. Yeah. You'll appreciate that one day."

With that he puckered up his lips and started kissing an imaginary girl. I hoped one day to grow up to be a great kisser like my brother. It seemed like I saw him kissing a different girl every day. Max didn't know it, but I saw him sneak girls into our trailer next to the cabin all the time. He was one of Finky's heroes. Which was good, because that stopped Finky and JoJo from beating me up sometimes. The only girl I had ever kissed, on purpose, was a blond English girl from across the street in Albuquerque named Cheri. And that hadn't gone very well. We had stolen a box of cigars from her dad and lit two of them up. We quit smoking when we started to get sick and then had tried to kiss. Her lips were real soft but she tasted horrible. I almost puked. I think she did too because she made a gagging face.

"But Finky isn't English, is he?" I asked.

"Probably."

"But his Grampa looks like us." Actually, my brother was lighter-skinned than me; he and my sister Anna even had red hair, but they didn't look English like Finky.

"Well, maybe his *other* Grampa is English," Max said.

"Yeah...you're probably right."

With that my brother grabbed me in a headlock until I started yelling and he took off laughing.

Anyway...the day Finky and JoJo came running up to us, Chato and I expected the worst.

"Hey, you turd farts, what're you doin'?" Finky asked, a little out of breath. He looked down at our old worn-out shoes and made a face. "When're you two little punks ever gonna get some new shoes?" He laughed and pointed at our shoes. "You been wearing them old things for years, man. You even wore them messed up things when you were in your sister's wedding, didn't you, you little turd? Man, you guys are gonna run out of cardboard!" He looked at JoJo and they both started laughing.

He was right. I *had* worn them when I had been the ring boy in my sister Rachel's wedding. Everything else had cost so much money that my parents couldn't afford to get me shoes. Which was OK with me, because I really liked the little white jacket I got to wear.

I put my wooden gun down to my side. "We're just playing army," I said, warily looking at JoJo, who already had his fists clenched by his side for absolutely *no* reason at all. He just *anticipated* that one of us was going to say something stupid so that he could pound us. "And besides, one of these days I won't *need* cardboard, 'cuz I'm gonna get new Keds," I retorted. I don't know why I said that. I knew my parents could *never* afford to get me new U.S. Keds. But I just hated it when Finky would say stuff to embarrass me.

Finky took a step toward me. I braced for the worst. He stopped and sneered at me. "Sheeeit!" he said. He loved cussing in front of me and Chato. "The day you get new Keds is the day I'll stick my head in a pile of crap!" Both he and JoJo got a kick out of that one, which was OK with me. I'd rather them laugh at me instead of hitting me.

"We just came back from the outhouse by the river," Finky said, still laughing. He grabbed his crotch and started moving his hips back and forth. "We saw Tina's butt, we saw Tina's butt." JoJo grabbed *his* crotch and they both kept laughing and singing over and over, "We saw Tina's butt, we saw Tina's butt."

Finky always liked to grab his crotch and move his hips when he was telling us something nasty. The first time I saw him do that, I went back to the cabin and asked my mom what that meant. Unfortunately, I asked during supper, and when I got up to demonstrate, my sister Sarai screamed at me to stop, my brother opened his eyes real wide and dropped his jaw like he couldn't believe that I was actually doing it; my dad just shook his head and closed his eyes and muttered something, and my mom jumped up and yelled, *"Cochino! Malcriado!"* She grabbed the fly swatter and let me have it right on my crotch hand. I was only seven years old at the time, and I didn't know what it meant, but I knew then it was something I should *never* do. Especially in front of my family. Especially at dinner. That was the same summer that Finky had taught me how to "give the finger."

Finky and JoJo finished their little dance and looked at us with big smirks on their faces. "C'mon you little, punk, Indian boys," Finky said, "you wanna see Tina's butt?"

"Indian boy" was one of Finky's favorite names for me and Chato because we were both dark and our hair stood straight up. Just like a paintbrush. But Chato's mom had at least let him get a flattop. My mom, on the other hand, had tried different things to keep my hair down, but they all made it look too greasy. One time she used *"Tres Flores,"* which my brother and I really liked because it made me look like a little *"pachuco."* But that, of course, didn't set right with my mom. She would not have her son looking like a *pachuco.* So instead, after my weekly Saturday night bath, she would put a *panial* on my head, tie a little knot in back of it, and have me sleep with it. I didn't like it because it looked like a little girl's bonnet; but when I objected, she would assure me that *nobody* would ever see me that way except our family. Those were the nights my brother would call me "Maria" instead of "Mario." My brother also used to tell me that I *was* an Indian. A Navajo Indian, to be more specific. He said that our parents had found me in a basket by the side of the road in Gallup, took it as a "sign from God" and adopted me. And even though my mother tried to assure me that I *wasn't* adopted, I always suspected I was.

"What're you guys, chicken?" Finky asked.

"I'm not a chicken," I said.

"I'm not a chicken, either," Chato said, holding on to his wooden gun just in case JoJo attacked.

"Well, let's go see Tina's butt then," Finky said, starting up the trail to the river.

"Wait a minute," I said, picking up my wooden gun, keeping an eye on JoJo.

"Don't you think she's done using the bathroom by now?"

Tina was a pretty hefty girl and I wasn't exactly looking forward to looking at her butt.

Finky stopped and walked back to where I was standing. "So what," he said, "maybe somebody else will go in there and we can see *their* butts!" He had put his volleyball face and beady eyes real close to my face and I could see the veins in his nose and cheeks.

"So what's the big deal about a butt?" I said, backing up.

Finky jumped back as if he had just put a bobby pin in a wall socket. "What?!" He spun around and looked at JoJo. "Did you hear that?!?" He looked back at me. "Did I hear you right?" he asked, like he couldn't believe what he was

15

hearing. "You don't wanna go look at some girl's butt? What are you, some kinda' homo or something?"

"No, I'm not a homo," I said, wondering what a homo was, and wondering if I should ask my mother.

"Well, then, why don't you want to see some girl's butt?"

"Because it stinks under that outhouse," I said. "And besides, you can't really see anything anyway."

"Sure you can," JoJo said, "but you got to put your head way, *way* under."

They both nodded at each other solemnly, as if they had just unearthed one of civilization's great discoveries.

I was beginning to regret *big time* ever showing them the discovery *I* had made two days earlier while throwing my knife. My dad had just bought me this beautiful Boy Scout knife with *everything* in it: a needle, spoon, fork, corkscrew, file, scissors, screwdriver, and about four different blades. He even had my *name* engraved on it! I had been practicing throwing it against a tree by the river when I decided to see if I could make it stick to the girls' outhouse. When I got there I looked around to make sure no one was watching, then I threw it as hard as I could and it hit the back of the outhouse with a loud "CRACK!" From inside the outhouse I heard a high-pitched scream so I hid behind one of the big logs by the river. A few seconds later, old *Hermana* Frita came out holding on to her roll of toilet paper and looking extremely frazzled. She hurriedly looked around and tried to run off, but she couldn't go very fast because her underwear was still around her ankles. She put her hand with the roll of toilet paper up in the air and started waving it. *"Quitate, Satanas! Quitate!"* she yelled, as she tried to shuffle away. *"Te reprendo en el nombre de Cristo!"* Poor *Hermana* Frita, she was looking at the outhouse with her eyes real wide and was rebuking Satan as she tried to pull up her underwear and hurry away.

And I would have thought it was real funny, if I hadn't been worried about my brand new knife.

As soon as she was out of sight, I made my way through the little trees and tall grass in back of the outhouse and searched the ground for my knife. I couldn't see it so I got on my hands and knees and tried to feel for it, and that's when I made the discovery that would forever change the lives of Juan "Finky" Malacara and Jose "JoJo" Baltazar. It would change mine and Chato's lives too, but not like those two guys'.

I was feeling around next to the wooden boards in back of the outhouse when I almost fell into a hole that was completely covered with long grass. It was perfectly camouflaged from the outside and was impossible to see unless you were right on it. I parted the grass and looked down into the steamy abyss and almost puked with the smell. It was horrible. It was the worst case of *asco* that I had ever had. My stomach felt even worse when I saw a faint glint at the very bottom. Like something shiny was looking up at me from the great beyond. And there it was. Beautiful. Brand new. Shiny. The knife of a boy's lifetime. Sitting very pretty, about ten feet down, on top of some really *foul*-looking stuff....and totally out of my reach. I was still looking at my knife when I heard the outhouse door open and somebody go in. I came back up for air and looked around. The small trees and tall grass made it impossible for anybody to see me as long as I didn't stand up. That's when I decided this might be the only time I would ever get to see some other girl's butt, so I took a deep breath and twisted my head under the wood as far as I dared to go. And there it was. Sure enough. I could barely see it, but there it was. The faint outline of somebody's rear end. I was beginning to see stars from holding my breath when I heard a really loud *pedo* and something whizzed right by my head and plopped at the bottom of the abyss. I yanked my head out quick. I didn't want anything wet to land on me and I thought to myself that what I was doing was really pretty sick. Especially at the church's campground. I still didn't know a lot about the deep things of God, but I *knew* He couldn't be very pleased with me. If the rapture that my mom *always* told me about would have happened then, everybody else would have gone to heaven, and I would have been left behind with my head under an outhouse. So I said goodbye to my knife and very quietly snuck back to the log by the river to wait and see whose butt I had kind of seen.

When the door opened I got even *sicker.* Old *Hermana Frita* had apparently decided that the outhouse was clear of Satan, because she had come back to finish her business. I couldn't believe that I had actually been gazing at some seventy-year old woman's wrinkled old *nalgas.* I put my head in my hands and tried as hard as I could to put the image out of my mind. But it was no use. When I closed my eyes, there they were, staring right back at me. I knew right then that there *was* a God. And that He had definitely punished me. And here it was, two days later, and I could *still* see the faint outline of that old ladies bottom. When my dad asked about the knife later that same day, I lied and told him I had lost it in some deep water in the river. I *hated* lying to my dad. He was Conference Superintendent, so he had to put up with *everybody else's* crap. And here was his youngest son, *lying* to him. So now, not only was I a pervert, but I was also a *liar* too. I was *really* in trouble with God now. But I just couldn't work up the courage to tell my dad what had really happened. The denomination couldn't give him much money, so I knew he had sacrificed just to buy me that knife. And there it was, at the bottom of the outhouse, just because I hadn't been content enough throwing it at a tree.

When we got to the river we saw Tina and her sister, who was almost as big as she was, walking down the trail, so we knew that *she* wasn't in there. Finky told us to hide behind the big log and wait for someone to go in. I turned and sat down on the rocky river bank and regretted ever telling Finky about the secret outhouse hole. I didn't feel like putting my head under that outhouse no matter *who* went in there. I didn't even care if Virgie Medina, the most beautiful girl in the campground *and* the universe, went in there. I *still* wouldn't do it. I just had a bad feeling about the whole thing and turned to tell Finky that I didn't want to do it when I heard him gasp and grab his head like he had just drank an Icey real quick and had gotten brain freeze.

"Oh, mama, oh, mama, mama, mama, ay, ay, ay, ay, ay!" he said, almost crying. "I can't believe it! I just can't believe it!"

He grabbed me by the front of my shirt. "Guess who just went into the outhouse. Oh, my God, you little turd head, I just can't believe my luck! Somebody up there loves me!"

"Who?" We all asked, knowing that Marilyn Monroe had *never* come to the campground.

"Virgie," he said, wiping the sweat from his forehead. "Virgie Medina. Can you believe it?"

I went numb. Completely numb. I wondered how I could still be standing without legs. Where were my arms? Yes, I wanted to tell him. Yes, I could absolutely believe it. The way things were going right now, you bet I could believe it. Virgie Medina. Thirteen years old and the object of every desire *and* fantasy I had ever had. Sitting bare-bottomed in an outhouse with a drafty secret. My stomach sank. My heart beat hard against my chest. I felt like wetting my pants. But I knew my mom would be real upset if I stained my sister's panties.

"C'mon, let's go!" Finky said excitedly. "Let's go before she leaves!"

He crouched down and started for the outhouse with JoJo close behind. He turned around and saw me and Chato still standing by the log. He came back and grabbed my arm. "C'mon, you little turd," he hissed, pulling me toward the outhouse. "You're gonna do this with us! Or I'll tell everybody you're a homo."

My legs felt like lead and I stumbled after him. I wondered if being a homo felt as bad as this. Chato grabbed on to the back of my shirt and followed us.

JoJo was already behind the small trees on his hands and knees, quietly moving back the long grass from the hole. I looked around nervously and crouched down. I didn't *even* want to get caught. If my mom ever found out, I hoped they would bury me by the river. I grabbed Chato and motioned for him to crouch down.

Finky knelt down by JoJo, moved the grass aside and put his head into the hole. At the same time JoJo decided that there was room for him too, and *he* put *his* head in the hole too. They were both jockeying for position with *both* their heads in the hole when all of a sudden someone huge and wearing blue overalls just *exploded* through the the small trees screaming *"Satanas! Quitate! Quitate, Satanas!!! Te reprendo! Te reprendo!! Quitate! Quitate! Quitate!"* It was old toothless Flotches, old *Hermana* Frita's slightly retarded, older brother. He had been waiting at the outhouse for two days for Satan to show up so that he could chase him away from the outhouse for good. He even brought a homemade whip made of vines so that he could nail Satan good and was waving it around his head, cracking it. When he burst through the trees, I thought <u>he</u> was Satan and he had come to take us to hell for putting our heads under an outhouse to look at girls' butts.

Both Chato and I screamed and fell back into the grass when Flotches came flying through the trees. When *we* screamed, we heard *Virgie* scream from inside the outhouse. When I heard *her* scream, I stained my borrowed underwear on both sides. And from the look on Chato's face, I knew that he had done the same thing in *his* underwear. I looked down at Finky and JoJo struggling to get their heads from under the outhouse but they couldn't because Flotches kept hitting them hard on their butts with his whip while he screamed *"Te reprendo, Satanas! Quitate de aqui! Quitate! Quitate de aqui. Te reprendo! Te reprendo! En el nombre de Cristo! Quitate!!!"*

Everything was happening so fast, but it still seemed like it took me forever to get to my feet. Flotches was screaming at Satan and whipping Finky and JoJo; *they* were screaming from under the outhouse, Virgie was screaming from *in* the outhouse and Chato was screaming as I started to drag him to his feet. I knew that we had to get out of there quick; it would only be a matter of minutes before someone heard the screaming and a big crowd would gather to see what was going on.

Flotches was so worked up now that his toothless jowls began to foam and he was beginning to get hoarse from rebuking Satan so loud. As we turned to run to the river we saw him raise the whip high and bring it down so hard on Finky and JoJo that the ground gave way and both of them disappeared into that great black hole. We heard them scream on the way down and then we heard a big "SPLAT!" and some gurgling sounds and that's all we stayed around for.

We both ran straight to the river and dove in. There were big rocks on the bottom and I scraped my nose on one of them, but I didn't care. I came up quickly for air and was still so scared that I was still peeing in my pants. But that was OK because I was in the water now and I knew it would wash away. My view was partially blocked by the logs, but I could see a few people starting to gather around the outhouse. About a half minute later I saw Virgie's two hung-over big brothers running up to the outhouse and I thanked God that I was semi-hidden by the logs. From what I could see they looked very upset and I was *extremely* happy that I was in the river and not up there with everybody else. Chato came up for air and came and stood next to me; the big rubberband was still holding his glasses tightly to his flattopped head. The cold, somewhat murky water came up to our waists and I could feel the current pulling us to the much quicker rapids downstream. The snowfall had been heavy in Chama that year, so even though we were close to the edge, the river was still much deeper and swifter than usual. I was under strict orders not to even play *close* to the river.

"What do we do now?" Chato asked. His eyes were real wide behind his glasses, and he was shivering.

"Nothing," I said.

"Nothing? Waddaya mean, nothing? The whole *camp's* gonna be at that outhouse in about two minutes. Your dad's gonna be here, Mar!"

21

When Chato mentioned my dad, I just groaned and knelt down under the water. I *knew* my dad would be there in a few minutes. He was the 'Big Cheese' in camp. He *had* to be there for a disaster of this magnitude. What if someone had seen us running from the outhouse? What if they were already telling my dad? And what if they were telling Virgie's *brothers*! I groaned again under the water. Would people come to my funeral? Would they want to come to the funeral of a pervert *and* a liar? Would my mom mention my underwear predicament at the memorial service? Would my brother cry for me and regret telling me I was an adopted Navajo? Would they let Tippy come to the burial? Could Jesus ever love someone like me? Would He want a little ten-year-old boy in heaven that had put his head under an outhouse and had seen old *Hermana* Frita's butt? Would Virgie's brothers get the electric chair for murdering a ten-year-old boy? Should a ten-year-old boy have this much stress?

I came up for air and felt the cool water tugging at my legs. I wished that I could just float away. The sound of the rapids downstream made it hard to hear what was going on by the outhouse but I could see that there was a great commotion and that many more people had gathered and more were coming from every trail. It was somewhat comforting to know that we were still partially hidden by the logs and apparently hadn't been discovered yet. I was getting ready to stand up when all of sudden it hit me.

"C'mon!" I whispered to Chato.

I grabbed his arm and put him on his back and we both started to float downstream.

"But the rapids!" he said, grabbing my arm.

"Don't worry, the big rocks are flat. We'll go right over them. Besides, do you want to take your chances in the rapids, or go up to the outhouse?"

At that point, I think that both of us would have rather taken our chances with a *tidal wave* then go up to the outhouse. He didn't say anything to me in response; he just squeezed and shook my arm and we both started to float feet first downstream.

****

"Don't try to get up; just keep floating or you'll hit your legs on the rocks," I said. I knew. "The Flats" was one of the places that I had almost drowned several times. I didn't want to tell him that our only chance would be to grab the big tree branch that was hanging over the water. And that was only if we were lucky enough to come up for air after that big drop straight down from the flat rocks.

The water was getting louder and swifter now, so even if we *wanted* to go back, we couldn't. As we got closer I told God that I knew I didn't deserve any favors, but I would really appreciate it if He could make sure that Chato and I grabbed that branch; but if not, could He make sure my mom didn't cry too much and could He tell her how sorry I was to always make her worry so much. And could He take care of Tippy. And if I, by some miracle of unbelievable proportions somehow made it to heaven, could I *finally* have a pair of new shorts? And then I thought, 'would I even *need* new shorts in heaven?' It's crazy what goes through your brain when you think you might die.

The sound of the rapids was rumbling now and I could see the water turning white and foamy. I grabbed the back of Chato's shirt and we both yelled as we slid down that big flat rock. And then everything became real quiet as we flew through the mist of the big drop. It was like we were suspended in the air in *real* slow motion. Then we slammed into the churning water and we were under it, trying like crazy to come up from that terrifying thunder and I was not wanting to let go of Chato because I had gotten him into this in the first place. I could feel him struggling too and I could also feel the current trying to keep us under water *and* send us downstream at the same time.

I finally came up for air and I tried to pull Chato up, but he had become very heavy. I saw the branch coming up quickly and I knew I had to grab it. As I reached for it, Chato came up and grabbed me by the arm. When he did that, he turned my back to the branch so that when I reached up for it the back of my hand hit it and we both watched helplessly as it passed from our reach. Then I knew we were in *real* trouble. In about one minute we would be in rapids that were ten times crazier than the ones we had just passed. My brother had told me to never, *ever,* go near them because he knew of people that had actually *drowned* there. I tried to pull Chato closer but he was getting heavier and his head kept going under. He came up and grabbed me with both arms.

"I don't want to die, Mario!" he cried, holding me tight. "I don't want to die!"

I was going to say something when he went under again. I went under to try to bring him up, but I was so tired that I could feel myself being pulled further down and I knew that I was not going to come back up. It was so strange. There was no fear. Just incredible, overwhelming fatigue, extreme sadness, a strange quiet, and just knowing that you're going to die. Well, as much as a ten-year-old can know about dying. I remember thinking, "I'm sorry, Mom. I'm sorry, Dad." That's it. Real simple. Nothing heavy. My lungs felt like they were on fire and then the second that I finally let my air out, the most remarkable, incredibly *awesome*, unbelievably miraculous thing happened.

When I talked to Chato about it later, he couldn't believe it either. It was like this light, this really *bright* light, came on *under* the water. I swear. Like a million spotlights. At first I thought we *had* died and maybe, just *maybe*, by some kind of big spiritual mistake or incredible miracle, we were actually entering Heaven. But *then,* we felt ourselves being

pulled *out* of the water! At that moment I didn't know if I was more ecstatic about knowing that there was a chance we weren't going to drown after all, or experiencing that absolutely *stunning* feeling, that's the only way I can describe it-- *stunning*-- that the things my mom always told me about day after day, night after night, year after year, might, just *might*, actually be *true*! She had always told me that miracles would happen if only I had the faith of a child or the faith of a mustard seed. Well, I didn't know what a mustard seed was, but I *was* a child, only I never felt that I had *any* faith. I had always *wanted* the stories about Jesus to be true. I truly *wanted* the Bible to be true because she really *believed* in it so much. And unless I *had* died and was experiencing some kind of strange, dreamlike thing that only recently-dead people can experience, then here it was, an actual *miracle*, happening to Mr. Faithless, the unlikeliest person in the whole world, a liar and a pervert, and an outhouse criminal--a miracle of such enormity, that 99.999% of those people up in that big Tabernacle would never, *ever*, even come close to it. Wow!

We couldn't see *who* was pulling us out, but whoever it was, wasn't pulling us out by the back of our shirts, we were being *scooped out* of the water from *underneath* by what looked like these incredibly *huge* hands! I felt like that lady that I had seen pictures of that was being held in King Kong's hand. Only *bigger*! That's how *massive* this hand felt. At least, I *think* it was a hand. And another crazy thing was that I wasn't choking on the water! As a matter of fact, it felt like I was *breathing* the water! It was crazy! Later, on our way back to the camp, Chato told me the same thing. He said that as soon as the light came on, *he* was breathing underwater *too*! He said that's why *he* thought *he* was entering Heaven! I know it sounds crazy, but it's absolutely true!

Anyway, this giant hand, or whatever it was, put us on the dry river bank and we just laid there, on our stomachs, relieved beyond imagination to be out of the water, and wondering if what had just happened to us had really *happened*! I opened my eyes just in time to see this *huge* shadow come over us; it looked like the shadow of a wing of an incredibly *gigantic* bird, so I rolled on my back to get a better look and about fell back into the water when I saw this big Indian standing over me.

"Hey!" I yelled, "Waddaya doin'? Waddaya want'?" I struggled to get to my knees.

Chato heard me yell and he tried to get up, but was so tired that he fell back down again by the edge of the water.

The Indian squatted down close to us on the balls of his feet and studied us both. "You guys OK?" he asked, reaching out his hand. His voice was soft and even and I was surprised that I could hear him perfectly, even with the noise of the rapids. He was dressed in worn, loose fitting jeans, old, worn-out cowboy boots, a silky, bright red cowboy shirt and a turquoise velvet suit jacket. His long, jet black hair was in a braid and he was wearing sunglasses, but I could see the outline of his eyes, and they looked like they were softly *glowing* behind the lenses, and when his big hand touched my shoulder I smelled the sweet aroma of apples on his coat. He smelled like my grandmother's kitchen. He didn't smell like *any* of the Indians I had talked to on West Central Avenue in Albuquerque.

"Waddaya want?" I asked, backing away from his hand. Chato was on his feet now and I went and stood in front of him.

"I just wanted to make sure you two were all right," he said. He hadn't stood up yet, but he was *still* taller than us.

"Did you see what happened? Who pulled us out? Who are *you*?" I asked, still trying to shield Chato.

"Yeah, I seen everything," the Indian said. He stood up and when he did, he blocked out the sun. I had never seen Wilt Chamberlain in person, but I couldn't imagine him being taller than *this* guy! "I followed you from the outhouse, all the way over here."

Chato and I both groaned. If this big Indian had seen us, that meant somebody else probably did too.

"Waddaya mean, you followed us from the outhouse?" I asked.

"Just what I said. I followed you from the outhouse, I didn't let Old Flotches hit you or Chato with his whip, I made sure you didn't crack your skull open on that rock you didn't see when you dove into the river." He let out a big sigh. "And once again, I didn't let you drown." He turned around and walked to a big rock up the bank and sat down. Chato and I looked at each other, then slowly followed and sat on a log to the side of the rock he was sitting on.

"You've definitely kept us busy, kid," he said.

Us? You mean there was more?

"Waddaya mean, *us*? Who are you, anyway?" I asked.

He leaned towards us. "You're not going to believe this, kid, but..." He scooted closer. "I'm one of your angels."

"What!?!?! An *angel*? But you're a big Indian!"

"Well, that's what I look like to you. If I showed you what I *really* looked like you might freak out."

"Freak out? What does *that* mean?"

"Oh, yeah. I forgot. Never mind. You'll say it a lot one day."

He didn't look like any angel I had seen in the Bible or in books at the library. I didn't see any wings. He wasn't wearing a long white choir robe, and he didn't look English like all those other angels. He was dark. Just like me.

"Are you really an angel?" I asked. Chato held my arm tight and he just sat there with his mouth open and his eyes real wide behind his big glasses.

"Yup."

"Do all angels look like Navajos?"

"Nope. Only the good looking ones." When he said that, he smiled. His teeth were real white and even. They looked just like Max's, only bigger.

"Am I a Navajo?"

"Nah, you're not a Navajo, kid. Although your hair certainly makes you look like one." He reached over and rubbed my wet hair. I didn't move. His hand was *very* big. I wasn't sure if what was happening was real, so I thought I'd better ask him some angel questions.

"Is there a God?" I asked.

"Oh, yeah. There's a God all right."

"Is He 'Assembly of God'?"

"Nah. He's not very religious. He's just God."

Wow! God wasn't religious! How did He get to be God if He wasn't religious? How did He get to be God if He wasn't *"Assemblies of God"*?!? If this wasn't a dream, and I *did* get to tell my mom and dad about it, this thing about God not being religious or Assemblies of God would be something I would probably keep from them. I didn't think they would be able to take the news. As I was thinking about this heavy bit of information, I looked down at the Indian's boots and noticed for the first time that his boots and pants looked wet up to his knees, like he had been standing in the water.

"Is there a heaven, angel? Is my little friend Jimmy in heaven?"

Jimmy was a little Navajo friend of mine that had lived by my house in Albuquerque. He and his brothers wanted me and Max to go swimming with them one day last summer in the Rio Grande River underneath the West Central Bridge. My mom didn't let us go and we found out later that day that Jimmy had drowned. I cried a lot for him. He had been a real good friend and had hung out with Tippy and me all the time and I missed him very much.

"Yup. There really is a heaven," he said. He looked up to the sky, then looked back at me. "Yes", he said, nodding. "Jimmy's there. He's up there."

"Well, I was just worried because he wasn't Assembly of God."

"You don't have to worry, kid; your little buddy made it. As a matter of fact, there's a whole bunch of people in heaven that aren't Assembly of God."

"Really?"

"Really."

Wow! People made it to heaven and they didn't even have to be Assembly of God! Wow! How was I going to tell *that* to my folks? I wonder if my dad knew all this, but just hadn't told me yet.

"Well, is Jimmy OK? Is he doing OK up there?"

"Yeah. He's doing great."

I nodded but was very careful not to move anything else but my head. I was still a little afraid and very much in awe of all that was happening. I also didn't want to move too fast just in case this was all a dream. I didn't want to do anything that would accidentally wake me up. If it *was* a dream, it was the *best* dream I ever had! Even better than the one where I married Virgie in the Tabernacle. That one was a little strange, though, because my mother sang "You Ain't Nothin' But A Hound Dog" at the wedding reception and Jose and Joey did a drunk version of "The Star Spangled Banner," but it was still a good dream. I looked over at Chato and all he could do was *still* stare wide-eyed behind those thick glasses, which had managed to stay on this whole time, with his mouth open, at this big stranger. He hadn't said a word this whole time.

"Is it a beautiful place? My mom says it's beautiful."

"More than anything you can imagine, kid. More than you could ever imagine."

"Have you met Jesus?" I asked.

He looked over my shoulder and smiled at something, or someone. "Yeah, I sure have."

I turned around to see who or what he was looking at, but all I saw was the river. "Is He nice?" I asked, turning back to him.

"The best."

"Is He who my mom thinks He is?"

"Way more than your mom could ever hope for."

"Does He look like any of the pictures?"

"Like, did He really have a beard, or was He tall, or did He have crooked teeth, or something like that? Is that what you want to know?"

"Well, yeah, you know. What did He look like? His hair, the color of His eyes, you know, stuff like that."

"You mean now, or when He was here?"

I hadn't thought about that. "You mean He looks different now?"

"Oh yeah, way different."

"Well...uh...I mean what did He look like when He walked around with people down here. 'Cuz He looks English in all the pictures. Was He English?"

"You mean, did He have white skin like Finky or Cheri?"

"Yeah. You know. Was He English?

"Nah, He wasn't English. As a matter of fact, He was kinda brown. He spent a lot of time outside, you know."

"Really? Was He really brown?"

"Yup. He sure was. And He didn't have blue eyes either. They were almost black."

Wow! Jesus was brown and His eyes were almost black! Wow!

"Well, how come in most of the pictures of Him, His eyes are blue?"

"That's because when an English guy paints Him, His eyes are blue. And when a brown guy paints Him, His eyes are black."

Hey. Yeah. I hadn't thought of that either. But it sure made sense. I guess a person could pretty much make Jesus look like anything they wanted to. But at least now I had a little bit to go on. I didn't think my angel would lie to me.

I hesitated before I asked the next question. Even if this was a dream, I wanted the answer. "Does He like me even though I put my head under the outhouse and looked at old *Hermana* Frita's butt, and I lied to my dad?" I cringed a little waiting for the answer.

He sat up straight and put his hands on his knees. "Well, Mario," he said, real serious-like. My heart started pounding and I held my breath. I *knew* I was in big trouble. "He thinks that thing that whizzed by your ear cured you *forever* from putting your head under the outhouse anymore." He started laughing and he hit his thigh with his hand. "As a matter of fact," he said, still laughing, "He thought it was pretty funny when Old *Hermana* Frita blasted that loud *pedo* and almost

31

nailed you. We all did !" He laughed loudly and shook his head like he couldn't believe that I had actually had my head underneath an outhouse. It *was* pretty funny. *And* sick! But what I couldn't believe, was that *Jesus* laughed at things that I laughed at too! Or maybe He just laughed at little boys who almost got nailed by *pedos*! Wow! Now that was *really* crazy! Wait till I told Max! Unlike the English, Spanish people laughed at *pedos*' all the time! We thought they were hilarious! My dad specialized in ones you couldn't hear but would make you puke if you were unlucky enough to be close by. Max and I were in awe of him and thought he was a true artist. We hoped one day to be just like him and we worked hard at it on a daily basis. My mom said she wished we worked just as hard at being like him spiritually. I didn't know if me or Max would ever become preachers; we didn't know a lot of preachers' kids who, for whatever reason, had followed in their fathers' footsteps. But if I ever did, I hoped I would be just like my dad. I had always thought that he must be kind of like Jesus *anyway*, and now I was *sure* of it! Because just like Jesus, he could be the "Big Cheese" in charge of everything, hearing all the complaining and taking care of everybody's problems, but he was still able to laugh with me and Max at things little boys laughed at. I just couldn't believe it! Jesus laughed with little boys at funny things! Just like pals! Wow! Jesus Laughed! And so did angels! Wow!

The Indian angel quit laughing. Then he paused, and continued more quietly. "But He *was* a little disappointed that you lied to your dad."

I could feel the tears welling up in my eyes. I knew I was going to cry, but I didn't care. It seemed like I was always getting into some kind of trouble, and I *did* do some crazy stuff, but even so, I still <u>hated</u> lying to my dad, and I felt terrible about it. My lower lip started shaking and I could feel the hot tears slowly rolling down my cheeks.

He leaned back and put his big hand into his pocket. "But just to show you how much He *does* like you, <u>and</u> forgives you, He wanted me to give you this."

When he said that, he took my hand and opened it, and dropped a shiny metal object into my open palm. I gasped. My heart stopped. Time stood still. There it was. Beautiful. Brand new. Shiny. The knife of a boy's lifetime. I turned it over to the inscription side just to make sure, and sure enough, there it was, in real neat handwriting, "Mario Santos." And it was *clean*! I couldn't believe it! I just couldn't believe it! Chato even got up and came and touched it like *he* couldn't believe it either. He picked it up reverently and began to flip out some of the blades. "Wow, Mario," he whispered. "It's your Boy Scout knife! It's really your knife!"

"I cleaned it up for you too, kid. Didn't think you'd want it with all the, uh, the uh...uh..the *poop* all over it."

"But how..."

The Indian. My *angel*. *One* of my angels, is what *he* said, stood up from the log. "Finky's head landed right on it." He smiled and chuckled softly when he mentioned that. "But I made sure I got it before it was buried too deeply."

Chato and I both gasped at the same time. Finky! JoJo! Virgie! The outhouse! We had temporarily forgotten all about the trouble we were in!

"But what about..."

The angel started walking up the trail toward the camp. "Don't worry about Finky, *or* JoJo, they're not going to bother you two guys anymore." He stopped and turned to look at me. "And don't lie to your dad anymore, Ok?"

I started following him up the trail. "But you didn't..."

He held up his hand. "Don't worry, kid. We're never going to leave you. We've been assigned to you from the beginning. A special assignment, I might add." He started walking back towards me and when he got to me, he squatted down and put both his big hands on my shoulders. The smell of apples was in the air. It was a great smell. "You wanna know how much He *really* likes you? Huh? You wanna know?" I could see his eyes glowing a little brighter behind the dark glasses. "He didn't let you *or* your mom die when you were born, although the one from the other side wanted both of you dead. That's right, kid; there's another side. And the one filled with hate from *that* side wants you bad."

When he said that I got the chills. I could feel the little hairs on my neck stand up.

"But he can try all he wants," the angel said, "and he *will* try, again and again and again, for the rest of your life, but he can't touch you. Why do you think you never drown, even though it seems like you try to every day? Why do you think your mom didn't let you go swimming with Jimmy? Man, kid, I didn't let you break your neck when you fell off the high chair. I didn't let Bobby's arrow puncture your heart, I didn't let the cars hit you when Cheri dared you to hide in that big cardboard box in the middle of the street." I remembered the arrow and the cardboard box, but I had never known that I had fallen off a high chair. He stood up and rubbed my head. I could feel it still wet from the river. "There've been too many times to mention right now. And somehow, I got this feeling there's going to be a lot more. Uh-uh, kid. When God wants you alive, *nothing* can make you dead. I know that's a lot of information for a ten-year-old, but I guess it was time for you to know." He started back up the trail. "C'mon, I'll walk you back to the camp."

I turned around and grabbed Chato's hand. "C'mon, we gotta go see what happened!"

Chato pulled his hand back and looked at me uncertainly. "Are you sure we should go back there? What if Virgie's brothers see us?"

"So what?" I said. "We'll just come up the front of the trail and act as if we've been in the river the whole time." I looked down at our clothes and held my arms open. "We're all wet, ain't we? Nobody'll ever know!"

"Finky will," Chato said.

He was right. But I didn't think the Fink would tell. Besides, my angel said not to worry about Finky. My *angel? My Angel*!!! I turned to look back up the trail. He was gone! My angel was gone! Had it all been a dream? Had I imagined the whole thing? Had I finally lost my mind? Had putting my head

underneath the outhouse damaged my brain? Was this part of my punishment? I sat back down on the log and put my head in my hands.

Chato walked past me, then stopped and looked up the trail. "Where'd he go, Mario?"

I jerked my head up quickly. "You mean saw him too?!?"

Chato wrinkled his brow and looked at me. "What?"

"The angel! I mean the Indian! You know...the big guy! You saw him too?"

Chato walked back to me and put his hand on my forehead. "Are you OK, Mar?"

I hugged him real tight and laughed. "Heck yeah! Man, I thought I was going crazy there for awhile!" I pulled back from him. "Unless, of course, I *am* going crazy, and we're sharing the same dream." I held out my arm to him. "Pinch me."

He looked at me like I *was* crazy. But he reached for my arm and gave it a good pinch. It hurt. That was great! I reached out my hand before he could pull away and pinched *him*. He yelled and jumped back. "Hey! Cut it out, Mario! That hurt!"

I rubbed my arm where Chato had pinched me. "I'm sorry, Chato. But I had to make sure I wasn't going crazy?"

Chato sat down on the log rubbing *his* arm. "Has this all happened, Mario?"

"Yeah, I think so." I shaded my eyes and looked up to the sky. It seemed like the sun hadn't moved since we had been scooped out of the water and our clothes were still pretty wet. It felt like I had talked to the big guy for at least an hour, but the sun had hardly moved at all! Wow! Maybe it *had* really happened! I closed my eyes and tilted my head up to the sun. The heat felt good on my face. I noticed that the mosquitoes, which were usually horrible by the river, weren't buzzing around at all! Wow! What an incredible day! Besides the miracle of not drowning, would I be able to share *any* of this with my parents? I was trying to think of where all the places were that I had noticed the smell of apples, when suddenly the image of Finky falling headfirst into the great stink came into my mind.

Maybe if I was lucky, both he and JoJo had drowned at the bottom of that outhouse. I felt bad immediately after thinking that. Here I had just experienced a certifiable miracle from God, or at least I *thought* it was from God, and had been visited by an angel--at least I *thought* he was an angel--and now I was thinking murderous thoughts about somebody. Man, how come God even bothered with someone like me? I don't know.

"C'mon, Chato," I said. "we better go see what's going on in the camp."

"Are you really sure, Mario?"

"Yeah, I'm really sure."

"Because we could stay here till right before the service tonight."

That was an idea. But I knew we had to get back.

"Nah, we'd better go."

Chato let out a big sigh. "OK," he said, "are we going to sit in front tonight? The Ortega Brothers are singing and I want to be close."

"Yeah, I'll tell my dad to let us sit in front."

"Can Puggy sit with us?"

"Oh, yeah. Pug'll definitely sit with us."

"She likes the Ortega Brothers, huh?"

"Oh, yeah. Pug loves 'em. She'll be with us right in front."

That made Chato smile. Puggy was our good friend, and fortunately for her, she hadn't been part of this latest disaster. But the three of us loved it when the Ortega Brothers sang. Our favorite was the younger brother, Ricky. He had curly black hair and tattoos. He had been in jail before, and all the Bible School girls wanted to marry him. Actually, it seemed like Bible School girls wanted to marry just about *anybody*. Max said all they required was a "warm male body". I didn't know about any of that except that I had seen a few of them sneaking into Max's trailer next to the cabin during church services. So far, Max had avoided Brother Chinche and his flashlight. But anyway, we liked Ricky because he could play

37

two trumpets at the same time! And when they would play and sing *"Feelin' Mighty Fine,"* everybody in the Tabernacle would stand to their feet and dance around. It was great.

Neither of us said anything as we made our way up the bank to the trail and started walking back to the camp. Chato broke the silence by asking me if I had seen the bright lights too and wasn't it a crazy feeling to breathe water. We still couldn't believe it had happened. I wondered where my angel had gone to. I hadn't even asked him his name.

"Mario?"

"Yeah."

"Was that really a miracle?"

"I think so."

"Did all those things really happen?"

"Yeah, I think so. I don't think it was a dream." Neither one of us could still believe what had just happened to us.

We kept walking and I could see the smoke coming from the stoves and fireplaces in the camp. We were still too far to see the cabins.

"Mario?"

"Yeah."

"How come God saved us from drowning?"

"I don't know. Maybe one day we can ask Him." I had been thinking the same thing. And I wondered what the angel meant about the one "filled with hate." I was pretty sure he had meant the Devil, but I hadn't asked. I shivered when I thought about what he had said.

"But we're bad, aren't we, Mario?"

"What?" I stopped and looked at Chato.

"I mean, we were going to put our heads under an outhouse and look at a girl's butt, weren't we, Mario?"

"Yeeaah," I said, slowly.

"Well, if we were going to do something bad, how come He still kept us from drowning?"

I started walking up the trail again. "I don't know, Chato. My mom says even when we're bad He likes us. She said He even loved the guys that were hammering the nails in His hands. I don't know. I guess He just likes us. Or loves us." I could see the cabins coming into view. "We're almost there."

"Mario?"

"Yeah."

"Are we homos 'cuz we didn't look under the outhouse?"

"Nah. I don't think we're homos because of that."

"Mario?"

"Yeah."

"What's a homo?"

I had wanted to ask my angel the same question.

"Uh...I think it's a guy who rides on the railroad and then camps by the tracks."

"I thought that was a hobo."

"Yeah, well, I think a homo is a hobo who goes *home* at night, that's why they call him a homo."

"Ahhh, yeah, that makes sense."

The birds were chirping loudly and we heard a dog barking somewhere. There was a soft breeze rustling the leaves and tiny gnats looked like they were chasing each other through the massive beams of sunlight shooting down from the tops of the cottonwoods. The scent of something delicious frying made my mouth water. I was hungry.

"Mario?"

"Yeah." I was pretty sure the frying smell was freshly caught trout. Maybe it was coming from our cabin.

"Do all angels dress like Navajos?"

"Hmmm. I don't know, Chato. Probably not."

"I liked how he was dressed, Mario."

"So did I, Chato. So did I."

"He smelled good too, huh, Mario?"

I nodded. "Yeah, he smelled good, Chato. He actually did smell good."

We walked in silence. The smell of frying trout was getting stronger. I swallowed hard.

Chato reached out his hand and stopped me. "Mario." I turned and looked at my little friend. "Do I have an angel too?"

"Yeah. Of course you do, Chahts. And he's probably bigger than mine."

Chato's eye's got real big. "Yeah? Really?"

"Yup." I turned to start back to the camp and Chato stopped me again.

"Is my angel a Navajo too, Mario?"

"I don't know. Do you like Navajos?"

"I like Apaches better."

"Then yours probably looks like Geronimo."

"Really?"

"Yup. C'mon. We gotta go."

We were almost at the camp and could see that there was a great crowd of people gathered in the area of the outhouse. Nobody had seen us yet.

"Follow me," I said, ducking under the barbed wire fence by our cabin. "And if anybody asks, we've been in the river the whole time."

Chato nodded and quietly followed close behind.

We hid by the side of Max's trailer to make sure it was safe, and slowly made our way around to the fire pit. As we got ready to step onto the trail in front of our cabin, somebody grabbed me by the arm and turned me around. It was Max and his friend Rudy. We hadn't heard them coming.

"Where've you been?" Max whispered. "Mom's looking all over for you! She's worried sick, man! Dad's looking for you too."

"Why? What's going on?" I asked, turning back to the crowd around the outhouse.

"Yeah, right, you don't know what's going on," Rudy said, with a smirk on his face.

"How can I know what's going on if I just got here?"

Rudy shook his head and looked at Max. "I can't believe your little brother didn't have anything to do with this, man. He's *always* in the middle of things."

"Have anything to do with what?" I asked incredulously. "Me and Chato were in the river Max! We even almost drowned by the Flats!" This was one of the finest performances I had ever given. It was award winning. Great actors are nothing but superb liars. And actually, we *had* almost drowned.

"Well, a couple of your buddies are in some real deep caca, Mar, and what were you doing by the Flats anyway, I told you never to go there!" Max said, looking at me suspiciously. The four of us started walking towards the outhouse and pushed our way through the crowd to see what was going on.

When we got to the front edge I could see my dad patiently listening to old *Hermana* Frita as she tried to explain to the Superintendent what had happened to her and why her brother, old Flotches, had been looking for Satan at the outhouse. Big old Flotches was sheepishly standing behind her mumbling something about *Satanas*, but he was no longer holding the homemade whip. He had given it up to my dad who was holding it behind his back as he nodded and listened.

Standing on the other side of my dad were Virgie, her two older brothers and her mom and dad. They were trying to talk to him at the same time *Hermana* Frita was talking to him, which would have been very confusing for anybody else but my dad, who could listen to twelve people talking to him at the same time and *still* understand what each one of them was saying. I guess that came with having five kids and a wife and several thousand people looking to you for guidance. And that ability was coming in real handy now because Finky's Grandfather and JoJo's parents were *also* talking to him. And while all this talking was going on several men with sledgehammers were pounding the foundation of the outhouse to break it up.

Apparently, they had not been able to get Finky and JoJo out through the same hole that they had fallen in, and it was too deep for them to climb out, so, the men were getting ready to knock the outhouse over so they could have a clear shot at pulling both of them out with ropes. I couldn't believe they were still down there in that horrible, wet, putrid muck. Of course, even though a lot had happened to me and Chato, it didn't seem, by the sun anyway, that very much time had gone by.

With all this noise and confusion going on nobody had noticed that we were there, but when Virgie turned and saw me, I smiled and waved at her, but she narrowed her eyes, leaned over to her brothers, and whispered something. My heart stopped beating when she pointed at me and I thought I was going to wet myself again when Jose and Joey started walking towards us. I could never figure out why two brothers had the same name. I asked my mom, but she didn't know either. That's like two brothers named Miguel and Mikey, or Juan and Johnny, or Roberto and Bobby; it just didn't make any sense. This, however, was *definitely* not the time to ask.

"Where you bean, you leetle cheet?" Jose asked. Jose wasn't saved during the day, so he was *always* cussing, no matter who was around, even his parents. But his accent was so thick, his cuss words sounded funny instead of intimidating. He was reaching for me and I could smell the stale odor of beer on his breath, when Max stepped in front of me and pushed him back hard.

"Keep your hands off my little brother, you drunk, unless you want your ass kicked in front of all these people."

When my brother said that, I gasped. And I heard Chato and Rudy gasp too. Max <u>was</u> saved during the day. I even remember the day he was baptized in the river, and here he was, using the *a-s-s* word in front of people! I think even Jose was surprised because he backed up and didn't do anything. He was bigger than Max, but he knew Max wasn't afraid of him and I *knew* he didn't want to take the chance of getting thumped in front of all these people. Especially the girls, who all liked Max *anyway*. Now a crowd had started to gather around *us*!

"My leetle seester say chee hear heem een bock of de cheeter," Jose said. "And eef he wos der, hee's een beeg trable."

Max put his arm around me. "How could he be in back of the "cheeter" if he was in the river? Look at his clothes, man; he's all wet. Waddaya think, he *peed* all over himself?"

When Max said that some of the girls that had gathered around us giggled and that seemed to embarrass Jose and

Joey. Of course, Max didn't know how right he was. I *had* peed all over myself.

Jose was getting ready to say something else when a big cheer went up from the people around the outhouse. The men had succeeded in hammering the foundation loose and had pushed the small wooden structure over. When it hit the ground with a thud and a cracking wood sound, the cheer had gone up and the crowd had surged forward to the edge of the hole to get a better look at the two unfortunates at the bottom.

****

When the cheer had gone up, the small crowd that had gathered around us turned and quickly headed for the outhouse. Jose and Joey temporarily forgot about how to get around Max to murder me, and ran off to their sister's side to make sure they were with her when she confronted the two busted outhouse felons. Max and Rudy hurried to where my dad was standing, and I was getting ready to go too, when I felt a strong hand grab the back of my shirt and pull me back. I turned around and almost fainted when I saw my mom's face looking right at me. She also had a hold of Chato's shirt. Chato looked like he was getting ready to cry.

"Don't cry, Chato. Nothing's going to happen to you. Just go home. Your mother's waiting for you." My mother's voice was very soft, but *very* firm and businesslike. "Get out of those wet clothes, clean your glasses, eat some dinner, stay <u>inside</u>, take a nap, and get ready for tonight's service. Go on."

Chato looked at me and took off running to his cabin. He might have thought he was looking at me for the last time.

When I had seen my mother, my bladder had let loose *again*, but strangely enough, nothing came out. I was all peed out! I actually had the sensation that I was *peeing*, but nothing was coming out!

43

"Mom, I…"

"Shhh! Let's go. Hurry up! And don't say a word." She was almost dragging me as she was talking and I thought it wise to shut up. She had a very determined look on her face, and she seemed unusually calm. As she hurried us to the cabin, she was almost picking me up. I had never realized just how *strong* she was!

Right as we reached the cabin steps several screams and real loud "oohs" and "ahhs" came from the crowd. Somebody started shouting and I wanted to turn around, but her strong hand *threw* me inside the door and as I landed on my hands and knees by the rollaway bed that I no longer had to share with my sister Sarai, I heard the door slam shut.

"Hurry up and get out of those clothes, and then get in bed," she said. She went over to the stove and turned over the meat that was frying in a big pan. My nose had been right. She was frying some fresh rainbow trout.

"How come? I mean, how come I have to get in bed?" I said, picking myself up.

"Because you're not feeling well."

"I'm not?"

"No, you're not," she said. I nodded and sat on the edge of the bed and started taking off my wet and muddy shoes. I was actually feeling pretty good. I hadn't drowned; I had met a Navajo angel, *my* Navajo angel. My knife was safely in my pocket and Max had kept Jose from murdering me, but if my mom said I wasn't feeling good, then I wasn't feeling good. I knew this was not the time to argue with Cidelia Santos. I couldn't believe she was letting me take off my muddy shoes inside the cabin. She was a very *clean* woman, and she *never, ever*, let any of us come into the cabin with wet shoes, but this was just another extraordinary moment in what was turning out to be an unbelievably extraordinary day.

She removed one of the small, round, iron lids on the stove and put in two small pieces of wood to keep the fire going. I could hear the crackling sound of the fish frying and my mouth began to water as the delicious, smoky aroma filled the cabin.

Fatigue began to slowly creep up on me and I yawned wide, feeling relieved and thankful that my mother had made me come to the cabin. I felt safe in here.

I started to take off my wet pants when there was a loud knock at the door. My mom stood very still and took a deep breath. She closed her eyes, put her hands up to her head and lightly brushed her already immaculate not-a-hair-out-of-place with a neat little bun in the back hair, straightened out her apron, cleared her throat and walked toward the door. She remembered the fish and came back to the stove and moved the pan to the side where there was no fire. She tilted it on its side so the fish wouldn't soak up the grease. Then she went back toward the door, but before she opened it she put her finger to her lips and motioned for me to be quiet. There was another knock. This time louder and longer.

"*Hermana* Santos, are you there?"

My heart skipped a beat. It was Brother Chinche, the self-appointed camp Sheriff, Private Investigator, Police Chief, FBI, CIA, Gestapo, Secretary of State and Keeper of the Holy Flashlight.

I had asked my mom once why Brother Chinche didn't change his last name.

"Well," she had said, "he's as annoying as a bedbug. Maybe he wants people to think of him that way."

That was crazy, I thought. Why would anyone want to be called 'Brother Bedbug'?

There was another knock. "*Hermana...*"

"Yes, I'm here, brother. *Un momento, por favor.*" My mother bowed her head and whispered something to herself, then stepped out the door, closing it tight behind her.

I finished taking off my pants and my sister's borrowed underwear. I quickly put on my pajama bottoms, which were under the pillow, tiptoed quietly to the door and put my ear next to the keyhole. There was still some crowd noise and I could hear Jose talking very loudly to someone about his "seester," and I could even hear old Flotches yelling something about "*Satanas*" in the background. It was hard to understand

45

what was being said by everybody, but Brother Chinche I could hear very clear.

"*Y tu hijo, hermana, donde esta?*"

"Max is right over there, *hermano*, standing next to his dad." I put my eye to the keyhole right as my mother pointed toward the crowd by the outhouse. Brother Chinche was standing on the top step of the porch and he turned just as the crowd let out another loud cheer and started moving as a group across the trail, past the logs, down the river bank toward the water. My guess was they must've just lifted Finky and JoJo out of the muck and were taking them to rinse off in the river. I could make out the back of Max's head and Rudy's, but I couldn't see my dad.

Brother Chinche turned back to my mother. "Yes, I see Max, *hermana*, but I was wondering about your, uh...your little one. About Mario, is he, uh...is he here?"

"Yes, he is here, brother. Why do you want to know?" My mother was standing right next to the screen door, but she wouldn't open it to let him in. He, on the other hand, was not accustomed to having someone stand up to him, especially a *woman*, so he began to fidget and get a little nervous.

"Well...uh..well...yes...well...someone...said.." Brother Chinche knew he had to be very careful. This was no ordinary woman. This was the Superintendent's *wife*, so if he was going to make some accusations, he'd *better* be able to back them up, or his position as keeper of the Holy Flashlight, whether self-appointed or not, would be in serious jeopardy. Besides, he knew for a fact, *this* woman was not impressed or intimidated by him *or* his imaginary importance. He cleared his throat. "Well, someone..uh..some one said he might know something about..uh...about what...uh...well, about what happened here today. So I just..uh...I just wanted to ask..you know..uh...just ask him a few questions."

"Well, he's not feeling very good right now, brother. He just came in from the river soaking wet, so I made him take off his clothes and get in bed. Maybe if he feels better tonight, you can talk to him after the service."

"So, he's been in the river?" He tried to look around her, but she moved and blocked his view.

"That's right, brother," she said. "I understand he came close to drowning again today, and he's not feeling very good. So, if you'll excuse me, I'd like to go take care of him."

As I looked on through the keyhole, I was very much in awe of my mother and I was very happy that I was going to get to tell her about my miracle. If I could somehow convince her that I was really telling the truth, she would be very happy. My mother needed to hear something *good* about me, instead of always getting these knocks on the door informing her of my latest catastrophe. I wanted to wait to let her know about my angel. *That* might be a bit much for her. I wondered if I should tell her that Jesus was brown.

"He almost drowned *again*?!? I swear, *hermana*, your *jito* must have some pretty big angels."

Wow! How did *he* know?

"Yes, I believe he does, brother. And he keeps them very busy."

Wow! How did *she* know?

"*Bueno, hermano,* I'd better go check on him. I'm hoping he feels better for tonight's service. The Ortega Brothers are singing, and they're his favorites, you know. *Que Dios le bendiga.*"

"'*Si, si, hermana. Que Dios le bendiga tambien.* I'm sorry to bother you. I hope Mario is feeling better. *Buen dia.*" Brother Chinche smiled his thin-lipped phony smile, touched his hat and backed down the porch steps. I knew he was already thinking of a way to get me away from my mother tonight so that he could grill me. He kept nodding and smiling, then turned and hurriedly made his way to the big crowd that had gathered at the river bank.

The last time I had seen that many people by the river bank was last summer when my dad and several other ministers had baptized over one hundred people who had gotten saved at the camp meeting. I smiled, thinking that with Finky and JoJo, it was a *different* kind of baptism. And a different kind of salvation, too. I was trying to imagine the two of them washing off the gunk when my mother stepped through the door and almost knocked me over.

"What are you doing out of bed? Get back over there!" She pointed to the bed. "I told that mean, little man that you were in bed, and I'm not a liar, so get back in that bed!"

I hurried back to the bed and got under the covers. She had also told him that I wasn't feeling well, and I will have to admit that when I heard his voice, I really *didn't* feel well.

I watched silently as she put the frying pan back on the side with the fire. The pan quickly heated up again and the familiar crackle of the grease reminded me of how hungry I was. I knew she wanted to ask me about what had happened, but I also knew she didn't *want* to know. If she didn't know, then she wouldn't have to explain to anybody. And more importantly, she wouldn't have to *lie*. She hated to lie. She reached for the folded *trapo* on a small table by the stove and took out two beautiful, thick, fluffy tortillas. She put them on the stove next to the frying pan to warm them. My mouth was now flooding and my stomach was screaming. I knew I had to break the silence.

"Mom."

She turned the tortillas over, but didn't say anything. I tried again.

"Mom."

She ignored me again and reached up to a shelf above the stove and took down a shiny blue plate. Then she took the trout out of the pan and placed it on another *trapo* by the stack of tortillas to drain the grease. When the grease had drained she placed the trout on the plate, took the two warmed tortillas from the stove, grabbed a small saltshaker, and brought them over to where I was lying down.

"Sit up," she said. I sat up and put my feet over the side of the bed, and she handed me the plate and tortillas. Then she went to the small washstand by her bed and picked up the chair that was there and brought it to the side of my bed. "Here, use this as a table. I don't want you eating outside

48

right now. Brother Chinche might see you and come and bother you."

I looked down at the plate. The tail fin was fried real crispy, just liked I liked it. She always knew what I wanted. She knew that even before I ate the firm white meat of the rainbow, I would always eat the crispy tail, so she made it extra crispy, *without* burning the meat. I watched as she turned and went back to the stove. She took out another tortilla and put it on the hot, black metal. As I sat there watching her, a great wave of sadness came over me. In spite of the panties she made me wear periodically, I was very grateful for my mother. She made me happy; I made her sad. She brought much comfort and joy to my life; I brought much pain and misery into hers. She made me feel peaceful; I made her feel stressful. She gave me safety and contentment; I gave her heartache and disaster. It wasn't fair. I needed to make her feel happy.

"Mom," I said, still looking at the Rainbow's crispy tail.

"Huh?" She turned the tortilla over to warm the other side.

"Mom, how did you know I almost drowned?" I picked up the fish's tail and began eating it. It was crunchy and delicious. I groaned softly with delight. The sadness began to leave me. But I still wanted to make her happy.

She took a deep breath and let out a long sigh. "Because you *always* almost drown," she said. She didn't turn to me but kept looking at the tortilla warming on the stove. "Did you almost drown?"

I nodded and peeled some of the skin off the meat. "Yes. Yes, I almost drowned today, Mom." The skin was crispy too, and it tasted great. "I think today was the closest I've ever come. I really thought it was over today."

I looked up from my plate in time to see her shake her head. I watched as she went to the side cupboard and took the butter dish down. Then she picked up the tortilla and placed a small chunk of the butter in the center of it. I could see the butter melt as she turned and came and sat on the edge of the bed. She folded the tortilla so none of the butter could drip out and took a bite. There were tears in her eyes and they slowly made their way down her face as she chewed in silence.

When I saw her tears, I almost started crying too, so I quickly looked down at my plate and began to take the meat off the bones. It fell right off when I barely touched it. That's what happens to trout when it's expertly prepared. The meat falls right off the bone. I put a small chunk of the meat onto the tortilla and folded it and took a bite. The meat was very tender and tasted great with the semi-toasted tortilla. I was happy that my mouth was full because I didn't know what to say. I wasn't sure if this was a good time to tell her about the miracle or not, so we both just chewed in silence. I looked up as she wiped her eyes and cheeks with her apron.

"Brother Savage brought the trout this morning after you left. He said the fish were biting good today."

I nodded and took another bite. Brother Savage was an English who loved being around brown people. He played the banjo and was famous for singing a song at every camp meeting called "Forty Years Ago." I loved hearing him preach in Spanish. I was always amazed at English guys who spoke Spanish. He knew a lot of words, but could never roll his "r's". He was also a very good fisherman and would drop off three or four freshly caught trout to our cabin every time he went fishing. He wasn't the only one. We averaged at least seven or eight fresh trout every morning from different fishermen coming up from the river. My dad loved it. In the morning he would sit in the porch, drink his coffee, and wait for the fish. I loved it too. It was great. Being superintendent *did* have its advantages.

Thinking of my dad reminded me of the chaos he was dealing with down by the river and I glanced up at my mother to see if she was still crying. Her lower eyelids had tears, but at least they weren't running down her cheeks. I knew I had to say something to make her happy. I wondered if this was a good time to ask her what a homo was. Probably not.

I swallowed my tortilla and fish and smiled at her. I was getting ready to tell her about the miracle when we heard someone banging on the screen door of the porch. My mom had locked it to keep Brother Chinche from coming in and had forgotten to unlock it. She turned and looked at the closed cabin door without getting off the bed. I held my breath and in the silence between the banging I could hear my heart pounding against my chest.

"Mama! Maahm! Let me in! Who locked the door? Maaahhm!"

I breathed again. It was only my sister. My heart began to slow down. My mother stood up from the bed and walked toward the door.

"Stay under the covers," She said as she opened the door.

I pulled the blanket over my legs and watched as she walked to the screen door. Before she unlocked it, she looked around to make sure Brother Chinche wasn't around, then lifted the latch and let Sarai in.

"Maahm! What are you doing? Who are you looking for? Why is the door locked in the middle of the afternoon? It's because of Mario, huh. He did something again, didn't he? He had something to do with all the stuff at the outhouse, huh? Are the police going to come for him like they did when he broke out all the windows in that apartment building? Huh?"

My mother pushed her into the cabin. "*Callate*! Be quiet, Sara! No, your brother didn't do *anything*! And no, the police *aren't* coming for him! What's wrong with you anyway? Why are you talking like that?"

My sister was a real whiner and I loved to tease her, but she was crazy too, so I had to be careful because she *always* got even. Sometimes she would wait until I was sleeping to pounce. And I had the scars on my face to prove it. One time she talked me into letting two of her girlfriends carve their initials on my face. I had a big 'K' on one cheek and a big 'C' on the other. Yes, I was pretty dumb to let her do that. But she *was* crazy.

When she came through the door she saw me and her eyes narrowed to two thin slits.

"I knew it!" she hissed through clenched teeth. She started walking slowly toward me, like she was getting ready to capture me. "I knew you had something to do with this! Mom, Virgie told me that she heard Mario and Chato yell in back of the outhouse when Finky and JoJo fell in."

I looked down at my plate and put another piece of fish in the tortilla. "You don't know nothin'," I said, "and besides, how could Virgie know where I was, unless she was floating down the river with me and Chato. Do you see those wet clothes over there? Including your panties?" I pointed to the pile of wet clothes in the corner by the bed. "I don't know *what* Virgie heard, but Chato and I were in the river almost drowning." I put the food in my mouth and watched as she came closer.

I glanced at my mother. A very anxious look had come on her face when my sister had started talking, but she seemed to calm down when I had given my explanation. I'm not sure that she believed me, but I knew she wanted to.

"*Mi 'jita,* get away from your brother and let him eat. Here, come and have a fresh tortilla with butter." My mother took a tortilla from the pile and put it on the stove. "You'd better eat now, because with all that commotion going on out there, I don't know if you'll have time before the service. The Ortega Brothers are singing tonight, you know." She looked over to where my sister was and smiled. "Ricky's going to be playing the trumpets."

"I don't care, Mom," Sarai said. She was almost at my chair. "I just know Mario had something to do with all that out there."

I couldn't take it anymore. "I told you I was in the river almost drowning, Sarai!" I yelled, jumping up. The blanket fell to the side. "But you know what? Even if I was there, which I wasn't, but even if I was, so *what*? Why do you even *care* that Finky and JoJo fell headfirst into all that *caca*? You told me that you and Virgie *hated* them because they always say something nasty to you guys when you walk by them! What if I *did* push them into the *caca*!?! You should be hugging and kissing me! You should be congratulating me because those two bullies finally got what they deserved! But no! Here you are acting like you're Brother Chinche's main detective or something! Maybe you're Brother Chinche's bedbug wife and you don't even know it!"

"Mario!" My mother said. "That's enough! Don't talk to your sister that way!"

My cheeks felt wet and I realized that I had started crying. I wanted, so *badly*, right then, to tell them the truth. I wanted to tell them, yes, I was there. But, no, I did *not* put my head under that outhouse to see Virgie's butt. I wanted to tell them that I hadn't even *wanted* to be with Finky and JoJo, but I was there because I didn't want to be called a homo. Even though I didn't even *know* what a homo was. I *wanted* to tell my mother and sister the truth. But I knew I couldn't. After all, it was me who discovered that hole in back of the outhouse. And I would be eternally punished with the sight of *Hermana* Frita's wrinkled ol' butt permanently tattooed in my mind. That was punishment enough! No, I was going to have to stick with my story. So far my performance had been Oscar-worthy. I waited for the inevitable war.

My sister had walked to the front of my chair, but she didn't say anything. Her eyes were no longer thin slits and she didn't have that 'rage straight from hell' look on her face. As a matter of fact, she looked like she had a very *faint* smile on her lips. I thought 'Oh, my God! She's really gone crazy this time! She's thinking about how she's going to kill me!' I looked over at my mother by the stove. She was standing very still. She had my sister's just-warmed tortilla in her hand and she looked like she was holding her breath, waiting for the first punch.

Sarai walked right up to me and put her arms up and I instinctively ducked, thinking she was going to scratch me, or something. But instead, she put her arms around me and *hugged* me! She _HUGGED_ me! Sarai Santos actually hugged her little brother!!! I couldn't believe it! I just couldn't believe it! She had never even *touched* me except to hit me, or scratch me, or permanently try to *maim* me! And here she was...

hugging me! I was in complete and total shock! I looked over Sarai's shoulder at my mother. She had dropped the tortilla on the floor and was standing there with her mouth wide open, not quite believing the scene in front of her.

"You're right, Mar," Sarai said, still hugging me, "even though you weren't where you were, thank you. Thank you for doing what you didn't do."

Maybe all this was making me a little crazy, but I actually *understood* what she meant! She let me go, and I started breathing again. When I did, my heart skipped a beat. Sarai smelled like apples! Oh no! I hadn't noticed until now, but Sarai smelled like *apples*! Oh, my God! Oh..my..God! I sat back down on the bed in pure, unblemished, *immaculate*, yes, that's the word, *immaculate* and utter shock. I reached for the blanket with trembling hands and I wiped my eyes. Apples? *Apples*!?! A billion things started going on in my brain and I looked around to make sure that we were the only ones in the cabin. The smell of apples blended with the other delicious aromas in the cabin. This was absolutely crazy. I looked back at my sister, who was looking down at me smiling, and that's when I noticed that she had a shopping bag in one of her hands. It said J.C. Penney on the side. She turned around and started walking towards my mom.

"Where's that tortilla, Mom?"

My mother was still standing by the stove in shock, and hadn't even picked up the tortilla that she had dropped. Sarai walked by her, took a tortilla from the *trapo* and put it on the stove.

"*Mi 'jita*, what's in the bag?" my mother asked. She had come out of her semi-stupor and was bending over, picking up the tortilla she had dropped.

Sarai turned around and laughed. "Oh, yeah. I almost forgot. Ha! I had it in my hand all the time, and I almost forgot!" She walked back toward the bed and tossed the bag next to me. "Here. This is yours," she said, walking back to the stove. "Some really, *really* big Indian in a pretty turquoise jacket said to give it to you." She took her tortilla off the stove and buttered it. "His clothes were kind of crazy, but he *was* cute, and boy, did he smell great!"

She folded the tortilla and walked out of the cabin and right out of the porch. Just like that. Hurricane in, Hurricane out, as my dad would say. My mom had picked up the tortilla but still hadn't moved from her spot, but when Sarai walked out of the cabin, she slowly went to the door and closed it, then came and sat on the edge of the bed.

I was speechless. Some really, *really* big Indian. *Some really big Indian,* Sarai said, *with crazy clothes.* Of course, *she* would notice the beautiful shirt and velvet jacket. Did he always wear that? Oh, my Lord! It was true. Oh..my..God. If she only knew! My body felt numb. It was true! The miracle had really happened. Wow! The great Navajo. The Miracle. My brown Jesus. It was all real! I felt dizzy, so I closed my eyes and took some real deep breaths.

"Open it, '*jito*. But be careful. You never know."

I looked inside. There was a box and another package folded inside. My hand was still trembling as I took the box out. I looked at my mom. I had read the label, and I wanted to cry. I knew what it was.

"Open it," she said, "but slowly."

I nodded; some tears fell on the box as I slowly opened it. I removed the thin paper and stared unbelievingly at a gorgeous, white, brand-new pair of U.S. Keds. I looked over at my mom and she had covered her mouth with her hands and tears were streaming down her face. I looked back at the shoes and just shook my head. Finky didn't know it, but he had become a prophet. He had told me that same day that he would stick his head in a pile of crap the day I got new Keds. Well, I guess he called it. Wow. Had God known all this?

"What else is in there, *mi 'jito*?" my mom asked through her tears. I reached into the bag and pulled out the other smaller bag. My body was numb and tingly at the same time. I didn't think anything else could top the Keds. I was wrong. I turned the bag over and emptied the contents on the bed. I gasped. My mother let out a little scream. We couldn't believe it. There on the bed were five packages of brand-new boys' underwear. Real boys shorts! From J.C. Penney! Just my size. Three pairs in each package. Fifteen pairs of real...absolutely *authentic*, boys' underwear! No more panties! NO MORE PANTIES!! It was too much. It was all too much for this ten-year-old boy. I grabbed the blanket and lay down on my side on top of the shorts and started crying. I just cried. I felt my mother lay down by my side and heard her crying with me.

"*Ay, mi 'jito. Mi 'jito. Mi 'jito.* Thank you, Jesus. Thank you, Jesus."

She hugged me and kept thanking Jesus. Yes, thank you, Jesus. And thank you, my great Navajo. Would I ever meet him again? I was pretty sure I would. The plastic cover of the shorts felt good on my face. Is this how God worked? What part did Jesus have in all this? I knew I was going to have to tell my mom about everything. Even the part about Jesus not being Assembly of God.

I reached for my new gorgeous, white tennis shoes and stared at the little blue 'U.S. Keds' label on the back. I put my nose in one of them and breathed in deeply that beautiful brand-new canvas and rubber tennis shoe smell. Then I put both of them under my head for a pillow.

It had been an unbelievable day, and tonight the Ortega Brothers were singing. I could wear real shorts and new Keds to the service. Where was my Navajo? Was he talking to Jesus? Could *anybody* talk to Jesus? Would they be at the service tonight? Did Jesus wear bright red shirts and turquoise velvet jackets? Was He beautiful? What did He look like now? Was He still brown? Were His eyes still almost black? Did it matter?

I put all the packages of shorts close to my chest and that's how my mom and I fell asleep. With the delicious aromas of fried trout, fresh tortillas and apples in the air.

What a day. Wait till I told Chato. Wait till we both told Puggy.

****

The Holy Ghost,
A Green-Eyed Girl,
&
The Night
Me & Puggy
Saved Max

Puggy Miranda was the best football player I had ever seen. She didn't care if she wore a helmet or not. She would just put her head down and slam into anybody. She wasn't very fast, but she had some pretty fancy moves, and she was always the first one picked because nobody wanted to get hit by her, so they made sure she was on their team. She was also the only girl in the whole camp who wore pants. If you were an Assembly of God girl, you couldn't wear pants *or* makeup. If you got caught, then Brother Chinche and his deputies would embarrass you and your parents and then ask you to leave the camp. I had seen it happen. Sometimes I would see the girls around Max sneak on some lipstick, but they would rub it off real quick if they saw Brother Chinche coming up the trail with his big flashlight. He even carried it during the day. But Puggy didn't care. She told me she would *never* wear a dress to play football and if Brother Chinche tried to make her, she would flatten him. I believed her. And I think he must have heard about her threat, because he never embarrassed her or even told her to go change.

At last year's camp meeting, the kids from New Mexico were playing the kids from Colorado by the river in back of the cabins. Finky and JoJo were on the Colorado team and they were *all* bigger than us, but we felt good because we were faster...and we had Puggy. Max used to tell me that she was "the great equalizer." When he first told me that, he could tell I didn't know what he meant.

"It's something I learned in school," he said. "It means that it doesn't matter how big those other guys are, as soon as Puggy steps onto the field, then everything becomes equal."

He could tell I still wasn't getting it.

"Look," he said, "You're faster than Finky and JoJo and all those guys, but you're not meaner. But Puggy is tougher *and* meaner, so all of a sudden things are the same between you guys. In fact, even though all of you *are* smaller, now *you're* better than those guys. Understand?"

I nodded. Of course we were better with Puggy. Unbeatable, almost. But I disagreed with one thing. She wasn't meaner. I can't ever remember her being mean to anybody. The only thing was she didn't like Finky very much, she didn't like how he bullied me and Chato and the other smaller guy's, so she did take a lot of pleasure in slamming into him. Maybe that's what Max meant by her being meaner. As long as the other team *thought* she was meaner, that was OK by me.

Anyway, playing the other states in football, basketball and softball *and* army, was one of my favorite things to do at the camp meeting. The kids from the other states always had the latest shoes and clothes and even *haircuts*, but the New Mexico gang, with our cardboard-repaired shoes, our sisters' panties and our cereal bowl-on-the-head haircuts, pounded them on a pretty regular basis. I used to recruit the Madrid boys from Chama to play, because mountain kids were a lot tougher than the city kids and they loved to beat the city guys at *anything*. It meant bragging rights for the rest of the year.

So before I kicked off that day in back of the cabins, I gathered the New Mexico guys in a huddle and told them that Finky had called all of our mothers something horrible. I don't even remember what I said, but it was a lie, of course. What I wanted, was to charge up the team. Get them a little bit mad. It worked. Solomon and Sisto Madrid got so mad they started talking real fast in Chama Spanish and they looked like they wanted to cry and kill at the same time. I looked at Puggy and her nostrils had gotten real big and she was breathing hard and she had that crazy, glazed look in her eyes. I smiled and turned around to kick off. Moms are holy and sacred in New Mexico, so I knew the Colorado guys were in deep trouble.

I looked down the cow chip and dirt clod-filled, branch-and-log-strewn open space between the cottonwoods we called a "football field," spotted Finky, and kicked. The ball went right to him, and I watched and listened as Solomon and Sisto screamed something in Spanish, something my mother told me never to repeat again when I asked her what it meant, and took off insanely after their prey. I heard Puggy grunt and watched as she ran by me with her semi-long hair blowing wildly in the wind, and then I held back a little and let the rest of the team run by me, just in case Finky got past them, although I knew he wouldn't.

Poor Finky. Puggy was the first to get to him. I don't know what he was thinking, because he ran straight to her. I thought afterwards that maybe he didn't want anybody to make fun of him for running away from a girl. Maybe in a moment of real stupidity he actually thought he could run her over. Who knows why we do some of the stupid things we do. Anyway, Puggy looked like a wild bull when she lowered her head, and when her shoulder hit him square in the stomach, he let out this real high pitched squeak, and his face, which was pink, got real red. And then when she slammed him against one of the cottonwoods, his face got real white. Like milk. If I hadn't felt so happy about the bully being tackled, then I would've been real worried about him.

Everybody stopped running when she hit him and we just stood and stared. It didn't look good for Finky. The *sound* of her shoulder hitting him, not even the high-pitched squeak, but just the *"KA-BOOM"* of the hit, and then the sick *"CRUNCH"* of him hitting the tree made all the onlookers gasp. These interstate contests *always* drew a crowd, even when it was the younger guys playing. I looked over at the crowd, and some of the girls had turned away and were holding their hands up to their mouths. Of course, wouldn't you know, most of the girls were standing around Max and two of his Chama buddies, Floriancito and Buddy.

Well, when Puggy hit Finky, the ball *and* his shoes flew in the air. I had never seen that. A hit so hard, that it knocked the *shoes* off! And they were even *tied*! And before the ball *or* his shoes hit the ground, Sisto and Solomon both jumped on him. That's when he screamed *"MAMA!"* and started gagging like he couldn't breathe. Which of course, he couldn't.

Well, the ball hit the ground and rolled right in front of me. But nobody moved to get it. They were all looking at Finky and the three crazies on top of him. I didn't hear a time out, so I picked up the ball and ran to the small log that had been marked as the end zone, held up both of my arms and yelled "Touchdown!"

When I yelled "Touchdown!", Puggy, Sisto and Solomon jumped off of Finky and trotted slowly to where I was standing with both arms still up.

"You OK?" I asked Puggy.

"Heck, yeah," she said, with a big smile on her face. "But I betcha ol' Fink don't wanna play anymore."

We turned and looked as JoJo and a couple of the Colorado guys picked Finky up from the ground and were trying to get him to breathe. He looked like he was crying, but he was trying hard not to let anybody see. Solomon and Sisto kept laughing and telling Puggy things in Chama Spanish but they were talking too fast, so she just nodded and said "Yeah, you're right. Yeah, it was a good hit." That made them laugh louder and talk even faster.

Chama guys always talked in Spanish, but it was a different kind of Spanish that I didn't hear in Albuquerque. It was almost like their own secret language. My mom said it was called *"Manito."* And they took it for granted that all brown people talked in Spanish like they did. Which of course, wasn't true. We understood some of it, but most of us talked less and less anyway, because our parents wanted us to talk in English more so that we could talk without an accent. I think they believed that if we talked without an accent, we would have a better chance at succeeding in the English world. But that wasn't always true either, because I used to see English people get nervous around a brown person who could talk English better than they did. Like my dad. He could talk English better than the English. And I could tell a lot of them didn't like that.

Anyway, when Sisto and Solomon started laughing, that made the Colorado guys madder, because here we were, the small New Mexico guys with cardboard shoes, and with a *girl* even, and we had already basically won the game! Their best guy, and really, he wasn't a very good athlete, he was just big, was gone. And we could tell they didn't want to play anymore. They were afraid to get hit by Puggy. It was great. She was great!

The Colorado guys walked off the field and back to the cabins without a word, so the four of us put our arms around each other's shoulders and walked off too. Only we were a little happier. I even said something in Albuquerque Spanish to Sisto and Solomon. I made up most of the words, but it must have sounded OK, because it made them laugh. When we got to the fence Max came up to us, and about four or five girls who were with him, came up too.

"Way to go, kid," he said, putting his hand on my shoulder.

"Yeah," I said, a little embarrassed because I really hadn't done anything, except maybe tell a good lie to get everybody worked up.

"Great hit, Pug," he said, holding out his hand.

"Yeah," she said, shrugging her shoulders. She always got embarrassed around Max, and she looked at the ground and barely shook his hand.

Floriancito and Buddy said something in Chama Spanish to Solomon and Sisto which made Max and all of us laugh, although me and Puggy didn't know why *we* were laughing; we didn't understand what they had said, we were just happy, and that made all the girls giggle. When the girls started giggling, I looked over at them and was sure that I had seen two of them sneaking into Max's trailer during the church service the night before.

"You think the Utah guys will wanna play us?" I asked.

"I don't know, man. As long as you have ol' "Night Train" Miranda here, I'm not sure *anybody's* gonna wanna play you."

When Max said that. Puggy got even *more* embarrassed and put her head down again, put her hands in her pockets and started kicking the dirt. When she did that, the girls that were with Max giggled even *more*. I could never understand why Max's girlfriends giggled so much. About *everything!* He stood up; they giggled. He waved; they giggled. He smiled; they giggled. He frowned; they giggled. He tied his shoe; they giggled. He combed his hair; they giggled. He said something stupid; they giggled. He said something smart; they giggled. He didn't say anything at all; they giggled. Whew! If putting up with all this giggling was part of being that Latin Lover that Max told me all brown guys grew up to be, then I knew I was going to have a tough time. Max said it had something to do with being nervous before the kissing part. I don't know. I suppose I would find out one day.

Anyway, when the girls' giggling finally died down a little bit and Puggy was *completely* embarrassed, Max grabbed me in a headlock.

"Don't worry about these chicks, man," he whispered in my ear. "Remember I told you one day you'll *like* it."

With that he laughed, turned and put his arms around two of the girls and all of them started walking up the trail towards the Tabernacle. Solomon and Sisto laughed and said something in Chama Spanish and took off after them. I guess they thought they would get more entertainment around Max and the bigger guys than around me and Puggy.

When they all left, me and Puggy just kind of looked at them walking away.

"Do you think I'll ever be that weird?" I asked.

"Yeah, probably," she said. "Sarai told me that *all* guys end up like that. She said they get real stupid once the fuzz appears on their upper lips."

"Really?" I asked. I rubbed my upper lip. All I felt was dirt and sweat. I guessed I wouldn't be getting stupid for awhile. But you never knew about things like that. My dad had such a heavy beard, he had to shave twice a day. So maybe I was going to get stupid pretty quick.

"And how come Sarai knows about those things?" I asked, still rubbing my upper lip.

"I don't know. She says she just knows guys."

"My sister. Sarai Santos."

"Yup."

"She says she knows guys."

"Yup. That's what she says."

"My mom won't even let her *talk* to guys! So how can she know all about them?"

"I don't know. I guess you'll have to ask her."

Well, I knew *that* would never happen. I valued my life too much to ask my sister a question like that.

"Yeah, well, I guess I'll just have to wait and find out."

We looked at each other, shrugged our shoulders, and started tossing the football around, not really saying anything else. Actually, we would giggle sometimes too, but only when something really funny happened. Like if one of us would throw a really good, loud or stinky *pedo*. Now *that* was worth giggling about. Especially during one of the services in the Tabernacle. That was always a good way to get out of church, because our mothers would get mad and embarrassed, then tell us to go outside. Which was great, because then we could sneak around, following all the older kids sneaking around, hiding from Brother Chinche, looking for a place to kiss. But we would wait until the Special Music was over. We could *never* miss the music.

But right now, while everybody else was walking away, me and Puggy were just real happy we beat the Colorado guys. And I was real happy I had a friend like Puggy, who could be happy just tossing the football around with me, or sitting on a log and looking at the river flow by, or sleeping next to each other on the sawdust in the Tabernacle when our parents would get touched by the Holy Spirit and not finish till four in the morning. No matter where we were together, we were content just to *be* with each other. She even knew I had to wear my sister's underwear sometimes, but she had *never* told *anybody*! I loved Puggy. Not like a boyfriend- girlfriend kind of thing. But I just really loved her. Like a real special thing that we never had to say anything to each other. I had never felt like that about a girl or with any of my friends. I think she loved me that way too. So when she came knocking on the cabin door that same night of the outhouse fiasco, I was very relieved. Finally. Someone I could talk to about that whole incredible day's events. Maybe even tell her about my Navajo angel.

"Mom, it's Puggy. Can I let her in?"

I was on my knees looking through the keyhole when I felt my mother's leg push me out of the way.

"Mario! Stand up from there! Those pants are clean. I don't want you to dirty them before you go to church! Now move."

She pushed me again and I stood up and let her by to answer the knock on our screen door. She liked Puggy a lot too; of course it helped that Puggy's older brother Jesse had married my sister Anna a few years earlier. They had even been lucky enough to be Pastors at the little Chama Church when they were first married, so I knew that she trusted Puggy, but I also knew that she was still nervous about Brother Chinche ambushing me. So she wasn't taking any chances.

When she went by, I looked down at the freshly pressed, new pair of pants she was having me wear tonight and brushed the knees where I had been kneeling. Usually, I would feel pretty good about wearing my new pants, even though I had to wear them with my cardboard-bottomed shoes. But tonight, tonight was different. Tonight I felt brand new all over!

I brushed off my knees and followed my legs all the way down to my feet. There they were. My heart beat faster when I saw them. I still couldn't believe it. I closed my eyes, then opened them and stared in amazement at what was on my feet. And I wasn't dreaming. Beautiful. Gorgeous. Brand-new U.S. Keds. I was going to go to church in brand spankin' new U.S. Keds. On my feet! Unbelievable. *Reverendo* Macedonio and *Hermana* Cidelia Santos' little boy was going to go to church tonight, *not* with shoes held together with expertly placed string and extra heavy cardboard replacing the leather on the bottom, but with brand-new U.S. Keds. Wow! The real thing. Wait till I showed Chato!

And if that wasn't enough, underneath these brand-new pants--and this was *totally* unbelievable--I was wearing, for the very first time in my entire ten years, a brand-new pair of *authentic*, the absolute *real* thing, *not* my brothers' old sewn-up shorts, *not* my sister's panties, but my *own*, my very *own*, not somebody else's who got to wear them *before* me, but my very own, J.C. Penney boys', real cotton underwear. Mind boggling. A miracle of earth shattering significance. Now I didn't have to worry anymore about getting in an accident and having the ambulance guys see my sister's panties underneath my pants. Now, I *wanted* an ambulance guy to see my shorts! I was hoping to maybe somehow drop my pants in front of a lot of people tonight. And then I would just say something like "Oops! I'm so sorry! I didn't mean to drop my pants in front of you! Here, let me help you with that." That's how proud and amazed I was at what I was wearing tonight! I felt like one of those little English boys wearing all those new clothes in the Montgomery Wards catalogue. I felt like a million bucks. I had heard Max say that one time. Yup. That was it. Like a million bucks!

"Come in Puggy, he's in here. I want you two to go straight to the Tabernacle. I have to help Brother Chavez in the *comedor* tonight, so I won't be able to go to church. But I don't want Mario wandering around. I want you to promise me that you won't let Brother Chinche talk to him, OK?"

My Mom had already begun giving Puggy instructions as they walked through the porch and into the cabin. Puggy was wearing her church dress tonight and you could tell she wasn't happy about it. She stopped, closed her eyes, and put her nose in the air and sniffed the delicious aroma. The smoky, mouth-watering fragrance of fried trout and freshly-made tortillas still filled the cabin. Normally, Puggy would have looked at me and moved her eyebrows up and down real fast, motioning silently with her head at the tortillas underneath the *trapo* on the small table next to the stove, giving me the cue to ask my mother for a tortilla, because she just loved my mom's tortillas. But tonight when she opened her eyes, she saw me standing there with a *HUGE* smile on my face, pointing down to my shoes. When she looked down her eyes got real wide and her mouth opened wide. She looked back to me with a big surprised smile, then looked back down to the new shoes.

"Whoa, man, Mar! No way! When'd you get the shoes? Whoa!"

She knelt down and rubbed the front of both of them. I knew she wanted to smell them. Brand new tennies had a special smell.

"Wow. Wow! They look brand new!" she said, getting back up. She had that "Where in the heck did you get the money for new Keds?" look in her eyes, but I knew she was happy for me.

"They *are* brand new," I said, turning around so that she could see the blue Keds' tag on the back of the shoes.

"Sarai said a big Indian gave them to her, to give to *him*. They were even in a J.C.Penney bag," my mom said. She had already taken a fluffy tortilla from the *trapo* and was warming it on top of the still hot stove. "But Mario's been asleep until just a little while ago, so I haven't been able to really ask him about it. He didn't even wake up when his dad and everybody came home to eat." She picked up the tortilla and turned it over. I could tell it was getting toasty. I looked at Puggy. She was already licking her lips.

"A big Indian?" Puggy asked, not taking her eyes off the tortilla.

"Uh-huh, that's what Sarai said. A big Indian. Do know anything about that? Have you seen a big Indian talking to Mario?" My mother took the tortilla off the stove and put it on a napkin. She looked at Puggy for an answer while she buttered the tortilla. Puggy just shook her head, never taking her eyes off the tortilla.

"Nope. Uh, I haven't even seen a *small* Indian around Mario." My mother handed the hot tortilla to Puggy and we both watched as she closed her eyes and took a bite. "Thank you, Sister Santos," she said with her mouth full. "If I see a big Indian, I'll let you know. And I'll keep my eye out for Brother Chinche."

She turned and looked at me and then at the new Keds. There was butter dripping down both sides of her mouth.

"Hey, watch out," I said, moving a few steps back. "I don't want you dripping on my shoes."

Puggy tried to say something, but her mouth was so full of tortilla that I couldn't understand her.

I walked over to where my mother was putting food away. "Mom, does Max know I have new shoes?"

"Yes, he got real excited. But I told him not to wake you up. By the way, someone told me that he used a bad word today with those Medina boys. Did you hear him? The person who told me said you were standing right next to him."

Uh, oh. Someone had told my mom that Max had said the a-s-s word to Jose and Joey. It was probably Sarai.

"Uh...nah, he was just telling us about different words in the Bible. You know, like the word the Bible uses for donkey. Ass. You know, like where it says 'pisseth' instead of pee. You know, like..."

"OK. That's enough. Stop! I do know my Bible. You don't have to say anything else."

"Yeah, mom. It was kinda like a Bible study, you know?" Wow! I had actually said two bad words in front of my mom! And, I was lying to her again! I could feel the flames of hell coming through my new tennies. Any minute the devil and some demons were going to come up through the floor and take me down to burn with all the other liars in hell! But I couldn't let my brother get in trouble for defending me, so I considered it worth the risk.

My mother stopped for a few seconds and just looked at me. Was she thinking how could she have raised such a liar? Or had she really bought the story? She didn't say. She just shook her head, let out a sigh, and took a large blue bowl down from the small cupboard and put the rest of the tortillas in it. She covered them real tight with the *trapo* and put the bowl on a small table next to the stove. If we didn't come home too late from service tonight, I knew she would let me have one before I went to bed.

"What about this big Indian, *'jito.* Are you sure you've never seen him?" She took the little iron tool and lifted one of the heavy lids on the stove. She poked at the smoldering embers inside to make sure they were dying out. She didn't want to go to church and leave the fire going in her stove. I'm glad she was looking at the stove when she asked me that question, because I'm sure my eyes would have given me away.

"Uh, I uh...I don't know anything about a big Indian, Mom." That very same day God had saved my life with such an unbelievable miracle that even *I* couldn't hardly believe it! And I was *there*! Then, He sent a big Navajo, who said he was one of my angels, and had him give me *new Keds, and* new boys' underwear! And here I was, lying *again*! Was there ever going to be any hope for this ten-year-old sinner? Was God ever going to change me? Would He delay the Rapture until I could tell my parents the truth about everything? Or even about *anything*? I said a silent prayer and asked Him to please wait. I *knew* I was going to have to tell her the truth about today. Including the outhouse stuff. Even if she didn't believe me, I knew I had to tell her. This thing about God not being *"Assembly of God."* Wow! I wondered what she would do when she found *that* out! That was OK. Max used to tell me that the truth hurts sometimes, and I was determined to start telling the truth. But not now. Now I just had to get out of here so I could show everybody my new shoes and shorts.

"Well, I wonder who he was?" my mother said. She put the heavy lid back on the stove and took her apron off and folded it. She very neatly put the folded apron next to the blue bowl and straightened her dress. There wasn't even a hair out of place. She had just fed and taken care of her small army, including her little boy who *constantly* had her on edge, and she *still* looked like she had stepped right out of a Montgomery Wards catalogue for Chama people. She was the neatest and cleanest person I had ever known. She even waxed and polished the *vigas* on the ceiling of our house in Albuquerque! And here I was, the biggest dirt, dung and mud magnet in all of the history of Chama. Maybe Max was right. Maybe I *was* adopted. Both my mother and I knew that no matter even if I was wearing new everything, I was still going to come back to the cabin tonight being very close to filthy. It was sad, but I knew that even my new shoes were going to get a little dirty.

"I don't know, Mom. Did you tell Max I had new shorts?"

"Yes, I sure did."

"What did he say?"

"He said he needed some new clothes too. So he was hoping to meet this Indian. Do you need a napkin, Puggy?" my mother asked, getting a napkin from the cupboard.

I turned just as Puggy was stuffing the last of the tortilla into her mouth. She nodded her head and reached for the napkin. "Shan shu, shishu," she mumbled. I think she said, "Thank you, Sister," and when she did, a few specks of tortilla flew out flew out of her mouth and almost landed on my new shoes. I moved back another couple of steps. I wanted to keep them clean for as long as I could.

"You're welcome, Puggy," my mother said. I guess she had understood her. She turned back to the stove for one last look to make sure everything was put away. then grabbed her coat and put it on. She put her hand on the light switch and let me and Puggy go out to the porch before she switched it off.

I was almost at the screen door when I heard her call my name.

"Mario."

I turned to look at her.

"Yes, Mom?"

She slowly walked over to the big table on the porch and sat on one of the benches.

"Are you sure you don't know anything about this big Indian?"

"Maahm! I said I don't know."

"Well, it's sure strange that a complete stranger, a big Indian, would give you all those brand new things."

"Maybe it was a miracle. You're the one who taught me about miracles."

"Yes, but.."

"Maybe God saw my cardboard shoes, and He knew how much I hated to wear my sister's panties, and He felt sorry for me, and made a miracle."

"Yes *mi 'jito*. But..."

" Doesn't He specialize in the impossible?"

"Well, yes, but..."

"He didn't let me drown even though the river was real high. Right?"

"*Mi 'jito*, that's not..."

"Well, there you go. God made the impossible possible." And boy, oh boy, if she only knew how true that was!

My mother looked at me with her beautiful, sad eyes, shook her head, let out a long sigh, placed both her hands on my head, closed her eyes and began silently moving her lips. I knew she was praying for me. She *always* prayed for me.

When I would walk home from Lavaland Elementary School and would get about a block from my house on 59th Street, I could hear her praying. Actually, it was more of a wail. She would always open the windows when she prayed. Even when it was cold.

The kids that walked home with me would cross the street to avoid walking in front of my house because they seemed afraid when they heard her. They were especially afraid when they heard her speaking and crying in another language that didn't sound like English *or* Spanish. But the one thing that made *them* afraid was the one thing that gave *me* the most peace. And goosebumps. I loved hearing my mother pray in tongues. I think it was the *only* time I would sit quietly, just listening to her sing, cry and pray in tongues.

But that's why they made fun of me at school. Especially the Spanish kids. They were all Catholic and they called me an "*Aleluya*." I didn't care. I *wanted* to be an *Aleluya*. I had been to a couple of Catholic services with my parents, and I *never* wanted to be *that* boring. Nobody even *smiled* there. And it was *way* too quiet. But I did love the windows with all the pretty pieces of glass with pictures of people in them, and the little cushion things that were used for kneeling were pretty neat too.

Aleluyas, on the other hand, were very loud. They sang, jumped, shouted, danced, played trumpets and electric guitars, beat on drums and tambourines, shook the maracas, hugged, cried *and* smiled! And that was just during the song service! Anyway, I hoped one day God would let me speak in tongues as beautifully and powerfully as my mom. Of course, you couldn't tell that now, because I was a ten-year-old sinner who lied about *everything*! But maybe, just maybe, one of these days when I wasn't such a liar, God would let me speak in tongues. But right now, I just wanted my mom to finish praying so I could get out of the cabin. I wanted everybody to see my new shoes while there was still a little bit of light out.

She finished praying and then held my face with both her hands while a tear slowly rolled down her cheek to the corner of her mouth. When I saw that tear, I knew that was it. I hated to see my mom cry. I just couldn't take it. If I didn't say something now, I would go down in history as the worst son who ever lived. Oh well, "goodbye, life," as I once knew it.

"He's my guardian angel," I said softly.

Everything got real quiet. I needed to breathe, but my lips couldn't catch the air. I felt Puggy walk over to my side and she put her face real close to mine.

"What? Who?" Puggy asked. Her breath smelled like tortilla and butter. My mom still hadn't let go of my face.

"He's what?" Puggy asked again. Her eyes were real wide, but not as wide as my mom's, who also had that same exact look on her face that she had when the police had brought me to the door the day I had broken all the windows in the apartments in the vacant lot in back of our house in Albuquerque with a little rusty hammer that I had found.

"*Que?*" she asked, letting go of my face. "What did you say?"

"I said, He's my guardian angel, the big Indian."

I didn't quite believe that I was actually telling the truth. I knew there was some air in the porch, it was there when I had come out of the cabin, but my mouth couldn't find it.

"Actually, Mom, he said he's *one* of my guardian angels."

Was this really me? Why did I feel like I had left my body and my mouth was working on its own? Was I going to faint? Would someone call an ambulance? Would the ambulance guys like my new shorts?

My mother closed her eyes and slowly shook her head. "*Mi 'jito,* why? Why do you do this to me?" She got up quickly and started buttoning her coat. "I ask you a serious question, and all I get is a crazy answer. When are you going to quit lying so much?"

I stood there completely stunned. For the very first time in the ten long years I had been on this earth, I had finally told my mother the truth without having it beat out of me...and she didn't believe me! Maybe I should try again.

"Mom, I'm telling you the truth. He said he was one of my guardian angels." I hadn't moved from where I had been standing, and Puggy hadn't moved from my side. Her eyes weren't wide anymore; they had narrowed, like she was trying to figure me out.

"*Mi 'jito,* I told you never to make fun of the things of God," she said sternly. "I pray every day that God'll send His guardian angels to surround you. Why do you think you never drown?"

I jumped back quickly, almost knocking Puggy over. Had she really said that?

"That's what He said."

"What?" my mom said, putting her scarf over her head.

"He said the same thing. He said that's why I never drown. Mom, did I ever fall from a high chair when I was a baby?"

Now my *mother* stood there stunned with her mouth wide open. "Wha...Who...I never...Who told you that?" she asked shakily. Her hands had fallen to her side and she just stared at me.

"My angel. The big Indian." Wow! It was true! Wait till I told Chato!

"Mom." She still hadn't moved. I wanted to make her happy. "Mom, guess what? Jesus is real!"

She wasn't moving, so I walked over to her.

"And guess what, Mom," I said, grabbing her hand. "He's not English like all those pictures! He's brown like us! And he even has black eyes like me!"

She was getting ready to say something when we heard a real loud, "Ah-HAY-ya!!"

Me and Puggy recognized the yell, and we turned around quickly right as Chato and his little brother Beanie ran on to the top step of the porch. Beanie looked exactly like Chato, big black glasses, flat top and all, but about a head smaller. They both seemed very excited and were a little out of breath from running. Their mother, Sister Montoya, was walking quickly after them.

"Rafael! Benjamin!" she yelled after them. "Quit running! You're going to fall and get dirty! And don't run up on people like that! And don't get your little brother excited! You know how he gets!"

Beanie's small body did a little jerk and he let out another "Ah-HAY-ya!"

When Beanie yelled, Chato turned to him and gently put both of his arms around him. He put Beanie's head in his chest just as Beanie jerked again and let out a muffled yell.

"It's OK, Bean; it's OK," Chato said, still holding his brother's head. "Calm down. It's OK, buddy." He rubbed the back of Beanie's head as he talked to him. He was still rubbing his head and talking to him quietly as Sister Montoya quickly walked up to the porch a little out of breath.

"Rafael, please don't get him excited like that." She took Beanie and held him close to her. "He can't take it."

Sister Montoya never called Chato, "Chato." She always called him by his real name, "Rafael." And she never called Beanie, "Beanie." Always "Benjamin."

"He'll be OK, Mom," Chato said. He reached out and lightly touched Beanie's head. He loved his little brother. So did me and Puggy. We hated it when Finky and JoJo made fun of him and called him names like "freako" or "circus boy." Beanie had some kind of syndrome that made him jerk and yell. But we had seen him real excited before and he didn't even yell. And then sometimes he would. We liked to take him to church with us because for some reason, even though he was just a little kid, he threw the second most horrifying, sickening *pedos* I had ever smelled. My dad was first, of course. Chato said it was because of the medicine he had to take. He said it made him rotten inside. Me and Puggy had tried to talk him into giving us some, but he never did. We were always envious of the way Beanie could clear a room. I used to love to take Beanie and sneak up on Max and his girlfriends, but it didn't always work because sometimes Beanie would get too excited and yell, then everybody would scatter. He was a real little guy with a very powerful weapon. A gift, even. Me and Puggy figured Beanie had been blessed with really righteous *pedos* to make up for having that syndrome.

Sister Montoya held Beanie close for a few seconds and when he had calmed down, he went and stood by Chato and they both turned and looked at me through the screen door with real big smiles. It seemed a little strange that they would just stand there and smile at me. Sister Montoya stood there smiling too. Something was definitely up.

"Mario, come here quick! Look," Beanie said, motioning for me to come outside.

Chato didn't say anything. He just kept smiling.

I walked over to the screen door and opened it and looked down to where Beanie was pointing. My mouth opened and gasped. I heard Chato gasp at the same time. Then we both yelled "No way!!" at the same time. We looked at each other, then back down to each other's feet. Neither of us could believe it. We were *both* wearing brand new Keds!

I felt some hands on both of my shoulders. I had forgotten about my mom and Puggy. I looked at them and they were just standing there looking over my shoulder with their eyes real wide and their mouths wide open. Their eyes kept going back and forth from Chato's feet, to my feet, and back to Chato's, then back to mine. They couldn't believe it. I couldn't either. And from the look on Sister Montoya's, Chato's and Beanie's faces, they couldn't either!

Chato looked up at me and we both yelled at the same time, "All right!" Then everybody started talking at once. Sister Montoya came through the screen door and started asking my mom about a big Indian, Puggy and Beanie crowded around me and Chato, patting us on our backs and saying stuff like "Wow!' and "No Way!" and "Now you're really going to be able to run fast!" and "Finky's really going to be jealous!" I felt light headed, but at least I could breathe again. Was it possible to ever be this happy again? Was Heaven going to be like this?

I was thinking of Navajo angels with turquoise velvet jackets and real big wings flying me around the clouds when my mother's voice brought me back to earth.

"Mario!" She didn't sound mad, just kind of serious.

I turned around and looked at her. Sister Montoya was standing by her side with her arms folded and she was giving me that "We know you know something, and we want you to tell us right now" look on her face. My mom just had her normal, sad, and beautiful "It's only by the Grace of God and His miracle saving power that you're still alive" look, that she always had when I would come home after another near disaster.

"What, Mom?" I asked. Puggy, Chato and Beanie stopped talking and turned around and looked at the moms.

"*Mi 'jito,...*" she said quietly, searching for the right words.

I didn't say anything. I couldn't have even if I'd wanted to. I didn't know any words to describe what I was feeling. It was like my brain was foggy with all that was happening. It wasn't a bad feeling. Just foggy.

"*Mi 'jito,*...me and Sister Montoya have to go cook right now. Brother Chavez is probably wondering where we are. But when we get back tonight from the service...then we...we have to talk. OK?" I could tell that she was feeling a little foggy too.

"OK, Mom."

She finished buttoning her coat. "And remember, *do not* talk to Brother Chinche. OK? And do not, under any circumstances, go near that outhouse hole. Your dad says it's still uncovered and I don't want any of you to fall in. Is that clear?"

"Sure, Mom," I said.

Sister Montoya looked at me suspiciously, then walked past me to her two boys.

"And don't let your little brother out of your sight. You hear me?" she said to Chato, brushing down his and Beanie's hair with the palms of her hands. She reached behind their heads and adjusted the rubber bands holding their glasses. "And don't take your glasses off and lose them. They're the only ones you have. All right?"

"Of course, Mom. Besides, how can we lose our glasses with these big ol' rubber bands you have on them?" Chato said, putting his arm around Beanie. "And you know I always watch him good."

"Yeah, Mom," Beanie said, scrunching up his face. "You know he always watches me good."

She turned and looked at me and Puggy. "After the service, you guys all come to the back door and we'll have some hamburgers for you, OK?"

"Alright!" Puggy said, rubbing her hands. "The best hamburgers in the world!"

And she was right, boy. They were the absolutely, positively best, greasiest, grilled onion and mustard dripping down your chin, tastiest hamburgers that I had ever eaten.

The four of us watched as the two moms walked hurriedly down the little dirt road towards the Tabernacle. The sunlight was beginning to fade, and the musicians could be heard warming up over the loudspeaker. Pretty soon my dad would get on the microphone and announce that prayer was starting, and a few minutes after that the small trails would be filled with adults and children walking quickly to the church service, not necessarily to pray, but wanting to get there early to make sure they had a good seat. Especially tonight, because the Ortega Brothers were playing.

****

I closed my eyes and took in a real deep breath and held it. I loved the smell of Chama: cottonwoods, pine needles, the river and fireplaces mingling in with the different cooking aromas. I could hear the sound of the river even with all the other camp noises going on. The runoff had been very high, and I knew that me and Chato should be dead. I slowly let my breath out and opened my eyes. I didn't know what He looked like or where Heaven was, but after today, I knew I would never doubt that there was a God. Today had been crazy, and it still wasn't over.

"C'mon," I said, stepping off the porch. "We need to get a good seat."

"Wait a minute," Puggy said, grabbing my shoulder.

I turned around. She kept looking back and forth from me to Chato.

"What happened today?" she asked.

"Waddaya mean, what happened today?"

"OK, Mario. You and Chato have new Keds. You even have new shorts..."

"What!?" Chato said, interrupting Puggy. "You got new shorts too?"

"Yeah," I said, loosening my belt. "Real ones! Check 'em out!"

"Excuse me!" Puggy said. "I know you guys never think so. But I *am* a girl. So please don't take your pants off in front of me. Besides, there's people all around here, Mario. Are you crazy?"

I looked around. Sure enough, there was some people looking at us. This *did* seem like the perfect time to drop my pants. But because I respected Puggy so much, and because I knew she could drop me quick with a good body block, I re-buckled my belt. Right then my dad's voice came over the loudspeaker announcing that it was prayer time. We had about fifteen minutes before the Tabernacle filled up.

"I'll show you later, Chaht's. They're from J.C. Penney's."

"Really, Mar? Brand-new ones?"

"Yup."

"Wow."

"Thank you," Puggy said, as we started up the road. "Now tell me about today. How come you guys got all this new stuff? And what about this big Indian, Mario? Why did you tell your mom he was an angel? Are you lying again?"

"It's a long story, Pug," I said, looking down at my shoes. They were beautiful. I couldn't wait to show Max.

"Does that mean you're not going to tell me?"

"No. It just means that it's a long story. You know I'll tell you, Pug. Just not right now, OK? We gotta hurry and get a good seat. Ricky Ortega and his two trumpets, 'member?"

"Wait," Puggy said, stopping again.

"C'mon, Pug. We gotta hurry," I said, getting a little annoyed. I turned to face her and my heart skipped a few beats when I spotted *Hermana* Frita and her brother Flotches coming down the trail behind us.

I grabbed Chato and pulled him and Beanie behind one of the cabins. Puggy looked back up the trail and then slowly followed us.

"What are you guys afraid of?" she asked.

I didn't answer her and neither did Chato. We both peeked our heads around the corner of the cabin and watched as *Hermana* Frita and Flotches walked by. My heart stopped when Flotches pointed to where we were hiding and said something about "*Satanas,*" but *Hermana* Frita just kept walking and didn't pay attention to him. She wanted to get a good seat too. Both Chato and I breathed a sigh of relief, and leaned against the cabin.

"I said, what are you guys afraid of?" Puggy asked. She wasn't going to quit.

"Nothing," I said. "I just thought I had to pee real bad. That's why I came back here. But I guess I didn't."

"Is that why you pulled Chato and Beanie back here too? So they could watch you pee?" Puggy asked, narrowing her eyes at me.

"No. I just thought they might want to pee, too."

"Mario, you are such a liar! I know about the outhouse thing."

"What? The outhouse thing? What outhouse thing? Waddaya mean, you know about the outhouse thing? Waddaya talking about?"

"Yeah," Chato said, wide eyed. "Waddaya mean, you know about the outhouse thing?"

Puggy crossed her arms and shook her head. "You both are such pathological liars. Especially you, Mario. Aren't you afraid you're going to be lying when the Rapture happens?"

Yes, of course, I was afraid of that. But I figured if He didn't come back for His people when I had my head under an outhouse looking at people',s butts, then it looked like He would probably wait until I quit lying.

Chato and I looked at each other at the same time and I could tell he had the same question I had. Patha-what? That was a big word. And I knew a lot of pretty big words because my mom made me read a lot. That was my entertainment. My mom had even had me memorize four Psalms before I was even in kindergarten. So I knew some big words. But I had never heard of that one. Puggy must have heard that one on TV.

Puggy's family was one of the lucky Pentecostals who had a TV. We didn't have a TV in our house. My dad said the people would get mad because a lot of them thought it was a sin. *He* didn't think it was a sin. But he wouldn't do some things just because the people of the church thought it was a sin. He wouldn't even go to a movie, although he did let my two older sisters, Rachel and Anna, sneak out to see "The Ten Commandments." And it was a good thing Puggy's dad didn't think it was a sin; otherwise, I would never know what was going on with Annette and the Mickey Mouse Club. I used to daydream about being the first brown boy on there. That's why I liked Annette, because she looked brown. And, she was pretty.

I would ask her later about that "patha" word, but right now I wanted to know what Puggy knew about today.

"Don't worry about me," I said. "I'm going in the Rapture, even if I have to hang on to my mother's leg."

"Yeah, me too," Chato said, nodding his head.

"Yeah, me too. Huh, Chato?" Beanie said, not wanting to be left out.

"That's right," I said. "We're *all* going in the rapture. We'll just stick close to our moms in case it happens when we're still liars."

"You can't do that," Puggy said, making a face. "It's going to happen in a twinkling of an eye. Just like that." She snapped her fingers.

"That's OK. There's supposed to be a loud trumpet right before, right?"

"So," Puggy said, crossing her arms.

"So, when we hear it, we'll just look around for our moms and start running."

"What if your mom is far away?" she asked.

"She'll be close, and I'll be quick."

"Even if your head is under an outhouse?" Puggy asked, with a little smirk on her face.

My heart skipped a beat, and several seconds went by before I realized that I wasn't breathing. How in the world did Puggy know that I had my head under an outhouse? Was she bluffing to see what I would say? Who told her? I turned and looked at Chato, but I could tell by the look on his face that he was just as surprised as I was.

" Mario, I saw you guys from my porch," she said, shaking her head.

Ay, ay, ay! That's right! Puggy's cabin was right next to the river and her porch was the only one around with a perfect view of the outhouse! Did she see everything?

"I saw the whole thing."

Well, I guess I didn't have to ask *that* question.

"Don't worry. I'm not going to tell anybody."

She looked down at the ground and started moving a small rock around with her foot.

"And besides," she said, still playing with the rock, "I knew you and Chato didn't really want to go with Finky and JoJo. But I heard what he told you."

"You heard everything too?" I asked.

Puggy quit playing with the rock and looked up at me. "Mario, my porch has a screen on it, 'member? I can hear *everything* that goes on."

"So you heard everything?"

"Yup. Finky said he would tell everybody you were a homo if you didn't go with him and JoJo."

"You heard that too?"

"Yes, of course I heard it." She looked up and rolled her eyes, then put her hands behind her back and started playing with the rock again.

"Well."

"Well, what?" she said, still looking down at the rock.

I had to ask. "What's a homo?"

"Is it a hobo that comes home at night?" Chato asked. I had forgotten about him and Beanie.

Puggy looked up at me again. "Don't worry, Mario. You're not a homo."

"Really?" I asked, feeling relieved.

"Yes, really," she said.

"And you know what a homo is?"

"Yes."

"And I'm not one."

"That's right. You are definitely not one."

"How do you know?" I asked.

"Because you like girls too much."

"Really?"

"Yes, really."

Wow! It had to do with girls!

"Is Max a homo?" I asked.

Puggy laughed and twirled around in a circle. "No way!" she said, still laughing. "Never! Not that guy!"

Well, that was good. Because if Max wasn't a homo, then *I* didn't want to be one either.

"Well, then, what's a homo?" I asked.

"Yeah, Puggy. Is it a hobo?" Chato asked.

Beanie quickly walked up to his brother's side. "Yeah, Puggy. Is it a hobo?" Beanie asked.

"Huh, Pug, is it?" Chato asked.

"Yeah, Pug, is it?" Beanie asked.

Puggy looked at both brothers, then looked back to me. "Can we talk about this later?" she asked.

"Sure," I said. "Will you tell me what it means?" She must have found out what it meant on TV.

"Yup. Will you tell me what happened when you jumped in the river? I was really worried about you guys. The runoff is high this year."

"Pug," I said, putting my hands on her shoulders, "you are not going to believe me when I tell you. It was unbelievable. You're going to think I'm lying. And I don't blame you. Because I lie about everything. But I promise you, everything that I tell you is going to be the truth. Promise."

"Yeah, Pug, it's the truth," Chato said, coming to my side. "It was unbelievable."

"Yeah, Pug," Beanie said, walking right behind his brother. "It was truly unbelievable!"

We were laughing at Beanie when we heard my dad come on the loudspeaker and make the announcement that the service would be starting in five minutes.

"C'mon!" I said. "We're gonna lose our spot!"

I walked slowly along the side of the cabin back to the trail and made sure no one that we needed to avoid was coming, then motioned for the others to come. We were going to be late. We might have to use Beanie's "special gift" to clear a space for us.

The sun had almost gone down and most of the people were out of their cabins and were either already at the Tabernacle or were hurrying along one of the small trails to get there. It was beginning to get cooler, and with freshly bathed and washed adults and children hurrying past us, the chilly air began to be filled with the unique smells of church: soap, deodorant, all kinds of perfumes, Aqua Velva, Old Spice, Vitalis, *Tres Flores* and whatever other products people wore to make themselves smell good and more presentable. These church smells mingled with the normal delicious camp meeting aromas of fried food, woodburning stoves, and crisp, clean mountain air. Sometimes, the scent of roasting *pinones* would float from one of the cabins. I loved all the different smells. I would even day dream about them when I was in school back in Albuquerque.

We fell in step behind a group of older girls who seemed to all be talking and giggling at the same time. I heard Max's name mentioned a few times and also Ricky, the double trumpet player, and then one of them mentioned something about Finky and they all started laughing. The four of us didn't say anything because it was more fun to listen.

Two of the girls were dressed exactly alike with white blouses, white sweater vests and full purple skirts and they both had real pretty smiles. They were the Baca twins, Monica and Monique, from Salt Lake City. Every summer that we came to Chama, they were here too. Their dad was also a minister and they had always tried to get Max to look at them but he never did. Until this summer. For some reason they looked like they had grown up. Like, they had kinda filled out or something. *I* even liked looking at them, and I knew Max had noticed too, because I had seen him smile at them even when he was surrounded by the other girls. The problem for him, I think, was that *both* of them liked him, and he hadn't yet figured out how to be alone with one of them because they were *always* together. But I knew he would come up with a solution before the camp meeting was over.

One of the other girls turned around and spotted us walking behind them. She whispered something to one of the twins and they all stopped walking and turned around and started giggling.

"Hey, Mario," the twins said, at the same time. Wow! They even talked together. I couldn't tell them apart, so I never said their names.

"Hey," I said. The four of us stopped walking too and just looked at all the girls, who were looking at us and still giggling.

"Those are really nice shoes," they said, pointing down at my new Keds. "Are they brand-new?"

"Uh, yeah," I said. I looked over at Chato, and we both pulled up our pants at the same time so everybody could get a better look. I wondered if this was a good time to show them my new shorts? Nah. Puggy would probably deck me.

"We heard you had a big day today." When the twins said that, all the girls started whispering to each other, while they were *still* giggling!

"What? Whaddaya mean, a big day?" I said, letting my pant legs down.

"Oh, you know," they both said, at the same time, raising their eyebrows up and down like I was supposed to know some secret they knew. Or something like that. I don't know. All I knew was that these girls were driving me crazy. How in the world did Max put up with it? And how did one twin always know what the other one was going to say?

"Do you mean because I almost drowned again? Is that what you're talking about?" I asked. Hoping that it was.

"C'mon, Mario. We know about the outhouse thing." That made the girls quit giggling and just start laughing out loud.

"What outhouse thing?" I asked. Geez! Did everybody in the whole universe know what happened today? I looked accusingly at Puggy, who held up her hands and shook her head. "I didn't say anything to anybody," she said, shrugging her shoulders.

"Well, anyway, where's your brother?" The twins asked, still giggling. When they asked that, the other girls giggling went to an even *higher* pitch. Man, if all this giggling had to go on before the kissing part, I just *knew* I was in trouble. I might not *ever* get a kiss! I wondered if Max wore earplugs before he kissed. I'd have to ask him. But I *was* relieved that they had changed the subject.

"I don't know where he's at. He's probably up there finding a good place to listen to the Ortega Brothers. And if we don't get up there quick, we're going to have to stand outside."

When I said that, the girls all turned around and started running up the trail.

"We still want to talk to you about today, Mario. OK?" the twins said in unison as they ran after the other girls.

I looked at them running, and I just shook my head in amazement. "How in the world do they do that?" I asked, to no one in particular. "How does one twin always know what the other twin is going to say?"

"I don't know." Puggy said. "But if we don't hurry, we're not going to get a good seat either, and we'll end up cruising around the Tabernacle with all the Chama guys."

Puggy was right. Sometimes it was fun cruising around the Tabernacle with all the Chama guys, watching them pick fights with the guys from out of town, even while the preaching was going on. Come to think of it, I don't think I ever saw a Chama guy sit down in the Tabernacle even when there *was* room. This was their big time of the year too, and I don't think they wanted to waste it by going to church. They probably figured they could go to church *anytime*, but they weren't always going to get the chance to pick a fight with a Utah guy, or try to kiss a girl from Colorado. The camp meeting only happened once a year, so they were going to take advantage of it. But tonight was not the night to cruise. Tonight, the Ortega Brothers were singing, and we needed to get into the Tabernacle quick.

Right then my dad's voice came over the loudspeaker. He was opening the service in prayer and we were barely getting to the stairs at the bottom of the hill! Normally we would stop and look for empty Popsicle boxes to slide down the wooden hand railings, but my dad's prayer was almost over and the music was about to start. So we just ran up two stairs at a time, rushed past the *comedor* and it's delicious, greasy smells. We were in such a hurry that we didn't even look in to see if our moms could sneak us a few French fries. We quickly passed several families hurrying to get good seats too, turned the corner, and stopped dead in our tracks. The big side door was jammed with people trying to get in. I heard Puggy groan.

"I knew we should've come earlier, Mario," she said, shaking her head. "Man alive, we'll never get in there now. Look at all those people."

"C'mon," I said, grabbing her and Chato at the same time. I pushed my way through the crowd and headed for the left front window. Puggy, Chato and Beanie were following close behind. The left front window of the Tabernacle was Max's favorite window. He never sat in the church services either. But he always made sure he had a good spot to hear the special music *before* he took off with the girls.

There were four windows on each side of the Tabernacle, and the bottoms of the windows were about waist high to an adult, so they were perfect for those people who just wanted to look, but didn't want to commit. Especially the front windows, because they were close to the altar area where the bands played. And I knew Max and the Chama guys didn't want to sit in for the preaching, because sometimes the Spirit would move very heavily in there, and they were afraid they might get saved again. And if they went and did that, then they wouldn't be able to go around fighting and kissing. So they would usually wait till the last day of the camp meeting to get saved, because by then most of the people and the pretty girls had already left. That's why you could always find them cruising by the windows, or standing next to them.

Three years ago, Floriancito and Buddy had offered me a quarter and dared me to throw a lit cherry bomb into the right front window while Brother Savage was preaching. I knew I was going to get beat pretty good if I got caught, so I held out for three quarters. Back when I was a *little* kid, I would do *anything* for a quarter. Well, they gave me the quarters, then lit the cherry bomb. I took it and tossed it right through the open window and then took off running. I didn't stay around for the explosion.

I heard later that when the cherry bomb exploded, some people started screaming and thought that the Rapture was happening. Others thought it was the devil coming after them because of their sins. And then they all started running to the altar, crying. Old Brother Mares, who had been filming the service like he did every year, got real scared and dropped his camera with the four big spotlights that always blinded everybody, because the cherry bomb had landed right by his foot. And poor Brother Savage, who had turned even *whiter* when the explosion happened, let go of his notes and his Bible, fell to his knees and covered his head. He probably thought the building was falling. He opened his eyes in time to see the people rushing to the altar and got up a little shaky and began praying for everybody. They said he looked a little confused, but happy, because he had never preached a sermon that had caused so much conviction. Max told me later, when I had confessed to him that Floriancito had dared me to do it, that it was OK because it had been an "explosive sermon" and that people had gotten a "big bang" out of it. Sometimes Max was pretty funny.

So instead of causing a disaster, the cherry bomb incident (as it became known) actually got people *saved*! Can you believe *that*!?! My mom said that even when the Devil wanted something to turn out bad, God always made it turn out good. And that's why I only got *one* swat with the fly swatter instead of many. *Nobody,* including Brother Chinche and his police force, could in fact *prove* I had done it. Except my mom, of course, who didn't *have* to prove that I had done it, because she just *knew* that I had done it. But it's a good thing the Rapture *didn't* happen then because I would've definitely been left behind with all the Chama guys. Whew! Putting my head under an outhouse to see butts. Throwing cherry bombs in the Tabernacle. Lying about everything. Why in the world would God even *bother* with me? Why would He send a Navajo Angel to rescue me, and talk to me? Could He really save a ten-year-old kid like me? Wow!

Well, anyway, when we finally got to the window, I saw immediately that the twins and the other girls had beat us to Max and his buddies and were crowding around them. Max had his arm around one of the twin's waist and he was holding the hand of the other one. Oh, boy. I hoped he knew what he was doing.

The song service had already started and the lively sounds coming from inside made my heart beat a little faster. There was nothing like a good, old-fashioned Pentecostal song service.

I pushed my way to the front of the window right in front of Max. He looked down at me and saw me smiling and pointing down to my new Keds. When he saw them he got a big smile on his face and he let go of the twins.

"Hey, man!" he said, bending down to touch my shoes. "I heard. Brand-new Keds. Wow! That's crazy! Some big Indian guy, huh?" I turned around so that he could see the little blue Keds label in the back.

I turned back around and started unbuckling my belt. "Yeah, but he wasn't just some big Indian guy. You wanna see crazy?" I asked, getting ready to drop my pants and show him my new J.C. Penney shorts.

Max grabbed my belt before I could take my pants off. "Hey, hey! Not here, Mar. Not here," he said, in my ear. "Show me tonight when we get back to the cabin, Ok?"

"Are you sure?" I asked. I really wanted him to see my new underwear.

"Yeah, I'm sure," he said looking back up to the twins and smiling. I don't think they would have cared if I would've dropped my pants *and* my shorts, as long as they could stand next to Max.

"All right," I said, disappointed.

"You guys wanna get in?" Max asked, looking at the four of us. I could hear the music going full blast through the open window.

"Is there any room?" I asked.

"There's a few spaces on the front bench next to some Bible School guys, but you better hurry."

I didn't wait for him to finish; I had already climbed up the window and jumped onto the soft sawdust floor of the Tabernacle. The smell was great, just like a lumber yard, only with people smells. Puggy was next and Chato came right after her. She didn't care that she had a dress on because she always wore Bermuda shorts underneath just in case we had to play an emergency football game.

Max picked up Beanie and put him on the window sill.

"Hey, Bean Man. You gonna bless us with your "gift" tonight?" Max asked him, as he put him down on the sawdust. The girls heard him ask, so of course they started giggling again. Beanie's gift was well known.

"Yeah, pro'bly," Beanie said, looking back up at Max and smiling. "But only if I have to."

Max laughed and went back to the twins, and the four of us made our way to the front bench.

I turned to say something to Puggy but the music coming from the band and the singers on stage along with the steady roar of the clapping, shouting and singing of the congregation was so loud that even when I yelled at her I couldn't hear myself. It was great. Some people were already so full of the

Spirit that they were doing their little Pentecostal skipping dance in front of the stage. My dad called it the "Holy Ghost Two Step." I used to try it in front of the mirror when no one was watching. I almost had it down, but I wasn't quite ready to join the other dancers. Maybe one of these days. Others were twirling around in time with the music and Brother Mares was in his familiar place by the right front window and was wandering around blinding everybody with the lights on his movie camera. The Bible School students didn't even notice when we came and stood next to them. And that was good, because with all the coats piled up in the empty spaces on the bench, it looked like they were saving these places for somebody else.

I moved the coats to where the students were standing, hoping they wouldn't notice us, and when they didn't, I turned to Puggy and smiled. She smiled back and we started clapping and singing with everybody else.

"No hay Dios tan grande como tu,
no lo hay, no lo hay
No hay Dios tan grande como tu,
No lo hay, no lo hay.
No hay dios que puede hacer las obras,
Como las que haces tu.
No hay Dios que puede hacer las obras,
Como las que haces tu."

Then when that *corito* stopped, the band started another fast one. And then another, and another. After about the fourth or fifth song, the Bible School students finally noticed us, but by that time, even *they* were so much in the Spirit that they just looked at us and smiled. And they must've *really* been in the Spirit, because they *never* smiled at me. Especially when Beanie tagged along. That must be what my dad meant when he said that being in the "*Presence*" would change *anybody*. He said a person had to be dead not to feel it.

93

I asked him if all religions had the *"Presence."* He said they should, but they didn't. He said that most religions were afraid of the *"Presence"* because they couldn't explain *"Him."* He said even some Assembly of God churches didn't have the *"Presence."* He only said that to me, though, because the people in the church would have gotten mad at him if he would have told them. My dad used to answer me like that when I would ask him a question. Like he knew I would be OK with the truth about things. Almost like he was giving me information for future use. I had a feeling that he was going to be all right with the news that God wasn't Assembly of God. It was my mother I was worried about.

The band stopped playing fast songs and started playing slower worship songs, and the shouting and clapping and dancing of the people slowly turned to weeping and lifting up of their faces and hands toward the wooden roof. Some people got on their knees in the aisles and some even got on their faces on the wooden floor in front of the stage. This was the part of the service where I *always* felt the *"Presence."* I didn't know what it meant exactly, but I *did* know this was the *"Presence"* my dad talked about. I would get goosebumps sometimes. I heard him tell his good friend Brother Giron one time that the reason so many people come to this little mountain village every summer from all over was because the *"Presence"* was so real and heavy here.

I turned to say something to Puggy, but even she had her eyes closed. Chato and Beanie had their eyes closed too and the four of us were swaying from side to side in time to the music. Wow! Even though none of us was sure what it meant, the *"Presence"* even touched little kids who were always in trouble!

The worship leader had his arms lifted and was leading the congregation in one of my favorites:

"Paz. paz, cuan dulce paz,
es aquella que el Padre me da,
Yo le ruego que inunde
Por siempre mi ser,
Con sus
Ondas de amor celestial."

The song was about peace. And that's what I felt every time I heard it. I wish I could explain it. But I can't. Some things you just have to be there to know what a person is talking about. And that's why I thought every other church I had gone to was boring. Especially the times I had gone to a Catholic church. Whew! Those poor guys! How could they take sitting in there so long without the *"Presence?"* I guess they were one of the ones that were afraid of *"Him."* Before he drowned, I had asked my little friend Jimmy, who was Catholic, to go to one of our church services. I told him all about the music and the dancing and all the instruments and about the goosebumps and that it was a lot of fun. He said he wanted to, but he told me his mom wouldn't let him because church wasn't *supposed* to be fun. Whew! Those poor guys!

I sat down on the bench while everyone was getting "blessed" and just thought about how lucky I was that even before today when I wasn't absolutely sure about whether God existed or not, and even when I did all the crazy things that made my mom and dad worry about me so much, and even when I put my head under an outhouse, God *still* let me feel the *"Presence."*

This is how I felt whenever I heard my mom praying or singing in tongues when I came home from school. Just like this. Very peaceful. No talking. No moving around. Just being able to sit there and actually *feel* that heavy and powerful thing that surrounded the air in my living room and also here in the Tabernacle. Like someone real close to me that I knew real well, but I could never see or touch. When I asked my dad about how I felt, he said not worry about it, because even though I couldn't touch Him, He would *"always* reach out and

95

touch me." I guess that's why even Jose and Joey, Virgie's drunk brothers, could go to Foster's Bar in town and drink all day, then come and cry at the altar and get saved every night. Even *they* felt the *"Presence."*

The music had stopped but the people were still praising, praying and crying out loud. Some were praising in Spanish, some in English, and others were praising in tongues. It was just an incredible sound. Every time I heard it like this, It reminded me of what my Sunday School teacher, Sister Velma, had told us about the day the Holy Spirit had come into the Upper Room with fire and a "mighty rushing wind." And how everyone there, including Mary, the mother of Jesus, she said, had gotten baptized in the Holy Spirit and had started to speak in other tongues. And that the people from all these other countries who were in Jerusalem at the time heard what was going on and were "amazed," she said, that these other people who weren't even from their country were praising God in the other country's language! She also said that a lot of people didn't believe that the Holy Spirit could visit us like that today, because people are naturally afraid of something they can't figure out with their brains. And that's why they make fun of us and call us *"Aleluyas,"* she said, because we didn't *try* to figure it out, we just took a "simple step of faith and let it happen." I liked Sister Velma. She never tried to complicate things. She just always said it like it was. Like my dad. Of course, sometimes, she had to kick me out of her class because I was too *travieso.* But, anyway, that's what I thought of every time I heard all these different languages.

All the different voices in the Tabernacle gradually quieted down, except for one voice that sounded like it was coming from the back. It was a woman's voice, and she was crying as she spoke. It wasn't very loud, and even though it was coming from the back, you could hear exactly what she was saying. And she was saying it in tongues. Whenever this happened, I would always get the chills. I don't know why, but every time there was a true message in tongues, I just always got the chills. She sounded desperate as she gave the message. And then she finished, and everyone was very still, and waited. A few people coughed and cleared their throats, and some others were crying softly, but no one was moving around. Even the cruisers by the windows had stopped talking and giggling.

Sometimes I almost couldn't stand it during this time. The *"Presence"* had surrounded the air extra thick, and it seemed like it was getting harder to breathe. Like the air was pushing down on me. I looked at my dad on the stage, and he had his head bowed and his hands clasped together in front of his mouth. I bowed my head also and was thinking about where I would be right now if I would have drowned today, when all of a sudden this big, booming man's voice right behind me made me jump about a foot off the bench and made my hair stand up. It was a good thing I had used the bathroom before church or else I probably would have stained my brand new shorts. I heard a little squeak come from Puggy, Beanie let out a good "a-HAY-ya!" and even the Bible School students had jumped a little. But nobody really noticed us, because the man was giving the interpretation to the message in tongues and everybody was paying close attention to what he said because they wanted to hear what it was.

The interpretation was in Spanish and the part that I could understand what the man said had to do with the Holy Spirit letting us know that He was there and He was going to do great things in Chama, not necessarily at the camp meetings, but in the village of Chama itself. Some of them might not see it in their lifetime. But He *was* going to do it, because God said that Chama was special to Him, and all we had to do was "humble ourselves and pray." He said more, but that was the part I understood. When the man finished the people started clapping and shouting thanks to God. I looked at my dad and he had his hands lifted and he was shouting with everybody else. So I stood to my feet and started shouting too. I looked over at Puggy and Chato and Beanie and they were also on their feet clapping and shouting too. A good ol' *"Aleluya"* service--the only place in the universe where a kid could jump, clap, dance around and shout without getting into trouble! In fact, we were *encouraged* to do those things! Wow! And this was only the beginning! We still had the Ortega Brothers to go!

After awhile the clapping and shouting gradually died down and the people began to return to their places. Everybody had a big smile on their face. The Holy Spirit had spoken. No matter what happened the rest of the night, the Holy Spirit had spoken--And we had all been present to hear Him. How much of a privilege was *that*? Wow!

I turned to Puggy and saw that she and Chato and Beanie had sat down again. They had big smiles on their faces too. It hadn't seemed like it, but the entire worship service had taken a little over an hour. Some nights it took a lot longer, because *Aleluyas* loved to sing, but tonight I think the worship leader had been instructed to shorten it to give plenty of time to the special music.

The worship leader sat down and my dad went up to the microphone and told the people, wasn't it great that the Holy Spirit loved us enough to speak to us? There was more shouting and clapping as the people agreed with him. He held his arms up, and when it had quieted down again he made some announcements about the next days' business meetings and he reminded the people that the *comedor* had plenty of good food for after the service. Then he surprised us all by calling up Brother Savage to sing "Forty Years Ago" with his banjo, and said not to worry because the Ortega Brothers were going to be there shortly. Brother Savage singing was one of the big traditions at the camp meeting. We could never have a successful Chama without him singing "Forty Years Ago" at least two or three times. And normally everybody would love it, but tonight we were all waiting to hear the two trumpets of Ricky Ortega.

When Brother Savage finished, the Tabernacle was humming with anticipation, but my dad went to the microphone and drove the crowd a little bit crazier by bringing up Brother Giron to sing "Jericho Road," which was another great tradition, but you could sense by the little groan that went up that the congregation was getting a little restless. My dad looked like he was having a good time teasing everybody, but I hoped he wasn't going to bring up any more warm-up groups. At this moment he was pretty popular with the people. And I wanted to keep it that way. It helped a kid who was always in trouble, to have his dad not only be the "Big Cheese" in camp, but to be a *well liked* "Big Cheese."

Brother Giron finally finished and my dad went up to the mic, smiled at everybody, and said, "Are you ready?" And just as he was getting ready to say something else, my heart skipped a beat and a big buzz and a lot of "oohs" and "ahhs" went up from the congregation because right there in front of us, climbing up the steps and walking through the back door on the right side of the stage came Ricky and Art Ortega and their two uncles. Ricky was carrying his two trumpets and a small double trumpet stand and the other three were carrying their guitars. I heard the Bible School girls next to us sigh, "There he is!" and then start giggling. Of course.

Puggy nudged me on the side and we both smiled at each other. I looked past her and saw Chato and Beanie scoot to the front edge of the bench. Their legs didn't reach the sawdust, but they didn't care. They were ready to jump off when the trumpets started anyway.

Alright. We were ready. The Ortega Brothers. Brand-new Keds. Brand-new J.C. Penney boys' underwear. Brother Chinche and his flashlight nowhere in sight. No more warm-up acts. I was here instead of at the bottom of the river. I had a great big Navajo Angel who smelled like my grandmother's kitchen. My favorite band was getting ready to play. Wow! Was there a God, or what?!?

I looked back to the stage and listened as my dad introduced the group. He said something about "Michigan" and then everyone started clapping. The stage guys had put up three microphones. Ricky and Art had their own and the uncles shared one. I was disappointed that Ricky had on a suit instead of the white tee shirt with the rolled up sleeves he wore around the campground. I wanted to see his tattoos. Max said he had gotten them while he was in jail. The first time I had seen them, I had gone back to Albuquerque and asked my cousin Benjie to tattoo Virgie's name on my hand. He was as old as Max and he had told me one time that if I ever wanted a tattoo, he had some India Ink and a needle, and he would do it.

Well, we spelled her name out on the top of my hand with the ink and he started poking me with the needle. But before he could finish, my mom walked into the room and screamed at us and whacked us both with a fly swatter. So when I wiped off the ink and the blood, only a little bit of the "V" was showing. It wasn't a very good tattoo, but I was proud of it, and I hoped one day to show it to Virgie. Of course, that was going to be difficult, being that she never even *looked* at me, except to give me a dirty look.

The music started and everyone got to their feet and started swaying to the beat. The first three songs were Spanish ones and when they would finish one, first Art would say something and then Ricky would say something, like a joke or something or part of their testimony and then they would play another song. Then Ricky talked about when he was in jail, then Art talked about how he and his mom would always cry for him and pray for him and how one day Ricky made his mom real happy by throwing away his cigarettes. And when they got to the cigarette part, everybody would cheer and clap because cigarettes were a big deal with Assembly of God people, and how he finally gave up his life of crime and got saved. I had heard it before, but I never got tired of it. And neither did anybody else. It was great. I wondered if I would ever have a testimony. I didn't want to start smoking because it stunk. I got *asco* just remembering the taste of kissing Cheri after we had smoked her dad's cigars, but I thought maybe I should start anyway just so that I could quit and have a testimony. I wondered if Virgie would like me if I had a cigarette testimony. Probably not.

Art introduced his uncles and they said a little bit. Then Art asked, "Is everybody feeling fine?" When he asked that the Tabernacle went crazy. Then he asked it again and the people screamed even louder. When he would ask that, it could only mean one thing: They were going to sing "Feelin' Mighty Fine," my all-time, forever and eternity, favorite song. And the song in which Ricky picked up *both* trumpets and played them at the same time! This was also the place in the program when all the kids in the Tabernacle would run up to the stage to get a better look.

Me and Puggy got to the stage first with Chato and Beanie right behind us. We wanted to make sure we got to the best spot, which was right in front of Ricky and his two trumpets. When we got there, Ricky looked down at us and *smiled*! He actually *smiled* at us! I got so excited that I held up the back of my hand to show him my little one line tattoo. He must've thought I had something physically wrong with me that I couldn't put my hand the right way so he reached down and put the back of his hand on the back of my hand! Then he started moving my hand from side to side! Wow! There we were, me and Ricky Ortega, the best musician in the whole world, in front of everybody, shaking hands *backwards*!

His uncles started playing the guitars for the beginning of the song, so Ricky quit moving my hand, but before he picked up his trumpets, he smiled at me again and rubbed the top of my head. Wow! Ricky Ortega had rubbed my head *and* smiled at me! This was too much. I was smiling so much my cheeks were beginning to hurt. I even felt kinda dizzy. I looked at Puggy and she was smiling just as big as me and she was patting me on the back. Wow! Could life get any better? I turned back just as the group started singing the first verse. And me and Puggy sang right along with them. We knew the whole thing by heart. Sometimes in Albuquerque when we would play church, she and I would act like we were the Ortega Brothers and we would sing "Feelin' Mighty Fine" for the neighborhood kids. Except we would just fake like we were playing two trumpets.

It was nice and loud where we were standing, and I could barely hear myself sing:

"Well, I woke up this morning feelin' fine.
I woke up with Heaven on my mind.
I woke up with joy in my soul,
For I knew the Lord had control.
Well, I knew I was walking in the Light,
'Cause I stayed on my knees in the night.
And I prayed till the Lord He gave a sign.
And now I'm feelin' mighty fine.

Oh, well, I'm feelin' mighty fine.
I've got Heaven on my mind.
Oh, don't you know, I want to go
Where the milk and honey flow.
There's a light that always shines,
Deep inside this heart of mine.
Well, I've got Heaven, Heaven on my mind.
And now, I'm feelin' mighty fine."

After the first verse and chorus, the place was "rockin," as Max would say. Even though we didn't have a TV, Max always knew the latest things people were saying because he would listen to the rock- and -roll station with his friends. One time when we were in church in Albuquerque, the people had started dancing in the Spirit and he turned to me and said, "This place is rockin', man." I had nodded my head and acted like I knew what he was talking about, but I didn't. But now, with all the kids moving back and forth and clapping our hands, this must be what he meant.

The band started singing the second verse and I could feel the excitement level go up because we all knew that right after this Ricky would play his two trumpets.

"Well, I'm walking and talking as I climb.
I'm talking to Jesus all the time.
I'm taking that road to the sky,
Where I know I'll live when I die.
He's been telling me all about that land,
And He tells me that everything is grand,
And He says that this home will be mine,
And now I'm feelin' mighty fine."

They started singing the chorus and Ricky turned and picked up his trumpets. He blew into both of them to clear the spit out and he pushed the valves up and down to make sure they were working OK, then he put both of them to his lips and walked up to the microphone right as they were getting to the end of the chorus.

"...Well, I've got Heaven, Heaven on my mind.
And now I'm feelin' mighty fine."

Right when they finished singing he started playing both trumpets. I just couldn't believe it. Someone being able to play two trumpets at the same time. But there he was. Right in front of me. And boy did it sound good. Now people started jumping and shouting, and some were even twirling around. Old Brother Mares had jumped on the stage and was blinding everybody with his movie lights, but I didn't care. I even twirled around a few times. Ricky Ortega and his two trumpets. And I was two feet from him. The place was going crazy. I got tears in my eyes, and I thanked God over and over and over, for not letting me and Chato drown that day.

"As a matter of fact," I said, as the tears came down my cheeks, "Thanks for not letting me drown all the times I was *supposed* to drown." I was pretty sure He had heard me. He hears everything. Even when it's noisy.

Ricky finished playing the verse and when he started on the chorus his uncles and Art started singing along with the trumpets. So did everybody else. And when they finished, the

place *really* went wild. Ricky smiled real big and held up both trumpets over his head and me and Puggy started jumping up and down and clapping with the rest of the kids. I wondered if Heaven was like this. My mom told me that the Angel Gabriel played the trumpet. So maybe there was a band of a jillion angels in Heaven and a choir of another jillion angels and there would be a concert going on all the time. Wow! Maybe when Ricky got to Heaven, he could teach Gabriel how to play *two* trumpets. Heck, maybe they would even let him play in the band! Oh man, now *that* would be something to see *and* hear! Whew!

Ricky and Art both put their instruments down and so did the uncles. Then they took a step forward and held hands and lifted them over their heads and then they all took a bow at the same time. When they did this Ricky's head came real close to me and Puggy so we rubbed *his* head and patted him on the back. He looked up at both of us and smiled, then he rubbed *our* heads, patted our shoulders and then waved at the people as he and the rest of the band picked up their instruments, and walked off the stage, and right out the same back door that they had come in from.

My dad came to one of the mics and said something, but I couldn't understand him because I was still kinda' numb from the music blasting in my ears and Ricky rubbing my head. Everybody started going back to their chairs and Puggy grabbed my arm and pulled me because my legs weren't moving real good. She turned and gave me her raised-eyebrow look and motioned with her head and that could only mean "It's time to get outta here."

And she was right. This was the perfect time to leave. While everybody was going back to their seats we would just go right out the door and nobody would notice. My mom was cooking in the *comedor,* my dad was on the stage, my brother was occupied, as usual, with all his girls, and as long as my sister Sarai and Brother Chinche didn't see me, we were in the clear.

I grabbed Chato and Puggy grabbed Beanie and the four of us walked down the sawdust aisle right out the door. I looked around to make sure the coast was clear, then motioned for Puggy and the boys to come out.

****

The air was crisp and cold and the smells coming from the *comedor* made my mouth water. We would head there later to pick up those greasy burgers that Chato's mom had promised us. But right now it was time to cool down from all the heat in the Tabernacle, and cruise around with the rest of the cruisers and see who was trying to be with who tonight.

We headed towards the back of the Tabernacle and passed by Solomon and Sisto and some of the Chama guys who were following some giggling Utah girls and trying to talk to them. When Solomon saw us, he smiled real big and moved his eyebrows up and down like he might actually get lucky tonight and maybe get to hold one of their hands or something. But I could tell they didn't even understand what he was *saying*, so he probably was going to end up holding his own hand. Those poor guys. They would practically *beg* the girls to talk to them, and maybe, just *maybe*, the girls would stop and talk to them. That's why they all liked hanging around with Max. Because all Max had to do was walk somewhere and just *stand*, and he would instantly be surrounded by girls. I'm serious. I had seen it with my own eyes. All he had to do was *stand*, and *BOOM!* There were the girls.

Earlier in the week he had come to see me play softball against the Wyoming guys. I came up to bat and he came and leaned against the backstop to watch. I hit the first pitch and rounded first base and looked back to see if he had seen me, and there he was, surrounded by about ten girls, not even paying attention to his little brother. Although he did say "Good hit, kid," when I crossed home plate.

We smiled back at Solomon and I heard Puggy say "Oh, brother. That boy needs to get his hormones under control."

I stopped and looked at her. "What?" I asked.

"What," she said, rolling her eyes.

"What was that you said? Hor what?"

"Hormones," she said. We started walking again.

"What are those?" I asked.

"Yeah, Puggy. What's a horbone?" Beanie asked. He was walking close behind and was listening, as usual, to everything we said.

"HorMONE. M-o-n-e, not horbone, hor*mone*. And you don't need to be asking about any of these things, Bean. You're too young." Puggy turned while she was walking and rubbed Beanie's head. Chato didn't say anything, but I knew he wanted to know too.

"So what is it?" I asked, getting a little impatient. It was probably another word she had learned watching TV.

"Don't worry. If you're anything like your brother, you'll be finding out sooner than most guys." She looked at me, gave me her "oh, brother" look and shook her head.

"Is that bad or good?" I asked.

"Well, in your case, it'll probably be good."

"Yeah?" I asked, relieved.

"Yeah, but it all depends," she said.

"Depends?" I was worried again. "Depends on what? It's not like being a homo or anything, is it?"

We stopped walking and Puggy put both her hands on my shoulders. "No, Mario," she said, in her best mother's tone of voice. "It's not like being a homo. Everybody has hormones. But it all depends on how cute a person is. See all these people walking around wanting to kiss each other?"

I turned and looked at all the groups of girls and boys passing us by. Some were holding hands. Some were laughing. Some were sweating. The sweating guys I *knew* were in trouble. Max told me girls didn't like guys who sweated. He said it was like holding hands with a wet rag. And to always chew gum, because girls didn't like stinky breath either. I nodded my head. "Yeah, I see 'em," I said.

"Well," Puggy said, taking her arms off my shoulders and spreading out her arms, "that's what hormones are all about."

"It's about trying to get someone to kiss you?" I asked.

"Yup, mainly that's what they're all about," Puggy said. We started walking again. "And most of these guys have as many hormones as your brother; they're just not as cute."

"What? Wait a minute," I said, grabbing her arm and stopping. "So you think Max is cute, huh? How come you never told me?" I leaned closer to her. Chato and Beanie leaned with me. "Does anybody else know?" I whispered.

She looked at me like I was the dumbest guy in the world.

"Mario," she said, leaning *her* face even closer to mine, *"all* the girls think Max is cute. Besides," she said, taking my hand off her arm, "he doesn't sweat, and that makes him even cuter. C'mon," she said, turning to walk again, "if we keep stopping, we're gonna miss all the action."

"Does it count if you sweat jumping up and down, singing "Feelin' Mighty Fine?" I asked, keeping in step with her. I had definitely sweated tonight. I sniffed my underarms to make sure I didn't stink. Chato and Beanie did the same. Max told me to always use his Old Spice just in case.

"In case of what?" I had asked him.

"In case you get lucky, man." he said, laughing.

"Lucky? Waddaya mean, lucky?"

"Never mind. Just put some on. If some incredible miracle happens and Virgie actually talks to you, you're gonna wanna make sure that you're smelling good."

But tonight, I had been so excited about my new Keds and authentic J.C. Penney boys' underwear, that I had forgotten to put some on. But that was OK. The chances of Virgie talking to me were pretty slim, especially after she thought she heard me screaming in back of the outhouse today.

"Nah," Puggy said, "sweating in church doesn't count. Everybody sweats then. Only when you're trying to hold hands or get a kiss--try not to sweat then."

"So then you think I might actually get kissed one of these days?"

"You told me you kissed Cherie, didn't you? Or were you lying?"

"Nuh-uh. It was a real kiss all right." But I didn't really count that because we were smoking cigars. My stomach turned a little just thinking about it.

We rounded the corner to the back of the Tabernacle and almost ran into the three Madrid sisters with their purple and gold Chama Wildcats letter sweaters. I could not remember a year when the sisters were not in the back checking out the action in their letter sweaters. They looked like triplets, same big smiles, same big hairdos, same way of standing, but I knew they weren't. They were nice enough, and I loved their smiles. Maybe this was their year to get lucky.

"Hey, Mario," they said, at the same time. I thought maybe they had been hanging out with the twins. "You're not gonna throw a cherry bomb in the Tabernacle tonight, are you?" They put their heads together and had a good laugh.

"I wasn't planning on it. But if you got some cash, then maybe we can work something out," I said, holding my hand out.

"No way, you crazy little kid. '*Tu estas loco*.'" The older one said. Then they all laughed again.

Yeah, I thought, maybe I am loco. But I knew I wasn't loco enough to throw a cherry bomb in the church for less than two bucks. If I was going to get chased and whipped, then it was going to have to be worth it. Besides, I heard my dad was preaching tonight, and I would *never* throw a cherry bomb while he was preaching.

We left the laughing Madrid sisters and their letter sweaters by the two, big back doors and went around the corner to the baseball field side of the Tabernacle and saw a group of kids our age and a little bit older gathered around somebody, but we couldn't see who it was, so we pushed our way in closer to get a better look, and stood in back of this girl with long, jet black hair that everybody, but mainly the boys, were all trying to talk to at the same time. She had a bright blue dress on and every time she would say something, the older boys would laugh real loud like it was the most hysterical thing they ever heard, and then they would move from side to side and try to act like *pachucos* and give their best Max impression, and the younger guys like me just stared with a goofy smile on their lips. Guys my age *never* knew how to act around girls.

I looked around the group and froze when I spotted Sarai and Virgie looking at me. Oh-oh. I was in trouble. My insane sister standing with the love of my life who hated me. They both put their hands on their hips, narrowed their eyes and gave me their best "What in the world are *you* doing here?" look. I started to move back from the group when one of the older boys spotted me. He was one of the guys from Colorado that hung out with Finky and JoJo.

"Hey, Mario. Put your head under any outhouses lately?"

He turned to his friends and they all started laughing.

"Only when your mother goes in," I said.

I have no idea why I said that. I had never said that in my life. I had heard Finky say stuff like that. But I had *never* said anything like that. A gasp went up from the group. I even heard Puggy gasp. I felt my head start to get hot and my eyes started filling with tears. I *hated* to be embarrassed in front of my friends. *Especially* with Virgie and my sister standing there.

Right then, the girl with the long black hair and the bright blue dress turned and looked at me, and when she did, I heard a little groan come from my mouth and my head got even *hotter*. I had never seen a human being as beautiful as this girl. Not Virgie, not even the pictures my sister had of Marilyn Monroe. As a matter of fact, compared to this girl, Virgie, all of a sudden, looked kind of plain. Almost like an old, beat-up, Raggedy Ann doll, compared to a brand-new, beautiful doll. This new girl's eyes were almost the color of her dress. Only mixed with green. I had never seen a girl with eyes like that. I didn't know God could make someone this beautiful. My legs began to feel weak, and all I could do was stare at her. No wonder all the boys were standing around her.

The boy quit laughing, and after the shock of hearing what I had to say about his mother began to wear off, he started coming towards me.

"Whajya say?" he said, clenching his fists. I quit gawking at the girl and reluctantly looked back at the boy I had insulted. Even though he was bigger than me, I remembered that I had tackled him before when we had played football. He had gone down real easy then. If I could just tackle him before he swung at me, then maybe I could sit on top of him and hopefully get in a few good whacks before his buddies jumped on me.

"Maybe you could hear better if you took your head out of your ass," I said. There I went again! I couldn't stop! I just couldn't stop. Oh, my God! What was wrong with me? I was the Superintendent's son. I had just come out of church. The Holy Spirit had been moving heavy in there. I had *felt* Him! And here I was, cussing like Jose and Joey! Could God forgive me? Would He even *want* to now? Would He regret not letting me drown today? Was there a special place in hell for little preachers' kids who said the 'a-s-s' word? My heart was pounding hard against my chest. I couldn't believe that after being so close to making things right with God, here I was messing it up again!

Well, an even bigger gasp went up from the group after I said what I did. I looked over at my sister and Virgie and they were both looking at me with their mouths open and their eyes real wide. Even the boy with the clenched fists stopped and looked at me with his mouth wide open. I looked back at the girl with the blue green eyes and saw that she wasn't staring at me with her mouth open like everybody else. She was *smiling* at me! She was actually *smiling* at me!

I begin to sweat and to feel even weaker. And right before you're going to get jumped is not a good time to feel weak. And when the *new,* most beautiful girl in the universe was

smiling at you with the most gorgeous eyes ever created, was not the best time to sweat! Why was she smiling at me? No pretty girls *ever* smiled at me. At least not to my face. Puggy told me that a couple of girls had told her that I was cute, but I knew they only wanted to talk to me so they could meet Max. But for some reason, this beautiful girl was smiling at *me*! Just me! I saw the boy out of the corner of my eye. He was still coming at me, but I couldn't take my eyes off this girl.

She took a few steps towards me, crossed her arms, and then kind of leaned on one leg, and stood right in front of me. I mean, right in *front* of me! When she did that, the boy stopped coming at me, otherwise he would have run right into her, and it seemed like everybody had stopped talking.

"So *you're* the world-famous Mario," she said.

I *was*? Me? I knew that if I didn't start breathing pretty soon I was going to be the world-famous *dead* Mario. And I especially didn't want to die until I had asked God to forgive me for saying the a-s-s word.

She looked down at my feet, then back up to my face.

"Those are pretty nice shoes; are they new?" she asked, smiling.

"Uh...yeah...uh." She was so beautiful, and her smile had made me so weak and breathless, I had forgotten all about my new Keds.

"I've heard all about you, Mario Santos," she said.

You *have*? Oh, my God! She smiled real big and her teeth sparkled! They actually sparkled! And they were real straight! Unlike mine, which were all over my gums. Max told me that when I grew up, I was probably going to have a couple of teeth coming out of my forehead.

"Uh...I...uh," I heard myself mumble. I couldn't breathe, much less talk. Oh, man! I had forgotten to chew some gum! I felt the sweat drip off my nose. This was definitely not good. No gum, and I was sweating like a rainbow trout.

"Are you really as crazy as they say? Did you really throw a cherry bomb in the Tabernacle while Brother Savage was preaching?" she asked. Those were the straightest and most beautiful teeth I had ever seen! My mom told me one time that King Solomon's wife had teeth that looked like goats. I could never figure out how come a guy who had his pick of all the girls in the world would choose one whose teeth looked like goats.

"Well...uh...uh." I couldn't think. I couldn't *breathe*! If those unbelievable, blue-green eyes kept looking at me and those beautiful sparkling teeth kept smiling at me, then I thought I was going to faint. Or pee in my pants. Or both!

By this time an even bigger crowd had gathered around us, including the Madrid sisters, who were pointing at me and giggling. Fights, or even *almost* fights, always attracted a big crowd. Solomon and some of the Chama guys were there too, and I *know* they were hoping that all those Colorado guys *would* jump on me so that *they* could get in on the fight. I would hear Solomon and his brothers walk up to different guys and challenge them by saying, *"No te pongas chango, o te doy una banana."* I wasn't quite sure what it meant, but it had something to do with a monkey and a banana. Chama guys were crazy, and they *always* wanted to fight. That actually made me feel good, though, because I knew I wasn't alone anymore.

Right then one of the girls that was with the new, most beautiful girl in the universe gave me a dirty look, grabbed her by the arm and said, "C'mon, Bonnie, let's go. You don't want to be around him. He's *always* in trouble!"

Bonnie? The girl's name was Bonnie? Wow! A beautiful girl by the name of Bonnie was talking to me! I thought girls that were named "Bonnie" were only in storybooks, or little English girls that I would never meet. But here she was. A real live Bonnie! Standing and smiling right in front of me! And talking to me! Wow!

Her friend was right, of course. I *was* always in trouble. But for some reason, that didn't seem to matter to the girl with the blue-green eyes. She just kept smiling at me and making me feel all weak and tingly. Sweat and all. Normally, I would have thought that it was pretty impossible for a gorgeous girl like her to like me. Especially one with a storybook name like Bonnie! I mean, my hair stood straight up like a stiff paintbrush. I had enough teeth in my mouth for twelve humans and I was so dark that at night Max would tell me to keep smiling so that he could see where I was. But with all the miracles that had happened to me today, my Navajo Angel, new U.S. Keds, new *real* boys' J.C. Penney underwear, whew! I knew that *nothing* was impossible! But why was God being so nice to me? I had just said the 'a-s-s' word right after I had gotten out of church, and there He was, letting an incredibly beautiful little girl my age, named Bonnie, actually seem like she was interested in me.

I had completely forgotten about the boy who wanted to beat me up and I was trying to figure out what to say to this gorgeous girl besides the incredibly brilliant "Uh..well...uh... uh" that I kept hearing come out of my mouth, when I heard Solomon's voice shout out, "Chinche! Chinche! *'Aqui viene Chinche'*!"

My heart skipped a beat and I looked up just as everybody started yelling, and running in all directions. Most of them had started running towards all the parked cars in the softball field. Including the boy who wanted to fight me. I looked to where Solomon had pointed before he and the rest of the Chama guys had taken off, and sure enough, I could see four or five adult heads coming at us very quickly from the back of the Tabernacle, and I could tell by the shiny glint from his almost bald head, that one of them was my mortal enemy, Brother Chinche.

I looked back to the little girl with the impossibly beautiful eyes, but her friends were already dragging her past the softball backstop and down the hill toward the cabins. I knew I should be running too, but all I could do was just stand there, stare and wave at her. And she waved back! She actually waved back! Then she smiled at me real big with those incredible teeth. So I took a chance and smiled right back at her with all five thousand of my teeth! And she kept smiling and waving!

Wow! She didn't get scared when I showed her all my teeth! Wow! Then she disappeared down the hill and Puggy was grabbing my arm and running at the same time.

"C'mon, crazy boy!" she yelled. "You can wave later! Chinche's gonna get us!"

I heard Beanie let out a couple of loud "ah-HAY-yas" as he and Chato started ahead of us, running hard toward the back of the Tabernacle. We caught up to them just as they were rounding the corner. As I got to the corner, I looked back to see how close Chinche and his posse were, then gasped and almost fell down when I saw my Navajo angel, this time with a bright red jacket on, stick his foot out and trip Brother Chinche. I couldn't believe it! He just stuck his big ol' beautiful boot out and *tripped* him! I stopped running and just stayed there, standing and staring with my mouth open in amazement, and watched as Chinche's police force fell right on top of him in a tangled mess. When they fell, my angel looked at me, smiled and waved, then walked right through the Tabernacle wall! I mean, right *through* the Tabernacle wall! Just like that! Right through the wall! Like he did it every day! Like, "Hey, how ya doin', Mario, excuse me while I walk through the wall." This was *really* crazy!

"Did you see that?" I yelled at Puggy.

"See what? Why are you stopping?" Puggy asked, looking at Chinche yelling at his guys to get off him. "And who are you waving at now?"

"My angel! My angel, Pug! He waved at me! He tripped Chinche, then he just walked through that wall!" I said, pointing to the Tabernacle wall that he had just walked through.

"What? You're crazy, man! Waddaya mean, an angel walked through the wall?" Puggy asked, shaking her head and grabbing my arm at the same time. "Let's get outta here while Chinche's still down."

We turned the corner and started running again, and almost ran into the Ortega Brothers and their uncles who were standing by the same back door they had come out of after their concert. Ricky still had both of his trumpets and

Art still had his guitar and they were talking and laughing with some people I didn't recognize. Ricky looked surprised when he saw us, then smiled when he remembered me and he held out the back of his hand so that I could shake it again. He probably thought, "Hey, it's that little kid with the crippled hand." I wanted to stop and explain to him that the reason I had offered him the back of my hand was to show him my one-line tattoo, but Puggy pulled me again and we flew right past his outstretched hand, right past the *comedor* back door with its delicious, greasy smells and around the corner toward the front door. Chato and Beanie were waiting for us by the wooden stairs.

"C'mon, Chahts!" I yelled, still running. "We gotta get to the store!"

The four of us ran down the side of the *comedor* where there were no lights, past Brother Chavez' candy and soda window, and stopped when we got to the corner. We all got low to the ground and Puggy peeked around the side to see if it was safe.

"C'mon," she whispered. "It looks clear."

As we hurried to the front door of the *comedor,* we could see a big crowd still gathered around the Tabernacle windows. Some were listening to what was going on inside, and others were standing around laughing and talking. I wondered if anybody had seen my angel go through the wall. Probably not, or there would have been a lot of commotion. I also wondered if any of them had ever even *seen* an angel. They probably wouldn't understand him being a very tall Navajo, and where were his wings, they would ask. Maybe he was just hiding them underneath those beautiful jackets. If I had a chance, I would ask.

When we got inside the *comedor,* the only people around were Brother Chavez and Brother Boni. They were both behind the candy counter separating all the coins that had come in that day. I was relieved because I knew that my mother was cooking tonight back in the kitchen, and I didn't want her to see me.

Brother Chavez looked up and shook his head when he saw me. Brother Boni smiled and shook his head too.

"You better hurry up, *travieso*," Brother Chavez said, as he unlocked the little door to go behind the counter. "I just saw Chinche and his army run by the window."

Brother Chavez had a really neat, gravelly voice and he usually sounded grumpy, like he was mad at me for something, but I knew he liked me, because he was always getting me out of trouble. Like right now.

We went through the door and ducked down behind the counter. Puggy was the last one through, so she closed the little door and put the latch in. Brother Boni looked at me and shook his head again.

"*Ay, que muchito,*'" he said, putting a bunch of dimes in his left ear. "*Que vamos hacer contigo?*"

I don't know *what* you're going to do with me, Brother Boni, just please don't turn me in.

I loved the smells behind the counter: Paydays, Snickers, Big Hunks, Black Cows, Bazooka Bubble Gum. I don't know how, but it seemed like I could smell them right through their packages. Sometimes Brother Chavez would let me help him sell stuff, or he would have me go through the camp and collect empty soda bottles, and he would pay me with a push-up ice cream or a bottle of R.C. Cola and a bag of peanuts. Putting the peanuts in the soda was one of my favorite things to do.

I was getting ready to whisper something to Chato about my angel walking through the Tabernacle wall when I heard a bunch of heavy footsteps come through the front door. The four of us held our breath and looked at each other wide-eyed as the footsteps approached the counter. Chato covered Beanie's mouth just in case.

"*Hermano* Chinche," Brother Chavez said, barely looking up from his coins. "*Como va, mi hermano. Quieren comprar algo? Una soda o dulce?*"

"No, *Hermano* Chavez. I don't think we want to buy anything right now. I'm looking for Brother Santos' boy. Have you seen him?"

"*Hermano,* just find out where all the girls are, and that's where you'll find *El Max.*"

Brother Chavez and Brother Boni thought that was pretty funny, because they looked at each other and started laughing. I looked up at Brother Boni and saw him stuff a few more dimes in his left ear and grab some nickels and put them in his right ear while he was still laughing. How in the world did they stay in there without falling out?

"'No, hermano. No andamos buscando El Max. I'm looking for the little one, *El Mario. El travieso.* Have you seen him? We saw him run around this building."

"*El Mario?*" Brother Chavez asked. "*Que hizo 'hora?* Did he throw another cherry bomb in the Tabernacle?"

Brother Chavez and Brother Boni laughed at that one too, but you could tell Brother Chinche didn't think it was funny.

"No, *hermano.* He was fighting with some..."

"Fighting? That doesn't sound like Mario," Brother Chavez said.

"Well, he was. And I'm pretty sure he had something to do with that outhouse thing that happened today, so I really want to talk to him."

"Really?" Brother Chavez asked. "You think Mario had something to do with that outhouse thing? Boy, I bet that was one stinky situation!"

Brother Boni about rolled on the floor with that one.

"*Ay, que pestoso!*" Brother Boni roared. And then he and Brother Chavez both held their noses and they both started laughing *real* loud. I wanted to laugh too, but I thought I better not. I didn't want to get Brother Chavez in trouble, although Brother Chavez didn't seem to be too much afraid of Brother Chinche. I guess only little guys like me were afraid of him.

"How *is* the Malacara boy, anyway? Is he alright?" Brother Chavez asked.

"Well, yes, he is. He and the Baltazar boy are going to be fine. I just want..."

"*Mira, Hermano Chinche,*" Brother Chavez said, leaning across the counter. "*La hermana* Santos is in the kitchen. Let me get her, so that you can ask her."

"Oh no...no, no. That's not necessary, *hermano*. Don't bother her." Brother Chinche's voice changed all of a sudden. He even chuckled a little bit. Like he was nervous about something. He knew my mother was *definitely* not afraid of him. "No...just if you see him, let me know, *bueno*?"

"I'll tell you what, *hermano*," Brother Chavez said, standing straight up again. "*When* I see Mario, I'll tell him you're looking for him. Maybe he'll go try to find you. *Esta bueno*?"

"*Seguro que si'*. Just let me know, OK?"

The footsteps had started toward the door when I heard a familiar voice say, "Is everything all right, brothers?"

Uh-oh. My mom was out of the kitchen.

"*Si, hermana,*" Brother Chinche said, with his phony little laugh. "I was just asking Brother Chavez if he, uh...if he knew, or heard, uh..." By the shuffling sound of the footsteps, I could tell Chinche's army was backing up, trying to get to the door.

"Well, I stepped out here a minute ago and I heard Mario's name mentioned. Is he OK? Did he do something?"

"Oh, yes, I'm sure he's fine, *hermana*. I just wanted to ask Brother Chavez a few questions about, uh...well, just about things. Uh...*bueno, gracias, Hermano Chavez*, I'll check with you later."

I took a chance and very quietly pushed aside the boxes of Big Hunks and David Sunflower Seeds and peeked through one of the knotholes in front of the counter just as Chinche and his soldiers turned to walk out the door. They looked like they couldn't get there fast enough.

And then, when they were almost at the door, as if walking through the Tabernacle wall hadn't been enough, my Navajo angel and his bright red jacket, walked right through the front wall of the *comedor*, right next to the door! Even though the door was wide open, he just "BOOM!", walked right through the wall! Just like that! Like he knew that being able to walk through walls was one of the neatest things in all the world to do! And it *was*!

I watched in total amazement as he kind of skipped-hopped right in front of Chinche and his boys, held his long arms out and knocked all of them down! Just like that! "WHACK!" I mean, just "BAM!" Big ol' arms, and they all went down! Wow! What kind of angel had God given me? I was kind of beginning to love him!

After he had knocked them down, my angel smiled real big and then pointed right at the knothole I was looking out of! He knew I was watching! Oh, my God! He knew! Then he made a fist, put his thumb up, waved, and walked out the front door. Just like that! Wow!...WOW!

There was a lot of noise as Chinche and his troops yelled at each other and tried to untangle themselves. When Chinche finally got up from the bottom of the pile his head *and* face were as red as my Navajo angel's jacket. His glasses had fallen off when he fell down, and when one of his guys handed them to him he put them on and I could tell that both of the lenses had cracked. But he was too embarrassed that he had fallen down in front of Brother Chavez and my mom that he just left them on and almost ran out the door.

The rest of the troops didn't even bother to clean themselves off; they just hurried out the door after their leader, and then it got real quiet. I shifted positions and tried to see where my mother was, but I couldn't see her. I sat back down next to Puggy as quietly as I could. I saw Brother Chavez and Brother Boni exchange a glance, then they went back to counting their coins.

"*Hermano* Chavez," my mom said quietly, breaking the silence.

Brother Chavez cleared his throat, stopped counting and looked over to her.

"*Si, hermana,*" he said.

"Is Mario alright?" she asked.

"*Si, hermana,*" he said. "He's perfectly healthy and safe."

"Are you sure?"

"Positive."

"Do I need to know where he's at right now?"

No! Please don't tell her, Brother Chavez!

"Only if you want to."

There was another silence. Oh, please don't, Brother Chavez! Please!

"But he's safe."

"Perfectly," Brother Chavez said, with that great gravelly voice.

"He's not with a big Indian, is he?"

"*Que?* A big Indian? *No, hermana,* I didn't see no Indian with him. Big *or* small."

"Are you real sure?"

"*Oh, si, mi hermana.* I know what an Indian looks like, and when I saw him, he wasn't with no Indian. *Porque?* Did somebody see him with an Indian?"

"Well...let's just say this has been a very unusual day. Even for Mario."

There was a long silence, then I heard my mother let out a big sigh.

"OK," she said. "But please let me know if he's in some bad trouble. And please don't let that...that...that Chinche bother him."

"I'll always let you know when Mario's in bad trouble, *hermana.* And if I can help it, I won't let Brother Chinche bother him."

"*Yo se, hermano,* I know. Thank you so much. My husband and I appreciate all that you do for Mario."

"*Oh, hermana,* you don't have to..."

"No, brother. We hear--we hear a lot of things about our son, and I just want you to know how much we appreciate you. Mario's not the easiest boy to handle and we worry about him a lot. But he seems to like being around you very much and he also seems to trust you. And trust with that boy just doesn't come easy. So, anyway, thank you, brother. And you too, Brother Boni."

"*Oh, si, si, hermana,*" Brother Boni said, smiling big. I was surprised he could hear with all those dimes and nickels in his ears. "Mario's a good boy. *No mas que tiene...como se dice en ingles?* Energy...*si,* that's it! *El tiene mucho* energy!"

"Yes, that right, brother. I've never heard him described that way. But that's a good word for him."

I wasn't looking at her, but I could tell by her voice that my mom was smiling. That made me feel good, because she didn't smile a lot when I was the topic of conversation.

"*Bueno, hermanos,* I'd better get back to the kitchen. The service is going to be over pretty soon, and the people will be hungry. *Gracias,* OK?"

"*Si, hermana. De nada.* Don't worry about Mario. He'll be all right," Brother Chavez said. He and Brother Boni had their backs to us and they both waved at the same time.

I heard the door to the kitchen open and close, and after he waited about ten seconds to make sure my mom didn't come back out, Brother Chavez turned back to the four of us, still huddled behind the counter.

"You know, Brother Chinche's gonna be waiting for you, don't you, boy?"

"Yeah. You're right. Can we get up now?"

Brother Chavez looked around the *comedor,* then walked over to his little candy window and looked out.

"Looks pretty clear," he said, walking back to us.

The four of us got up slowly and peeked over the counter; the place was still empty.

"What did you do to make Chinche come after you with the whole army? Did you really get into a fight?"

"No, I promise. I didn't want to fight anybody."

"He's telling the truth, Brother Chavez," Puggy said. "It was the other boy that wanted to fight Mario."

Brother Boni had put all the coins in two bags and was getting ready to put them in the secret hiding place under a loose board in the floor beneath the tub of ice that had all the sodas in it. Sometimes I would help Brother Chavez move the tub and then he would let me put the money in the secret place after all the customers had left. Finky and JoJo had beat me up last summer because I wouldn't tell them where Brother Chavez kept the money. It had cost me a black eye and a puffy lip, but I hadn't told them anything. Tonight, I thought Brother Boni would probably wait until we left before he put the money away. I didn't think he wanted anybody else to know. Although he didn't know that I had shared the secret with Puggy. But that was OK. *Nobody* was *ever* going to get it out of her.

"Yeah," Beanie said, adjusting the rubberband holding his big black glasses tightly on his head. "It was the other guy, Brother Chavez. And he was a Colorado guy!"

Beanie made a face when he said that and everybody, including Brother Chavez and Brother Boni, laughed.

Brother Chavez looked towards the kitchen door then turned back to us with his finger to his lips. "Shhh!" he said. "I don't want your mother coming out!"

We quieted down, then Puggy said, "It was about a girl, Brother Chavez."

"What?" I said making a face and looking at her. "Are you crazy? It was not. That guy just doesn't like me."

"It was about a pretty girl with blue-green eyes named Bonnie," Puggy said, totally ignoring me. So she had noticed the eyes too. How could anybody miss them. "Mario just looked at her and the Colorado guy got mad, and started saying some not-so-nice things about Mario, so Mario told him..."

"OK, OK, Pug," I said, hoping to stop her before she got to the a-s-s part. "I don't think Brother Chavez is interested in all that stuff."

"Yeah, Pug," Beanie piped in. "Brother Chavez isn't interested."

"Thanks, Bean," I said, rubbing Beanie's head and looking at Puggy at the same time and telling her with my eyebrows raised that she really didn't have to say anything else.

"Yeah," Brother Chavez said. "I know who you're talking about. Her mother plays the piano. They're from Denver and they just got here today."

Puggy looked at me with her eyes wide. "Oh, no, Mar!" she said. "You like someone from Colorado! How are we gonna tell the Chama guys?"

Yeah. She was right. As usual. Chama guys didn't like anything or anybody that wasn't from New Mexico. It was a good thing she wasn't from Texas. That would have *definitely* been the end of me.

"Hey," Brother Chavez said, rescuing me from having to deal with the girl-from-out-of-state issue. "Those are pretty nice shoes you got there, buddy. You too, Mr. Chato. I guess you two won't be needing those popsicle boxes anymore for your holey shoes, huh? Heh, heh. Did you guys buy them at the same place?"

With all that was going on I had forgotten about my new shoes again. But when he said that I looked down at my beautiful Keds and smiled. Even with all the running, they still looked unmarked and brand new. No, Brother Chavez, thank God, we wouldn't be needing the empty popsicle boxes to cover the holes on the bottom of our shoes. I looked over at Chato and he was looking down at his new Keds and smiling too. I thought about showing Brother Chavez and Brother Boni my brand-new authentic boys' underwear, but I was standing next to Puggy, so I knew it wouldn't be a good idea. Maybe I would come back and show them when she wasn't with me.

"Yeah, we kinda' did get them from the same place, Brother Chavez," I said. Chato looked over at me and we both nodded and smiled at the same time.

"Didn't have anything to do with that big Indian your mother was asking about, did it?"

"Well...yeah. He's the one who bought them. I think."

"So there *was* a big Indian."

"Yup."

"Really? You're not lying?"

"Yup. And I'm not lying. The biggest Indian I ever saw, Brother Chavez. The biggest *guy* I ever saw."

"Yeah, he was *real* big, Brother Chavez," Chato said. He walked over and stood next to me. Beanie followed close behind. "And he smelled real good too."

"*Que?* He smelled real good? Waddaya mean, he smelled real good?" Brother Chavez asked. He put his elbows on the counter, put his left hand up to his chin and started rubbing it. Like he was trying to figure out if we were telling the truth. Brother Boni came over and stood right behind him, adjusting the coins in his ears so that he could hear better.

"Well, he just smelled real good," Chato said. "Like apples, kinda'. Huh, Mario?"

"Yeah, Chato's telling the truth, Brother Chavez. He smelled just like apples. Like my *Mamau's* kitchen." Brother Chavez knew my grandmother, and he knew that I called her "my *Mamau*."

"Mario said that the Indian was an angel, Brother Chavez." Puggy said. Almost like she was telling on me. I gave her another raised-eyebrow look.

"An angel? The Indian was an angel? Is that right, Mario? An Indian angel bought you and Chato new tennies. *Ay, Senor*, I don't know, buddy," Brother Chavez said. "You've told me some crazy stuff before, but man...this is, uh...this might be the craziest."

"Well, it's true, Brother Chavez." I said. "But it's a long story. And if I take the time to tell you all about it now, my mom might come out of the kitchen, or worse, Brother Chinche might come back, and I would just have to try and escape, and cause another big commotion."

Brother Chavez didn't say anything. He just kept rubbing his chin and looking at me. He stayed like that for awhile, then took a deep breath, stood up from leaning on the counter, and said, "OK, but sometime tomorrow or maybe even later tonight, I wanna hear all about it. *Comprende?* The truth."

"OK," I said, relieved. "The truth. I promise. But we're gonna go now, OK?"

I thought that if we left now, there would be plenty of time to go look for Bonnie. I didn't care if she *was* from Colorado. She had *smiled* at me! That was worth risking a run-in with Chinche *anytime*! I would just have to deal with the Chama guys about the Colorado issue later.

"C'mon, you guys. Let's get outta' here," I said. The four of us turned to leave and Brother Chavez said, "Wait!"

We turned back around and saw him reach under the counter and come back up with four Big Hunks.

"Here," he said. "You can collect bottles for me tomorrow. Be careful! Chinche's got spies everywhere!"

"All right! Wow! Thanks, Brother Chavez!"

We quickly went up to Brother Chavez, grabbed our Big Hunks and ran out the door to the same unlighted side of the *comedor.* We ran to the back of the building where the wooden stairs were and stopped. Puggy peeked around the corner, gave the all-clear sign, and the four of us ran down the stairs. A few of the cabins had lamps burning, but for the most part, the camp was dark, providing plenty of cover for us. I started to run to the north side of the camp where I had seen my blue-green-eyed girl go, but Puggy grabbed my arm and pulled me toward the trail that led to the river.

"What are you doin', Pug? That girl's over there by the Tabernacle. "

"And so's Chinche," Puggy said. "There's too many people on that side. Let's just go to the big log in back of your cabin. Eat our Big Hunks, and *then* we'll go look for that girl, OK? Maybe Chinche won't be around by then. Don't worry, Mar, she ain't goin' nowhere."

Puggy was right. Of course. The smart thing to do would be to let things calm down a little bit, *then* go look for that beautiful blue-green-eyed Bonnie.

"Yeah, you're pro'bly right," I said, walking back down the trail toward the river. "Let's go eat our Big Hunks."

We started down the trail, then decided it would be better if we walked in back of the cabins behind the fence, so that the trees and tall brush could hide us. That way we wouldn't accidentally run into anybody we didn't want to see. We also didn't want to run into one of the hungry bears that came down from the mountains and wandered into the camp periodically to go through the trash, or step in any fresh cow piles from the loose cattle that grazed back there, so we walked quietly and carefully until we got to the log.

The big, dried-out cottonwood log was directly behind our cabin and when we played football it was one of the out-of-bounds markers. The other out-of-bounds marker was the barbed wire fence, which was about twenty yards away. It was perfect because we could sit on it and see everything in the dimly lit camp, but because of the shade from the other tall trees, it was too dark for anybody from the camp to see us. It was also one of the favorite places for all the kids who wanted to kiss. But tonight, nobody was there.

We climbed on to the log, got comfortable and unwrapped our Big Hunks. I was still looking forward to a delicious, greasy burger later on, but this white, chewy, tooth-sticking candy with peanuts was a great appetizer. The sky was clear except for the smoke rising from the fireplaces and stoves, and the stars sparkled like little Christmas tree lights, their shine bouncing off the smoke, making the camp almost seem like it was shimmering. The sound of the river gushing with the run-off was like soft thunder, and we could hear the preaching from the Tabernacle still going strong. There was an occasional "moo" from the cows wandering in back of us, and every once in awhile we could hear voices and laughter coming from the campground, but other than that, the only sounds were candy wrappers being torn off and kids making chewing noises.

I was tearing off another piece of Big Hunk and thinking about how incredible it was that God had not let me drown earlier that day when I heard giggling close by. The giggling got closer and I felt Puggy put her hand on my arm.

"Shhh!" she said, putting her finger to her lips. The four of us quit chewing and quietly jumped off the log. We knelt down behind the tall grass, and I picked up some of the candy wrapping from the ground that I had torn off and wrapped the rest of my Big Hunk and put it in my pocket. Puggy still had her finger on her lips so that we would be quiet, and she handed me the rest of her candy to keep because she didn't have any pockets, and then we all four very slowly put our heads over the grass and peeked to see who was making all the noise.

Sitting up on the log we could usually see who was coming down the trail. But kneeling on the ground we could only see right in front of us. Whoever it was must have come from somewhere else in the camp, because we hadn't seen them coming down the trail. I was trying to figure out where they had come from when all of a sudden I saw Max and the Baca twins come giggling and strolling around Chato's cabin and headed right for Max's trailer! Max had his arms around their waists and he didn't look like he was having any trouble at all trying to choose which one he was going to be with. He would put his face close to one, and she would giggle and make an "uhmm" sound, then he would turn and put his face close to the other one and then she would make the same sounds.

"It's Max!" I whispered excitedly, turning to Puggy. "And he's kissing the Baca twins!"

Puggy's eyes got real big and she made her Shut up-and-don't-even-say-a-word face, this time drumming her finger on her lips to make sure we didn't say anything.

Chato had his hand over Beanie's mouth to make sure no accidental "a-HAY-yas!" came out, and I could see that he was just as excited as I was that we were going to get to see Max in action without being told to "Get outta here!" This was like getting up close to Ricky Ortega as he played two trumpets at the same time. Like watching Mickey Mantle play center field, like watching Johnny Unitas play quarterback. IN PERSON! Maybe I was going to learn something tonight.

I watched as Max led the giggling and "uhmming" twins to the entrance of his trailer. He looked around to see if anybody was watching, then he pulled the canvas flap up so that the twins could crawl in.

I heard both of them giggle and say, *at the same time,* "Nobody's going to catch us, are they, Max?"

"Nah," Max said. "Everybody's in the Tabernacle, and Chinche's chasing my little brother around somewhere, so we're safe."

The girls giggled and crawled in and Max crawled in after them and closed the flap.

I was slowly getting up so I could get closer to the trailer when I heard a familiar high squeaky sound and turned around just in time to see Puggy and Chato put their hands over their noses and crawl quickly away on their knees a safe distance from Beanie. Uh-oh. Beanie had let loose of some of his "gift." He had been so good all night. The "gift" had not been on display during the church service, and he had even kept it in check underneath the candy counter. But I guess he just couldn't hold it any longer.

"I just couldn't hold it anymore," he whispered, with a big smile.

"That's OK, Bean," I whispered back, covering my nose. "Just don't cut loose when we get close to Max's trailer, OK? We don't wanna interrupt 'em."

"OK," he said. Then he let go of another high squeaky one. He must have been saving them all night.

I crawled as fast as I could over to where Puggy and Chato were. I had barely caught a whiff, but even that little whiff almost made me puke. Max was right when he had said Beanie was a true artist.

I remembered the time last summer when the four of us had been in children's church and Sister Archuleta had made us sit in the front row with the Vigil sisters, Becky, Sylvia and Doris. She must have thought sitting next to them was going to make us behave. The Vigil sisters *always* behaved. My mom used to tell me, "Why can't you behave like the Vigil sisters?" What my mom didn't know was that only *two* of the Vigil sisters behaved; the younger one, Doris, acted like us when her sisters weren't around. She had these really neat glasses that were pointed on the ends, but she didn't have a rubberband holding them up like Chato and Beanie.

Well, Sister Archuleta finished the lesson then got to the real quiet altar call part where we were supposed to bow our heads and not look around and lift our hand if we wanted to accept Jesus in our hearts, when a long, high, squeaky sound came from Beanie's direction on the front row.

"Oh, my God!" Becky had screamed, covering her mouth, like she was getting sick.

When she had screamed, Sister Archuleta, with her eyes still closed, had lifted her hands to heaven, thanking God because she thought one of the kids was accepting Jesus and getting *"en bendicion."* She opened them just in time to see Becky and Sylvia and Doris run right past her and the rest of the kids rushing to the exits.

"Kids! Kids!" she yelled, "Come back! Where are you going? Come back. You need Jesus!"

She was right. We sure did need Jesus. But right then, needing fresh air was an even bigger priority.

We were standing by the front door laughing when Doris came walking right up to us and then smacked *me* on the arm!

"Whatja do that for?" I asked, rubbing my arm. "I didn't do anything."

"That's for letting Beanie make my sister sick!" she said, crossing her arms.

"Waddaya mean, letting Beanie? I can't control his *pedos.* Get mad at him, not me."

"He's too small to get mad at," Doris said, still crossing her arms and making a mad face at me. "Besides, that's for all the other times you torment us and we *don't get* to hit you."

Right then Becky, who looked like she had gotten over being sick, and Sylvia, came and grabbed Doris by the arm and took her away. But not before they all three stuck their tongues out at me. I got in trouble even when I *didn't* do anything!

Anyway, Beanie's "gift" was well known.

"Is he about done?" Puggy asked quietly, looking at Chato.

"I don't know," Chato whispered, shrugging his shoulders, "sometimes he can go all night."

"Wow!" I said, a little envious. "How do you guys stand the smell?"

"My mom puts him by the window with a little fan blowing it outside."

"Even when it's cold?" Puggy asked.

"Even when it's freezing," Chato said, "but Beanie's used to it. He just dresses real warm and then flaps the covers when he needs to air out."

Me and Puggy both nodded, trying to picture in our minds what went on in the Montoya household every evening.

"Has your mom ever given him Enz?" I asked. The little green pill was my mother's favorite for my dad and me, although it didn't seem to work on my dad very well.

"Yeah, your mom gave her a whole bottle. But his *pedos* still smelled the same. Only with a little bit of spearmint in 'em."

I nodded. I knew the smell very well.

I was thinking about suggesting to my mom the idea of putting a fan by my dad when Beanie came crawling to where we were.

"I think I'm done for awhile," he said, with a big satisfied smile on his face. "And I think the smell stayed over there."

"Good," Puggy said. "It's nothing personal, Bean. I just don't feel like vomiting right now."

Beanie smiled and nodded. "I know Pug. It's OK."

We crept closer to the trailer and we could hear the giggling and the "uhmming" getting louder.

We quietly made our way right next to the fence, which was about ten feet from the trailer, and we could hear everything real clear. The girls kept saying things like, "Ooh, Ma-ax," and "Are you sure no one's going to see us, Max?" and, *at the same time!* "Do you really love us both, Max?" I'm not lying! I swear! They really said it, at the *same time!* And then Max said, "Of course I love you guys; you believe me, doncha?" Wow! Even though they knew he had been with a bunch of other girls all week, *in the same trailer* and would probably be with some different ones again tomorrow night, it sounded like they believed him! Incredible!

What a great lesson! Apparently all you had to tell a girl was what she wanted to hear and you could kiss her all night! Wow! I would definitely remember this!

But what if Max really *did* love them, and the reason he was with the Baca twins was because he was planning on taking them both to Salt Lake City and marrying them?

He told me one time that a guy could marry as many girls as he wanted in Salt Lake City because it wasn't against the law. He said you could have all the wives you wanted, but you just couldn't drink coffee or Coca Cola, or smoke cigarettes. I told him it sounded like a pretty good deal to me as long as they were pretty and they didn't mind me hanging out with Puggy.

One time I was watching my mom put *masa* and red chili on some *ojas* for tamales and I asked her about what Max had told me, and she said that King Solomon had taken seven hundred wives and three hundred concubines for himself. I asked her what a "concubine" was.

"She was kind of like a real close girl friend," she had said.

"You mean he had seven hundred wives *and* three hundred girlfriends?" I asked.

"Yeah," she said, shaking her head. "That's what the Word says."

"Wow! Was he from Salt Lake City?" I asked.

"No," she said. Then she handed me a fresh "*masa* only" tamale, and told me she would finish the story later.

Well, maybe Max wasn't going to marry the Baca twins; maybe he was just so busy that he had to take two girls at a time now.

I motioned to Puggy that I wanted to crawl through the barbed wire so that I could look through one of the holes in the canvas and maybe pick up some valuable pointers on kissing.

She put her hand on my arm and whispered, "I don't think it's a good idea for you to look inside the trailer."

"Why not?" I said, quietly.

"I just don't think your brother would appreciate his little brother spying on him while he was with two girls in the privacy of his own trailer, that's all."

"What, are you gonna tell him?" I asked.

"What, are you crazy?" she said, shaking her head. "If you want to find out about all this stuff, just ask him. I'm sure he'll be happy to give you some pointers."

"But this is a chance of a lifetime, Pug. He's got two girls in there! We get to see Max in action with two girls! When is *that* ever going to happen again?"

"Well, with him, probably tomorrow night."

"C'mon, Pug. It's gonna be OK. We'll just peek, then get outta there. OK?"

"OK," she said, "but I'm not gonna look."

She shrugged her shoulders and placed her foot on the bottom wire and held the one above it with her hand, and I went through with Chato and Beanie following close behind. I held the pointy wires open for Puggy, then the four of us very silently made our way to the trailer. The giggling was still going on and I could see that Max had his little lamp on, because the light was peeking out through the holes. I guess it was important to have some light on to see who you were kissing. Of course, with two girls who looked exactly alike, it probably didn't matter.

To be safe, Chato had put his hand over Beanie's mouth again, and we quietly and slowly walked to the corner of the trailer that was by our cabin's front porch. I was just getting ready to look into one of the holes by the corner when I glanced up in the direction of the Tabernacle, and my heart stopped. There, quickly coming down the dusty trail with flashlights beaming in our direction, was Chinche and his posse! I ducked back down and motioned for Puggy to look. She gave a little gasp when she saw them and looked at me wide eyed, grabbed my arm and whispered, "Let's go!"

She was right. We still had a chance to get back into the trees and Chinche would never find us. But if I didn't do or say something, Chinche would catch Max and the Baca twins, my dad and mom would be extremely embarrassed, and Max would be in a ton of trouble. But if I *did* do something, I would be in trouble with Max for sneaking up on him and his girlfriends, and Chinche would have a clear shot at me.

Oh, well, I couldn't let my big brother get caught. Chinche would just have to try and catch me.

I hit the side of the trailer hard with my hand and put my mouth to the hole I was going to look in and whispered as loud as I could, "Max! It's Chinche! He's coming down the trail!"

Some "Oh, my God's" and "Oh, no! What am I going to tell my mother?!" came from the girls inside the trailer, then Beanie let out two very loud "a-HAY-ya's!" and the four of us jumped up and ran to the trail in front of my cabin, turned to face Chinche, and stopped.

When Brother Chinche saw us, *he* stopped, and he looked like he was stunned. Like he couldn't believe that his luck was finally changing. He just stared at me for about five seconds, then he got a real big smile on his face and a crazy look in his eyes, pointed at me with his flashlight, and yelled, "Forget the trailer! *Alli esta el travieso! Agarralo!*"

When he yelled, Beanie let out another couple of "a-HAY-yas!" then we turned and started running toward the river. When we passed Puggy's cabin I looked back to make sure Chinche and his posse were following us, and when I saw that they were about ten yards behind us, I turned and started running to the high grass around to where the outhouse used to stand.

"Are you crazy, Mario? Where are you going?" Puggy asked, running right behind me.

"Just follow right behind me, Pug. And I mean, *right* behind me! OK?"

Nobody knew the area around the outhouse better than me, even in the dark.

We got close to the tall grass where the outhouse had stood, and I could see the outline of it laying down behind *Hermana* Luz's cabin. They still hadn't put it back up. That was good. This plan just might work.

We ran through the grass right up to the hole where the outhouse had stood. I put my hand out to make sure Puggy didn't fall in, then we hurried to the other side, turned around and stopped.

"Why are we stopping, Mario? C'mon! Chinche's gonna get us!" Puggy said, tugging at my arm. Beanie let out another "a-HAY-ya!" and came and stood real close to my side.

"Why are we stopping, Mario?" he asked. He grabbed me tightly around my waist and his little body jerked as another "a-HAY-ya!" came out.

"Watch," I said, hoping that my plan would work. I was counting on Brother Chinche wanting me so bad, that he would run straight to me.

When Chinche and his posse saw me, they started running hard. "Don't let him get away!" Chinche yelled, coming right at me, just like I thought he would.

Brother Chinche was the first to fall in the hole and he made the same "SPLAT!" and gurgling sounds that Finky had made earlier that day. The rest of his posse quickly followed, and when the last two men came up and tried to stop at the edge, a real tall man wearing a beautiful red coat who was following close behind, gave them a push and they joined Chinche and the rest of the gang at the bottom of the hole.

My angel walked over to where I was, put his arm around my shoulder and we both looked down into the hole. There was a lot of commotion going on down there and the smell was terrible.

"You're never going to let me relax, are you, kid?"

"Were you with me all the time?" I asked, still gazing into the hole.

"You mean forever, like since you were born? Or just like right now?

"Like right now," I said, looking way up at him.

"Yeah," he said, pulling me away from the hole. "I was with you. I've been with you all day and all night. I told you before: I've *always* been with you. Let's get outta' here. It stinks."

"You mean you've been with me all night?" I asked, moving out of the tall grass to the light in front of Hermana Luz's cabin.

"Yup," he said, walking with me, his huge hand still on my shoulder.

"Even when we were by the Tabernacle?" I asked. I could see his face better now that we were getting into the light.

"Yeah, that's right." He stopped walking and squatted down and looked at me. "You didn't think I was gonna let that Colorado guy beat you up in front of that pretty girl, did you?"

I smiled at him. "I think she liked me a little bit," I said. "She didn't seem to mind my hair and she didn't even get scared when she saw all my teeth."

"Yeah, that Bonnie girl is special alright." He laughed and stood up.

"Do you think I'll ever get to meet her?" I asked.

"Oh, you don't have to worry about that," he said, rubbing my head with that enormous hand. "You and that blue-green-eyed Bonnie are *definitely* gonna meet."

"Really?"

"Really."

"Hey," I said, remembering my brother. "Is Max OK? Did he and the Baca twins get away?"

"Yeah, he's OK," he said, laughing. "They should be gettin' to the Tabernacle about right now."

We were getting close to the trail that headed back to the Tabernacle and I was getting ready to ask him another question when I remembered I wasn't alone. I stopped and looked behind me at Puggy and saw that she and Chato and

Beanie, who had been following close behind without saying a word, were now just standing very still with their eyes and their mouths wide open staring up at my Navajo angel.

"You're letting them see you, aren't you?" I asked.

"Yeah, this way they won't think you're completely crazy and a total liar." He walked over to them, squatted down and stuck out his hand. "Hey, guys," he said, "I'm one of Mario's angels. How ya doin'?"

Beanie was the first to reach out for my angel's hand. His small hand barely wrapped around two of my angel's fingers. "Are you really an angel?" he asked.

"I sure am, Bean," my angel said, putting his face close to Beanie's.

Beanie let go of my angel's fingers and then walked completely around him, like he was looking for something. "Well, how come you don't have any wings?" he asked, crossing his arms and making a face.

"Oh, they're back there," my angel said, standing up. "You just can't see 'em." He stuck his hand out to Puggy and she reached out to his very slowly. Like she wasn't sure.

"Hey, Pug," he said, "so I finally get to meet the best football player in Chama."

When he said that, Puggy smiled, but she still didn't say anything.

He looked over at Chato. "How them shoes fit, Chato?" he asked. "Are they the right size?"

I walked over to Chato, and we both lifted our pant legs to show off our brand- new U.S. Keds. We looked at each other and smiled. We both knew that even if the shoes had been twelve sizes too big, we *still* would have worn them. The sound of voices laughing and talking made us look up the trail, but they were still too far away to see who they belonged to. I thought of my new underwear, and I turned to thank my angel. But he was gone. Poof! Just like that. I looked all around, but he had disappeared.

"Hey, come back!" I yelled. "Come back, angel! I don't even know your name!"

It was no use. He was gone. Or at least we couldn't *see* him. But he did say he was always with me. That made me feel good.

"Wow," Puggy said, looking around for my angel. "You weren't lying, Mar. Is he really an angel? He smells just like your gramma's kitchen."

"I told you I wasn't lying, Pug," I said. I looked around, hoping to see him.

"Yeah, Pug," Beanie said, looking up at Puggy. "He told you he wasn't lying."

The voices coming from the trail were getting closer, and we could even hear some muffled yells coming from the back of Hermana Luz's cabin. Maybe the people coming down the trail would discover Chinche and his posse and help them out of their hole. But I didn't want to be around for that.

I motioned to the others to be quiet and to follow me, and we hid in the bushes in back of the Archuleta cabin that was across from *Hermana* Luz's.

I looked through the bushes and saw nine or ten Bible School kids walking down the trail past us toward the river. I heard Max's name mentioned by some of the girls, with giggling right after, of course, and something about the twins, but they walked by us before I could make out what they said. Pretty soon they would discover Chinche, and I didn't even want to be anywhere *close* when that happened!

When they were safely past us, we ran to the front of the Archuleta cabin and down the trail and we didn't slow down until we had touched the rail of the wooden stairs at the bottom of the *comedor.* We turned back to make sure no one had followed us, and when we didn't see anyone we sat down on the first step, out of breath and completely exhausted. This had been quite a night. Even for me.

I wiped my face with my shirt and brushed off little specks of dirt that had gotten on my new Keds. I was careful not to smudge them, but even with the dirt, the beautiful white canvas and brand-new shoelaces seemed to glow in the soft night light. The preaching was no longer coming through the loudspeaker and a few families walked past us down the stairs, talking quietly and done for the night. But it sounded like there was still a good old-fashioned *Aleluya* altar call going on. We could hear coming from the loudspeakers the guitars and piano, the crying, the singing, the shouting and the laughter. No memorized prayers here, boy. These people talked to God like He was their friend or something. Like they knew Him personally. If I could just quit lying, then maybe one day He could be my friend. I think, maybe, He already was. At least He seemed interested in me. I mean, I had an angel and everything, right?

"I'm hungry," Puggy said, interrupting my thoughts.

"Yeah, me too," Chato and Beanie said at the same time.

I turned and looked at my friends. "Do you think God likes me?" I asked.

"What?" Puggy said, squinting at me. "Waddaya mean, does God like you?"

"Well, waddaya think? Do you think He likes me?"

"Of course He likes you, Mario!" Beanie said, getting up and standing in front of me with a scrunched-up face and his arms crossed. "He gave you a real big Navajo angel with a pretty red jacket, didn't He?"

Puggy and Chato started laughing, and so did I. Beanie was right. If God *didn't* like me, why would He even *bother* giving me an angel? I stood up and rubbed my stomach. The grease from the *comedor* was calling my name. My mouth watered just thinking about it, mixed with mustard and onion bits dripping down my chin.

"OK, but listen," I said, "nobody says anything about tonight to *no one*! Understand? Especially about my angel, OK?"

Everybody nodded. "Nobody'd believe us anyway," Puggy said, shaking her head. "C'mon. The food's gettin' cold!"

We raced up the stairs to the rear kitchen door. Our mothers would be happy to see we were all in one piece and hopefully they would already have the burgers and fries waiting for us. We might even be able to beat the crowd.

And tonight I definitely didn't have to worry about Brother Chinche bothering me, or Finky and JoJo picking on me. Was this incredible, or what?

Whew! I reached the top of the steps and stopped. I felt light-headed. A Navajo angel, new U.S. Keds, new J.C. Penney real boys' underwear, Big Hunks and greasy burgers, freedom from bullies, a brown-skinned and black-eyed Jesus, and a beautiful blue-green-eyed girl from Colorado who seemed to like me. Wow! Yes, Beanie, it did look like God was smiling down on me!

Man! Would there *ever*, I mean *EVER*, be a day like this in my life?

Hey, maybe Bonnie would be in the *comedor*!

Yeeaaah!

The Yanks,
German Browns,
Brujas,
&
Big Bennie's Funeral

My dad was a Yankee fan. I mean a *real* Yankee fan. He just loved the Yankees, and not just when they were winning, which was often, but even those rare times when they lost. I'm not sure how it happened that a guy who was born in the tiny New Mexico village of Ensenada (or Cincinnati, as he called it) became a fan of a team a couple of thousand miles away in New York City, but he just loved 'em. He even got my mom to love the Yankees. I remember a lot of times, before I had started going to school, and Max and my sisters were in school and my dad was once again on the road helping start a church somewhere, that she and I would sit at the kitchen table with our ears real close to the radio and we would listen to the games. If it was anybody else but the Yankees, we wouldn't listen, but if it was the Yanks, then we were in the kitchen. My dad said that's why we always liked to eat when we were listening to ballgames, because we were always in the kitchen. He was probably right.

My mom and I would both get real excited when Mickey Mantle would step up to the plate. She would stop whatever she was doing. Even if she was right in the middle of rolling a tortilla, she would sit down, still holding her rolling pin, lean her head in towards the radio, and listen with anticipation. Mickey was the only one that could make my mom stop rolling a tortilla. When he was batting, she would just *have* to sit down and listen.

"It's gonna be a homer or a strikeout," she would say.

"He's already struck out two times," I would say.

"That's OK," she'd say, "he's due."

He's due. My mom was the only mom in the world, in the *universe,* who would say, "He's due." She would listen to my

145

dad and the announcers do baseball talk, and then she would say something like, "He's due."

"Hope so," I'd say.

"Did you put your left sock on first today?" she'd say.

"Yup," I'd say.

"How about your left shoe?"

"Yup. Left shoe too."

"And did you hang the towel back up with the tag on the inside?"

"Yup. I even checked it before the game to make sure."

"OK, then. He's due."

My dad was an incredible man of God. And my mom was the most powerful praying woman I had ever seen. I know that I was only ten years old, but I had been around a lot of ministers and people who claimed to be Christians, and I had to say, my parents were the best I had ever seen or would probably *ever* see. They never even *talked* about anybody! Except maybe to tell me to stay away from Brother Chinche. You could just tell that they loved God very much. But even though they loved God a lot, and they even prayed a lot, when it came to the Yanks, they still had their little superstitions.

I asked my mom one time if God had a favorite team.

"Probably not," she said.

"Do you think it's OK with Him if I pray for the Yanks?" I asked.

"Sure you can," she said. "I do."

Wow! My mom, who was always praying for me and my dad and everybody, even prayed for the Yanks!

"Really?" I asked.

"Yeah," she said, "but only if they're in the World Series."

Well, that made sense. That's when they would need it the most.

And my dad sat me down once and told me that one time before the Yanks played a doubleheader, that he had put his left sock on first that day and also his left shoe, which he never did, and they had won.

And he said last year, when the Braves were up three games to one in the World Series, and things didn't look too good for the Yanks because Lew Burdette was pitching against them, he went to use the bathroom, and after he washed his hands, he said he remembered hanging up the towel with the tag on the inside, and the Yanks won the next three games to win the Series. And since then, he made sure that he hung up all the towels in the house with the little tags on the inside. Of course, that only affected a few towels, because most of them were so worn out from use that not only were the tags gone, but so were the little bumpy terrycloth things. My mom didn't throw things away until they started shredding. If I ever got a job, I was gonna buy her a thousand towels.

"So," my dad said, "make sure you put your left sock and your left shoe on first and that the towel in the bathroom is hung up with the tag on the inside when the Yanks are playing."

And, so, that's what I still do.

Mickey, of course, never made things easy for me and my mom. We could almost hear the "whoosh!" of the bat as he would take a gigantic swing and miss and we would both put our heads on the table and groan. But then we would hear the loud "*crack*" of the bat, and just by the sound you knew it had been hit hard, and we would both jump to our feet with our arms raised in the air. Then my mom would turn into the announcer and say, "It's a hard shot to right field! It's going.... It's going....It's GONE!!! The Mick has done it again!"

Then we would jump around the kitchen cheering and she would give me a big hug and then go back to her tortillas or whatever else she was doing. I loved seeing my mom like that. It made me happy to see her happy. The whole house seemed happy when the Yanks won. The only one who wasn't happy was my oldest sister Rachel. She was the one person in the family who didn't like the Yankees. Even crazy Sarai would get happy. Of course, with Sarai, you never knew. One minute she could be smiling at you, and the next she would be carving her friends' initials on your face.

But my big sister Rachel, she was a Cleveland Indians fan, and she also loved the Albuquerque High Bulldogs. Which was very weird because Cleveland never won *anything*! At least the Bulldogs won state championships every once in awhile. I think she just liked how Rocky Colavito looked. She probably figured that because Rocky Colavito was cute, that must mean the Indians were good. Which, of course, was far from the truth. The Indians usually stunk. Plus, she always liked to be different anyway. She even married a *Baptist*! Whew! That was crazy. An *Aleluya* marrying a Baptist! Wow! I guess it was OK, though. I never heard my parents say anything about it except to pray for them. Her new husband seemed like a nice guy. He let me be the ring boy in their wedding even though I had holes in my shoes. And he coached me one time in Little League. So I guess it was OK that she married a Baptist.

Sister Velma told our Sunday School class one time that Baptists were one of the ones who were afraid of the Holy Spirit. She said that the original Baptist, the one who ate grasshoppers, he wasn't afraid of the Holy Spirit, but the ones alive today, even though they knew their Bibles real good, they were afraid of the things the Holy Spirit could do. That made me sad for my sister, and I just hoped one day Rachel's husband wouldn't be afraid anymore. Because if *he* was afraid, then my *sister* would be afraid, even though she knew better.

Sister Velma said that some people were afraid to let the Holy Spirit do what *He* wanted and instead did what *they* wanted. I hoped I never got that way. Even though I couldn't stop lying, and even though I had my head underneath an outhouse, I still hoped I would always let the Holy Spirit do whatever He wanted with me.

Anyway...my dad loved the Yankees. And he just liked all kinds of sports. He was even my Uncle Manuel's manager when my Uncle Manuel boxed. He said my uncle was undefeated in the Chama Valley until he boxed a big Apache from the Jicarilla Reservation. He said my uncle didn't feel like training because he didn't think anybody, including a big Apache, could ever beat him. Well, my dad said that by the third round my uncle was so tired he couldn't even put his hands up, and The Apache nailed him with a solid right and knocked him out. That was the end of my uncle's boxing career.

But as much as my dad loved sports, the sad part was that he could never participate. He'd had an accident when he was young and he couldn't turn his neck and he was bent over a little bit and he walked with a limp.

He told me that when he was thirteen, he was sitting on a high fence at a Tierra Amarilla playground watching a baseball game. He said the batter hit a foul ball right at him, and when he tried to get out of the way, he had fallen off backwards and had broken his back. And back in those days, when a person got hurt, they would just carry them home, put them in bed and hope they got better.

There were no hospitals in the mountains, and even if there was, my grandmother couldn't have afforded it. So they just put him in bed, broken back and all, and he healed that way. With a bad neck, a bad back and a bad leg. Without a doctor and without medicine. He said that when he would be hurting too much, my grandmother Euphemia (she's the one who told me never to talk about witches on Friday) would give him a couple of shots of whiskey and roll him up a couple of Bull Durhams to smoke.

"But don't ever tell anybody, Ok, '*jito*?" he had said, "especially don't tell church people; they would never understand about the whiskey and the Bull Durhams. OK?"

"OK," I said, "but you weren't saved back then, were you?"

"No, I wasn't," he said. "I was still praying to them deaf little *santos* on your Grandmother's wall. But I still don't want you to say anything, OK? Church people get a little funny."

I told him I wouldn't, and I never have. Not even to Puggy. It got me mad to think that the church people would get mad at my dad for something he did when he was thirteen. And not even to get drunk, like Jose and Joey. But just to help him with his pain, which must've been bad with a broken back.

I wondered what God considered worse: drinking a shot of whiskey and smoking a Bull Durham or looking at *Hermana* Frita's rear end underneath an outhouse.

Just thinking about my dad's back made me love him even more. He must've been real tough to have gone through that. And I never heard him complain, not once. But the best part was that he didn't let his limp or his back keep him from doing great things. My mom told me that even though he limped and he couldn't turn his neck, he never asked anybody for any special treatment.

About two weeks before this summer's camp meeting, I was in the kitchen with my mom as she was preparing the evening meal. I started asking her about the "old days" in Chama, and how did my dad become a minister.

She said that several years after he had broken his back, he was working in the box factory, and as a teenager had organized the workers and formed a union. That's why the Catholic Church in Chama was grooming him to be a priest, she said, because he was a great organizer and they knew the people would follow him. But before they could send him to one of their seminaries--That's a Catholic Bible School, she'd said-- he saw my mom, fell in love, attended one of the *Aleluya* prayer meetings at my *Mamou's* (That's what we called my mom's mom) house, had his Holy Spirit experience, and that was the end of him wanting to be a priest. Which was a pretty big deal in Chama. Because, according to my mom, being Catholic in Chama didn't even have anything to do with believing in God; it was just a way of life.

"That's just the way it is over there," she said, as she started cleaning the beans. I don't know what it was, but my mom and I always seemed to have our best conversations around something that had to do with food. And it was usually in the kitchen.

"Waddaya mean?" I asked, watching her as she expertly separated the little rocks from the beans.

"Well, people have been Catholic over there for so many years, that it's just kind of like a way of life more than anything that has to do with God or the church."

She put the rocks in a little pile away from the beans, and then swept the beans into a big glass bowl.

"You mean they don't have to believe in God?" I asked.

"Well, no, that's not it exactly. I'm pretty sure most of them believe in God," she said, getting up and walking over to the sink. She turned the water on and started rinsing the beans. I got up with her so I wouldn't miss anything she said. This thing about Catholics was real interesting. Almost all my friends in Albuquerque were Catholic, and even though they made fun of me for being an *Aleluya,* I still wanted to know more about them.

"It's just that I think it's more important for them to be Catholic than it is to believe in God. Do you understand?"

"Not really," I said, shaking my head.

"Look," she said, turning the water off. "You know my cousin Antonio that owns that bar by your *Mamou's* house in Chama?"

I nodded my head. I liked my mom's cousin Antonio. His breath smelled a little stale, like Jose and Joey's, but every time he saw me he would smile, rub my head and give me a quarter.

"Well, you know, he gets drunk a lot, and he likes to get people drunk, and I don't think he even knows what the inside of the Catholic church looks like down there, but he still won't let your *Mamou* talk to him about God, because he's Catholic, he says, and he won't let anybody, especially an *Aleluya,* tell him anything about God."

"But he's nice," I said.

"Well, yes, he's nice alright. But being nice doesn't have anything to do with it."

She poured the water out of the bowl, holding the beans in and not letting them spill with her free hand, then filled it up again and put the bowl on the counter. I knew she was going to let them soak for a while before putting them on the stove.

"It's kind of like trying to change the color of your skin," she said, walking back over to the table. I walked back with her. She sat down and uncovered another bowl that I had missed because I was so interested in the beans and what she was saying. As soon as I saw the black and green skin of the roasted green chili, my mouth began to water. Soft, creamy beans and green chili. The fresh tortillas would soon follow. The kitchen was a good place to be when my mom was cooking.

"You wanna help me peel these?" she asked, putting a couple of handfuls of chili in an empty bowl.

"Yeeaah!" I said, licking my lips and rubbing my hands together. I sat down and she put the bowl of chili in front of me. Then she spread a few sheets of newspaper, put them in the middle of the table and handed me an empty bowl.

"Put the stems and the peelings on the newspaper," she said, "and put the clean chili in the bowl."

"I knooow, Mom," I said, rolling my eyes. I must have seen her do this a million times. I loved peeling chili. My fingers would tingle afterwards. I picked up a chili and started peeling. "So waddaya mean about the color of my skin?"

"Oh, yeah," she said. She sat down on the other side of the table and started peeling. "Well, it's like being Catholic in Chama is like the color of your skin. That's just the way it is. If you're brown, you're brown. If you're pink, you're pink. You just don't change. It's just the way it is. It doesn't really have anything to do with God; it's just the way they are. Like your cousin Antonio, almost all of them will never go to the Catholic church, except maybe for a funeral, but they say they're Catholic, and that's the way they'll live, and that's the way they'll die.'"

I peeled the first chili and put the meat with some of the seeds in the empty bowl, and put the skin and the stem on the newspaper. When green chili was roasted and steamed the right way, the skin peeled off real easy. And my mom, of course, always did it perfect.

"So what happened when my dad became an *Aleluya*?" I asked.

"Well," she said, putting the chili she had peeled into the bowl. She wiped her hands, stood up and went to the fridge. "People got real, real upset. Especially your dad's family."

She opened the fridge and took out a good-sized pork roast, got a knife from the drawer by the sink, and came back to the table. She stayed standing and started cutting the pork and putting it into two piles. One pile, the biggest, had bite-sized chunks of just the meat. The other pile, the smaller one, had little chunks of meat *and* fat. The smaller one was my favorite, because that was the one she would use to fry real crispy, little *chicharrones*. And when they were done frying, she would take them out, put them into a separate plate, and use that grease to brown the rest of the meat.

"So what did his family do?" I asked.

"They disowned him," she said.

I stopped peeling chili and looked at her.

"They disowned him?" I asked. "What's that?"

She put the small pile of *chicharrones* in a plate and walked over to the stove. She placed the meat with the fat in a pan that had been heating up over a gas flame. The crackling sound of the meat hitting the hot *manteca* made my mouth water even more. I could already taste the crispy pork fat wrapped inside of a freshly buttered tortilla. She fanned the smoke coming from the pan with a *trapo* and came back to the table.

"That means," she said, sitting down, "that his mother no longer wanted him as her son. And his brothers and sisters no longer wanted him as their brother."

What!? I thought. How could his family do that?

"But I thought my "G" (that's what we called my grandmother Euphemia, my dad's mom) loved my dad. She acts like she does every time we see her."

153

The half peeled chili was still in my hand, but I couldn't think of anything else except for my "G" not wanting my dad. That was his *mom!* How could she *not* want him!

"Of course she loves him. Your dad is her baby son." She grabbed a handful of chili and put it in front of her. She picked one up and started peeling it. "But she and your uncles and aunts were very hurt and angry with his decision. Plus, I'm sure they were real embarrassed too. Him not being a Catholic anymore, that was a very big deal down there, *mi 'jito*. His family and those priests had some pretty big plans for your dad. But God just had bigger plans."

"But she wants him now, right? I mean, she wants him as her son now, right?"

"She sure does. It's taken a while, but his family more or less accepts what he is and what he's doing. In fact, I think your "G" is pretty proud of him. Your dad only went up to the eighth grade, you know. And even though he didn't become a priest like she wanted, he's still a minister. And here he is, the Superintendent of the Central Latin Conference of the Assembly of God, letting God use him to start a bunch of small works around this part of the country, that hopefully, with God's help, will turn into bigger works."

When she said that, my mom stopped peeling chili and looked over at me and smiled real big. I think she was more proud of my dad than my 'G' was.

"But my G's an *Aleluya* now, isn't she? I mean, she goes to church with us and everything when we see her, right?"

My mom raised her eyebrows and picked up a chili and started peeling it.

"Well, I don't know," she said slowly, with her eyebrows still raised. "Your G's a pretty feisty ol' girl, and you just never know with her. But at least she does go to church."

I started peeling my chili again and didn't say anything. Wisps of smoke coming from the frying pan on the stove floated gently to the ceiling, and the only sound in the kitchen was the crackling of the *chicharrones* frying in the *manteca*. The mouth-watering aromas of fried pork fat and freshly roasted green chili would soon be joined by the equally delicious fragrances of fresh tortillas and beans. But even as incredible as these familiar smells were, and as much as I was looking forward to enjoying the food, I just felt real bad for my dad having to go through all that with his family. And he never even *said* anything about it!

"Well," I said, "He must've loved you a lot to go through all that."

My mom smiled. "Yes, *mi 'jito.* He loves me alright. But he didn't go through all that just because he fell in love with me. He also the loved the Catholic Church, he loved his family, and he loved all those people in Chama." She finished peeling one of the chilis and then stopped, wiped her hands on the *trapo* and looked at me.

"*Mi 'jito,* when your dad walked into that prayer meeting at your *Mamou's* that night, something happened to him that no human or no church or no religion could ever do to him. He came into contact with the mightiest power in the universe, the Holy Spirit. A power he had *never* experienced before! And once that happened, he was never, *ever,* going to be able to settle for anything less. He fell in love, alright. But he fell in love with God that night a lot harder than he fell in love with me. *That's* why he left the Catholic Church. *That's* why he was able to take his family disowning him. It wasn't because of me. It was because of God."

When she finished talking, she picked up her *trapo* and wiped her eyes. When I saw her tears, it made me want to cry too. I *always* wanted to cry when I saw her cry. But at least this time it wasn't me who was making her cry. These tears were different. Kind of like a happy cry. If that was possible. All I knew was that if I didn't say something, then I was going to have to borrow her *trapo.*

"Mom, do think my "G" still rolls her own Bull Durhams and drinks whiskey?"

My mom put the *trapo* down and looked at me like she was surprised.

"What?" she said, wrinkling her eyes. "What do you mean, Bull Durhams?"

"Well, yeah. You know, does she still smoke Bull Durhams and drink whiskey?"

"Who told you that?"

"Uh..I don't know," I said. I didn't want to tell on my dad. "Probably Max." Uh- oh. I hope Max didn't hear about this. "Maybe it was Sarai." I said, hoping to throw her off. I would rather get Sarai in trouble than Max.

"Sarai told you your "G" smokes Bull Durhams?" my mom said, squinting her eyes and leaning towards me. "Are you lying again?"

"Uh..I...uh." Why had I said anything? Why hadn't I just let my mom cry like she wanted? Now, here I was, lying again!

"Uh..I uh..I just can't remember right now," I said, hoping she would change the subject. "Maybe my "G" did. Yeah, maybe she did. Do you want me to peel some more chili, or can I go outside and play?"

She kept looking at me with that "Where in the world do you come up with these kind of things?" look. Then she put another handful of chili in front of her and started peeling. "Go ahead. Just make sure you get back here in time to eat. And if you see your sister, tell her to get in here. I need her to help me. And don't worry about your "G" and her Bull Durhams. I'm pretty sure she doesn't smoke them anymore."

I went around the table and hugged her. "I love you, Mom," I said. "One of these days, a miracle will happen and I promise I'll never lie to you again."

"Praise God!" she said, lifting her hands and face to the ceiling. "Now *that* will be a great, great day!"

And I had kept my promise. Well, almost.

It had been six days since that incredible Saturday when Finky, JoJo, and Brother Chinche had become instant legends by getting real acquainted with the outhouse by the river. Chato and Beanie had already left for home, and so had Puggy and her family. The camp was pretty much empty now, except for Brother Chavez and Brother Boni and the two or three families that had stayed behind a few extra days to help my dad clean up the grounds and secure the cabins for next years camp meeting.

I had finally told my mother about my angel, and about everything that had happened. I hadn't realized how great it was to just tell the truth. I was going to tell her the truth even if she didn't believe me. At least *I* would know it was the truth.

She had stayed real quiet. Even when I told her that God didn't have a religion. I had been nervous to tell her that He wasn't Assembly of God, but she took it real well. Almost like she already knew. And when I told her that Jesus was brown and not English, and that He had black eyes like me, she smiled. She didn't ask me any more questions about my angel, but I would catch her just staring at me sometimes. I knew she had told my dad, but it was strange that he hadn't asked me anything yet.

But here it was Friday, our second to last day in camp, she was in our cabin with Sarai making some fresh tortillas, Max and his friend Rudy were fishing by the bend near Brother Finkenbinder's cabin because he had told my dad that he had seen the Game and Fish guys stocking the river right there this morning. My dad had gone to see what Brother Chavez and Brother Boni were doing. I had wanted to go with him, but he said he would be right back. He said to wait for him because he had a surprise for me. So I grabbed a hot tortilla, a toasty one that my mom had made especially for me, melted some butter on it, and made my way to the river.

Was there anything more incredible for a ten-year-old kid who was almost always in trouble, than sitting on a big log, all by himself, not having to worry about bullies or Brother Chinches to come along and mess things up, *not* in trouble (at the moment anyway), with a delicious, toasty tortilla, with new U.S. Keds and new J.C. Penney boys' underwear, next to the most beautiful river in the world? Probably not.

The sound of the water hitting and then rushing past the big log was as delicious to my ears as the tortilla was to my mouth. I wiped the butter that dripped down my chin with my finger and licked it, not wanting to waste anything. The water looked a little green, not quite clear. Perfect for fishing. I had heard Max tell a girl one time that he "wished this moment could last forever." I think I was having that kind of moment. I looked toward the bend and saw Max with his fishing rod making his way carefully out about knee-deep in the river. The water was still swift and I didn't think Max was crazy enough to go too far out, but there was a big pool in front of him and I know he wanted to drop a worm in there. Rudy was standing on the shore looking like he could use some help putting the worm on his hook.

I put the last of the tortilla in my mouth, licked my fingers again, and thought about all the things that had happened at this summer's camp meeting. Except for the outhouse thing (or the "Outhouse Incident," as Brother Chavez was calling it), things had gone pretty smooth. I had met a beautiful, green-eyed Bonnie who didn't care that I had several rows of teeth or that my hair stood straight up like a paintbrush. She had even sat next to me in children's church the next day. I could tell that all the other little boys and girls, and even the teacher, Sister Archuleta, were kind of in shock that a pretty girl was actually sitting next to *me*! Mario, The Terrible! Especially the Colorado guys. If they didn't like me before, then they were going to *hate* me now. It was the absolute best day of all my ten years on earth.

I had sweated, but not bad, and I had made sure my breath didn't stink by putting the whole pack of gum in my mouth. Bonnie said maybe she would see me again one of these days, but she didn't know when, then her mother had pulled her into their car and they had zoomed away down the dirt road and over the small ditch by the Elk Horn and down the little highway to Denver. I had a real good feeling that I *was* going to see her again. Or maybe it was just wishful thinking. Her mother seemed a little bit nervous when she looked at me. I waved at her and smiled, but she didn't wave back. I guess she had heard some stories about me.

Brother Chinche had been in church the next morning, but when he saw me he quickly turned the other way and kept walking. I heard my dad telling my mom that the Bible School students had helped pull him and his posse out of the open outhouse hole, but not to worry because he probably wouldn't be bothering me anymore.

Max (who thanked me and Puggy for saving him and the Baca twins by giving us each a dollar) said that Finky and JoJo and their families had left early the next morning, which was OK with me. I guess they were pretty embarrassed by what had happened. I didn't care if I ever saw those two guys ever again for the rest of my life. Except maybe to walk back and forth in front of them with my new U.S. Keds. I still couldn't believe it. New U.S. Keds. I looked down at my brand-new tennies and smiled. There were a few smudges, but they still looked pretty new. How crazy was that? A Navajo angel who dressed with all the colors that I loved, buying me new U.S. Keds! And new J.C. Penney boys' underwear, which I was wearing right now! Maybe he *didn't* buy them. Maybe he just turned invisible and walked into the stores and just picked them up! And then saving me from drowning! Wow! Just *thinking* about that whole day was too much for me! Unbelievable! I wished he would show up again. I had a lot of questions.

I heard a yell and looked up the river just in time to see Max's fishing rod bend over double as a big trout had gone after his worm. He hurried as fast as he could over the slippery rocks back to the shore. He didn't want to lose the fish, but I knew he didn't want to go floating down the river either. The fish was putting up a great fight and the rod was bent over so much I thought it was going to break, but Max finally got back to the dry rocks and slowly brought the fish to the shore. It was flopping all around and Max was yelling and laughing at the same time. I could tell it was a huge fish even from where I was sitting. I jumped off the log and started running down the trail to where Max and Rudy were fishing. When I got there, Max was already back in the water casting his line back out to the same pool and Rudy was still trying to figure out how to put the worm on the hook.

"What're you doing here, you little *travieso*?" Rudy said, looking up from his mutilated worm.

I didn't answer him. Things were going too perfect today to spoil it by arguing with an incredibly stupid guy like Rudy. Why in the world did Max have dumb guys like this as friends? Whew!

I walked over to one of the gunny sacks on the rocks that Max had put his fish into. I got down on my knees and opened it and looked inside. The big one Max had just caught was in there still jumping. And there was a bunch more, all a pretty good size. I guess Max and Rudy had been busy.

"Whoa!" I said, turning to Rudy. "How many of these are yours?"

"None of your business," he snapped. He angrily threw away the remaining pieces of that poor worm and reached down to the Folgers can inside the big tackle box for another fresh one.

Well, I guess that meant that *Max* had been busy.

Max yelled again and I looked up to see his rod bent over again. The trout jumped high out of the water and was giving Max all he could handle. What a beautiful sight. Max let some of the line go, then started bringing the trout to the shore. As I was standing up I heard Rudy cuss. It was terrible to go fishing with someone and watch them catch while you suffered with nothing on your line but moss. Although, I did have to admit that I was enjoying watching Rudy suffer.

"Hey, kid," Max said, putting the flopping trout on the dry rocks. "You wanna help me? Grab this thing and get the hook out."

I happily got back down on my knees again and grabbed the fish with my hands *and* knees. This was no stocker; this was a beautiful, solid, gold and orange, spotted German Brown with that incredible hooked jaw. I put my thumb in one gill and tried to put my fingers around to the other gill, but the fish's head was too big. So I put my fingers into its mouth and took the hook out with my other hand. Some of the worm was still on the hook and my fingers were bleeding a little bit from the teeth. But that was OK. It was for a good cause, and I didn't even want to lose this fish. Not only was it gorgeous, but it was also the biggest one I had ever seen. Had to be at least twenty seven, twenty eight inches, easy.

When I took the hook out, I put my free thumb into the other gill and lifted the fish to my face. I loved the smell of fresh trout. I stood up, still holding the trout to my face, took a deep whiff, gave it a kiss right on its beautiful hooked jaw, and then put it into the gunnysack.

"Your little brother's weird, man," Rudy said. He had stopped torturing his worm long enough to watch me kiss the trout.

"Yeah?" Max said. He walked over to the coffee can and picked out a worm. "Betcha he wouldn't be taking a half hour to put a stupid worm on a hook." Max looked at me and started laughing.

"How many ya got?" I asked, picking up the gunnysack. Boy, it was heavy. I put it over my shoulder and turned around a few times. They'd better start doing something with these fish, I thought, or this sack's going to be too heavy for even *both* of them to carry.

"Well, let me see," Max said, quickly putting the worm on his hook. "I've cast nineteen times and guess what?" He looked at me and smiled real big. "That's right, I've caught nineteen fish."

I walked to the edge of the river, careful not to get my new Keds wet, bent down and put my hands in the cold water to wash the trout's blood off. Well, that's only eleven over the limit, I thought. Maybe the Game and Fish guy wouldn't come by today.

Max must have read my mind, because he said, "Don't worry, kid; the Game Warden prob'ly won't come by today."

He laughed and started walking back into the water. "And if this dumb guy," he motioned with his head over to Rudy, "would stop assassinating his worms, even *he'd* be catching.

I don't know how it happened, but I think every fish in the Chama River is at this spot. And I'm not just talking about stockers either. Watch this."

He walked out about waist deep and cast into some small rapids on his right and let his hook float into the big pool. The line was barely at the beginning of the pool when the tip of his rod bent over again. He let out a yell and started bringing the fish to shore.

"See what I mean?" he said, walking the battling trout carefully back to where I was standing.

"You wanna help me again?" he asked. The fish was almost on the rocks again.

"Yeah," I said.

I waited until Max had the fish safely away from the water, then I got on my knees again and grabbed the fish. It was a beautiful Brookie this time, with bright orange gills, but not as big as the Brown.

I took the hook out, lifted it up and kissed its pretty gills, and put it into the sack.

"I've never seen a Brookie down here," I said, going back to the river to rinse my hands. "They're usually up higher."

"Yeah, that's what I'm talking about," Max said. He walked over to the sack and whistled when he looked inside. "Man alive! I think every fish in the world is in that pool today. Maybe it's something in the water. Maybe it's like a big trout convention, or somethin'. Shoot, I don't know. But I ain't complainin'!"

"What if the game warden *does* come?" I said. "What're you guys gonna do then?"

"Then I'll just say they belong to Rudy." Max said, pointing to Rudy and laughing.

"Yeah, real funny," Rudy said, throwing another demolished worm on the rocks.

Max walked over to the tacklebox and picked up a little clear plastic container. "Here you go, Rood," he said, taking a little gold spinner out of the box. "I don't think I can stand seeing you murder any more worms, man. Besides, at the

rate you're going, I'm gonna have to stop fishin' and go dig up some more. And the fishin's too good to stop now."

He walked over to Rudy and grabbed his fishing rod. Rudy didn't say anything. He just stepped back and watched as Max tied the spinner on the end of his line. He actually looked relieved that he wasn't going to have to touch any more worms.

"See?" Max said, holding the little metal spinner up close to Rudy's face. "This little gold Mepp's gonna get you some pretty good-sized trout, man. And you ain't even gonna have to touch those poor little worms again, eh?"

Max laughed and so did I, and Rudy gave us both a dirty look. I had almost felt sorry for him until now. Man, fishing on the best fishing river in the world, and not being able to put a worm on a hook. Whew! How incredibly sad can you be?

"OK, you know how to do this?" Max asked Rudy as they both walked to the edge of the river.

"Yeah, I know how to do it. Just give me the rod, man."

Rudy walked into the river and stopped when the water reached his knees.

"Go out further, Rood," Max said. "That way, you can cast it way out there."

"No way, man. I'm not gonna drown."

"You ain't gonna drown, man," Max said, laughing. "The water's pretty smooth here."

"That's OK, man. I'm not crazy like you and your little brother. He's always almost drowning and you make me nervous walking out so far. I'm fine right here, man. Just leave me alone. Watch this."

He brought the fishing rod back and cast the little gold Mepp out to the middle of the pool. It wasn't a very good cast, but not bad, I guess, for a guy who was afraid to touch worms. He turned back to us with a big smirk on his face.

"See," he said, looking at us. "I told you I..."

He didn't have a chance to finish his sentence because right at his second "I", a trout hit that little gold spinner so hard, it knocked the rod right out of his hand and started it floating downstream.

"Agghhhhh!" he yelled, or something that sounded kind of like that, and then he dove; he just up and dove and did a big belly flop into the river after his rod. He floated with the current for a while, and when he came back up for air, he had the rod in his hand, but every time he tried to stand up, he would slip on the rocks and fall again.

"Help me!" he shouted. "Help me! I can't swim! I can't swim!"

"Then let go of the rod and grab that big rock!" Max yelled. We were both running along the bank trying to keep up with Rudy's head that kept bobbing up and down. But Rudy wouldn't let go of his rod.

"Let go of the rod, man!" Max yelled. "You gotta' let go of the rod!"

Rudy's head kept going under, and when he came up, he was gasping for air and choking on the water, but he would *not* let go of the rod.

I ran past Max and got to the big, round rock he was yelling about before Rudy did. I climbed to the top and lay down on my stomach, and leaned over as much as I could without falling in. In a few seconds he would be floating by. If he could reach up with his free hand, maybe I could grab it.

"Grab Mario's hand! Grab Mario's hand!" Max screamed at Rudy's head.

Rudy looked up at me and when he got close, he reached up with both hands and tried to grab my right hand with his free hand, but it was too wet and it slipped right out of my grasp. He groaned and started to float by, but I went over further and with my left hand I grabbed the fishing rod and held on. Rudy grabbed the rod with both hands and floated on top of the current and I felt myself being pulled down the rock and into the river. Oh, no, I thought, here we go again. And as I was getting ready to float downstream with Rudy, all I could think of was that my new Keds were going to get wet. Honest, that's what I was thinking about.

Right as I was about to go in, I felt two hands grab my legs and pull me up the rock. Max must've gotten there in time. Boy, I didn't realize how strong he was. He was pulling both of us up that rock, *quick,* like we were rags dolls. As I started going down the other side of the rock by the bank, Rudy was coming *up* the rock. And neither one of us was letting go of the fishing rod.

When my legs touched the ground, the hands let go of me. I looked up and saw Rudy laying on top of the rock, face down, with both of his hands still grabbing the fishing rod. Something started pulling hard on the rod, so I let go. I thought maybe Rudy just wanted it back.

I turned around to thank Max for saving us, but when I did, I saw him about ten yards back up the river on his hands and knees shaking his head. I walked over to see what had happened.

"What're you doing?" I asked. "How'd you get back there so quick? And what are you doing on your hands and knees?"

"Whadda ya mean, how did I get back here so quick?" Max said, getting up and wiping his hands and knees. "How did you get down that rock so quick? Is that some kind of new trick you learned, or what?"

"You mean you didn't grab my legs and pull me down?" I asked.

"Don't be funny, kid. I fell down running after you and Rudy. I thought you were both dead when I saw you going over that rock. But then, all of a sudden, I saw you coming back down. And quick, boy. I thought maybe that was something new you had learned."

Oh, my God! The hairs on my neck stood up, and I turned all around to see if I could see him. Or should I say, I turned around to see if my angel would let *himself* be seen. I mean, he let Chato and Puggy and Beanie see him, maybe, just maybe, he would let Max.

"Thanks," I said, looking up, "Thanks a lot!"

Max looked up and all around, then looked back at me.

"What? Who you talkin' to?" He asked.

"Well, uh," I said. I was getting ready to tell Max that it was my Navajo angel who had pulled me and Rudy over that rock when we heard Rudy yell. We looked back to the rock, and there was Rudy standing on top of that big rock, fighting with the trout that was still on the line! The fish was still on the line! Wow!

"Don't fall in, Rood!" Max shouted. "Come down off that rock, man. But slowly. Don't be in a rush. Just sit down and slide."

"I don't believe it," Max laughed, as we hurried back to the rock. "Ol' Rudy Fruity, who never caught a fish in his life, almost drowned, but he would not let go of his fishing rod, because there was definitely a trout on the other end. My, my my."

The fish was still putting up a good fight as Rudy slowly slid down the rock onto the bank. He was *not* going to let go of that rod. Rudy Fruity. I was going to have to remember that. It might come in handy one of these days.

The fish was getting tired, and little by little, Rudy was bringing him in. Finally, the fish flopped onto the bank, and all we could do was stare at it.

It was a beauty. A beautiful, fat Rainbow. I mean *fat*. The red and almost purple coloring was incredible. But all I could think of was, man, this fish almost made me ruin my new Keds.

"She's a beaut, Rood," Max said. Nobody moved. We just watched the fish flop a few times on the rocks.

"Yeah," Rudy said, quietly. He looked over at me. "Thanks, kid. I kinda' hate to say it, but I really owe you one."

He held his hand out to me, and Max nudged me to go shake it. I walked up to him and shook his hand.

"Whaddaya mean, you hate to say it?" Max said. "You shouldn't hate to say it. You don't owe him one, you owe him a million, man."

It was kind of awkward shaking the hand of a sworn enemy, but after you saved their life, it was definitely different. They even looked different for some reason.

"That's a great fish," I said. "I guess you can fish after all."

Rudy looked down at the fish. He still hadn't let go of my hand and he looked like he might cry. I hoped he didn't. Then I *really* would feel strange.

"Yeah, it is a pretty fish," he said. He looked back at me. "How in the hell...I mean, how in the heck did you pull us over that rock?"

"I didn't," I said.

"Whaddaya mean, you didn't? I was the one you pulled out of the river and over this rock, remember?" Rudy said. He let go of my hand and walked over to the fish. He bent down to pick it up, but you could tell he wasn't quite sure what he should do first.

" Here. Let me help you," I said, changing the subject. If I told Rudy a big Navajo angel had pulled us out of the river and over that big rock, then he might forget that I had just helped save his life and would start making fun of me again.

I kept the still-fighting trout down with one hand and took the little gold Mepp out of its mouth with the other. Then I picked it up and handed it to him.

"My mom says she prays to Jesus for miracles around her kids every day. I guess you and I just experienced one. Here. Just put your thumb or fingers up through the gills, and the fish won't slip out of your hands."

I cradled the big, squirming Rainbow against my chest as Rudy put his fingers in the gills. He held it up proudly, then kissed it on the side. " I ain't quite as crazy as you," he said, "but If I ever catch one cute enough, maybe then I'll kiss it on the mouth."

He laughed and so did Max. They don't come much cuter than that fat Rainbow you're holding, I thought, but I didn't say anything. This was Rudy's big moment, so I guess he could do or say anything he wanted. At least he seemed to appreciate what had just happened, and that catching a trout this size and almost drowning in the process wasn't an everyday occurrence. Except for me, of course. The drowning part, I mean.

"Hey," Max said, "There's a bunch more fish to catch. You ladies can talk all you want, but I'm gettin' back to that hole."

"Hey, you wanna fish, Mario?" Rudy said, holding his fishing rod out to me. "You can use my rod if you want."

Wow! That's the first time I had heard Rudy use my real name instead of calling me a bad word or something! I guess him thinking I saved his life really did something to him. Heck, I didn't even think of it as being *him* when I got on that rock to catch him. You just don't think of things like that during an emergency. It was probably because I had almost drowned so many times, and it was such a bad feeling, that I would have helped *anybody* get out of the river. Well, probably not Finky. Or JoJo. Those guys I think I would have just watched as they floated by. I might've even waved as they drifted by screaming for help.

"Nah," I said. "I don't want to get my new shoes wet. Maybe later, when I go put my old shoes on."

Max and Rudy looked down at my new Keds, and nodded. I thought this might be a good time to suggest to them that maybe later we could all go swimming at one of the safe spots up the river by the bridge, and that way I could show off my new J.C. Penney underwear. But then again, maybe me and Rudy weren't that good of friends just yet.

We turned to walk back to the pool where everything had started. Max picked up a water snake that was sunning itself on the rocks and acted like he was going to throw it on Rudy;, he laughed when Rudy almost fell in the river again getting out of the way, then he threw the snake into the middle of the river, where the current was real strong. The river took it swiftly, but it stayed on top of the water and I turned and watched as it made its way to the edge of the river and back on to the rocks downstream.

Rudy had floated downstream on the edge of the main current about fifty yards. It was a good thing he hadn't gone out to the middle or we would have never seen him again. Not alive, anyway. I looked around to see if my angel would make an appearance, but he wasn't anywhere around. Well, he was, but we just couldn't see him.

When we got back to the pool Max quickly went to the Folgers can and took out another worm.

"Times a-wastin'," he said. He put the worm on and started walking back out into the river. Rudy looked at his trout some more, like he still couldn't believe it, then put it in the gunnysack. I heard a faint yell, and I turned around and saw my dad standing by the big log where I had been, waving both of his arms in the air.

"Hey, I gotta go," I said, turning back to Max. "My dad's calling me."

"Wait a minute," Max said, "Do me a favor." He got out of the water and walked over to the gunnysack with the fish and picked it up. "You think you could take this to the cabin? Just tell mom to put 'em somewhere and that I'll clean 'em later. I just don't want the Game Warden to come by and here we are with all these fish, OK?"

I walked over and took the sack from him and put it over my shoulder. It was pretty heavy, but it was a good idea to get it out of there.

"OK," I said, and started walking up the rocky bank back up to the trail. When I got to the trail, I heard Max let out another yell, and I turned and watched as his fishing rod bent over again with another trout. Man, what was going on in that river? Or maybe it was just that spot. A dream come true for a fisherman. A few more fish and Max was going to be able to feed all of Chama.

I looked up the trail and saw my dad leaning against the big log I had been sitting on eating my tortilla. He said he had a surprise for me. Just thinking about what that surprise was made me walk faster.

When I finally reached him, my back was soaking wet from carrying the fish, and my legs felt like I had just run up a mountain.

"Hey, Dad," I said. I dropped the sack by his feet and let out a big "Whew!"

"Hey, buddy. What's in the sack?"

"Max and Rudy are fishing, and they asked me to bring these to the cabin and said they'll be over later when they finish to clean 'em all."

"Let's see," my dad said.

I bent down and opened the sack and brought the big one out that Rudy had just caught and held it up for my dad to see.

"Man, oh, man!" he said, "Are they all that size?"

"Pretty much," I said, taking Max's big German Brown out of the sack. I brought it up to my nose and breathed in its aroma. "You wanna smell?"

"Uh..no, that's all right. I can tell from here that it smells pretty good."

He knelt down on his good leg and looked into the sack.

"I wonder if those guys know what the limit is?" he said, getting back up. He got a worried look on his face and looked over to where Max and Rudy were fishing. "I just hope the game warden doesn't come."

I knew my dad wanted to say something to Max, because there *was* a legal limit, and he didn't want Max to get in trouble. But he hesitated because he saw what a great time his oldest son was having and also because he was born in this area, and I knew that all the guys who were born in these mountains, even the ones who were absolutely great Christians, like my dad, always kind of felt like they had some kind of special authorization, like from God or something, to get as many fish, or deer, or elk, or rabbit, or *whatever*, so they could feed their families. I know it doesn't make breaking the law OK, but that's how they felt. And they didn't like it when the game wardens would tell them what to do. Especially the English ones.

This summer, right before the camp meeting started, I was in town visiting my grandmother and playing with the Madrid brothers, Solomon and Sisto. Solomon told me that him and his dad and his brothers would kill a deer or an elk anytime they saw one. To prove it to me, we walked over to his house and he took me to a shack in the back. He let me inside and sure enough, there hanging from the beams on the roof were two unskinned deer and three big ones that were skinned. He said the big ones were elk. He said it was OK because there were fifteen kids and two adults in his family. The way I figured it, that was one deer or elk every two days just to feed that family. And they didn't just eat the meat. They ate *everything*! Brains, guts, eyeballs, *everything*!

So, anyway, that was one of the reasons I knew my dad wasn't telling Max anything.

I reached down, closed the top of the sack and put it over my shoulder.

"So, what's the surprise, Dad?"

"Huh?" he said, turning around.

"The surprise."

"Uh, oh, yeah. The surprise. C'mon. Let's go. Max'll be all right. Do you know if he even has his license? "

"I dunno, Dad."

"Oh, well. I think he'll be OK."

We walked up the trail and passed the spot that was now going to be in all the history books. Brother Chavez and Brother Boni had done a good job putting the outhouse back up. They had even made sure there was no hole in the back to tempt someone to put their head under. I know. I had already checked.

"Brother Chavez did a pretty good job on that outhouse, huh, Dad?" I said, as we walked by it.

"You don't really want to bring that up, do you? It's done. Finished. Right?"

"Yup," I said. "I just thought he did a good job. He even fixed some of the boards."

"Uh-huh. He sure did." he said. We stopped and looked at the outhouse. Brother Chavez *had* done a good job. He was a great carpenter on top of everything else.

"He even cut down the trees," my dad said.

"Yup," I said, nodding.

"That way *nobody* can hide back there," he said, looking down at me.

"Yup. I know what you mean," I said. Why had I even *mentioned* the outhouse?

"And nobody's gonna throw knives at it, especially when little old ladies go inside to use it, are they?"

"That's right, Dad," I said. "Nobody is. And if they do, it ain't gonna be Chato or me. Or even Puggy."

"Well, that's good," he said, "and I'm sure Puggy's real happy that you're including her."

We started up the trail again and then all of a sudden he started laughing. He just started laughing. *Loud*! That made me feel good. I loved it when my mom and dad were happy.

"What?" I asked. I think I knew what he was laughing about.

"You should have seen Brother Chinche when they brought him to me." When he thought about it, he laughed again.

He was still laughing when we got to the cabin. My mom and Sarai were outside in the screened porch, still rolling dough and making tortillas. The aroma from the fresh torts on the stove inside the cabin drifted outside to the porch. There was something else cooking too. And it smelled delicious.

I followed my dad up to the top step and stopped.

"What's in the bag, 'jito? And why's your dad laughing so much?" my mother asked. She had a flat piece of dough in her hands and was tossing it from one hand to the other.

"He's probably got a dead animal in there, or something." Sarai said. Even through the screen I could see her eyes narrow as she glared at me.

"Here," my mother said, handing Sarai the raw, flat dough. "Go put this on the stove and get the other one before it burns. Your brother hasn't even said anything to you, and you're already starting."

"She's right, Mom," I said. My dad opened the screen door and I walked in. I put the sack on the floor and opened it. "There's about twenty dead animals in here."

"I told you!" Sarai said triumphantly. "I knew it! I knew he had a dead animal in there!"

"And I told you to get that tortilla on the stove. Now go!" My mom pointed to the cabin door and motioned for my sister to get in there. Sarai stuck her tongue out at me, then walked through the door.

My mother walked over and looked in the sack. "*Ay, Senor!*" she said, her eyes opening real wide. "*Quien pesco estos?*"

"*Max, y tambien el Rudy,*" my dad said.

"But isn't this too many? Won't he get in trouble if he's caught?"

"*No te preocupes*, he'll be all right; he's not going to get into trouble."

"Macedonio Santos! What do you mean '*no te preocupes*'? Of course I'm going to worry. I know that you and a lot of other men around here think that river and everything in it, and everything that walks on four legs in those mountains, belongs exclusively to you; but the law says different, and they *will* give our son a ticket!"

"*Bueno, calmate.* Calm down. It's gonna be all right," my dad said. "Mario and I will go over there after I show him the surprise."

"*Ay*, yes, the surprise. How could I forget the surprise." My mom put her hands to her face and shook her head. She walked back to the table and started rolling out another tortilla. "One son going to jail and the other one learning how to kill things. You're right. I have nothing to worry about."

"Kill things? What are you guys talking about?" I asked.

"Sadie, Sadie," my dad said, walking over to my mom and putting his arm around her. "I've never let anything happen to your '*jitos*, have I? Huh?"

My dad was a pretty smooth guy. He never pulled out the name "Sadie" with my mom unless he was in deep trouble. Or if he was in a real good mood and he wanted to see her smile. This time it was trouble, and it didn't look like she was going to smile.

"You know I hate guns," my mom said. She put the rolling pin down and just let my dad hold her. "Just because everybody around here has a gun, that doesn't mean that my sons have to."

"Guns?!?" I said, excitedly. "Dad, what guns?!"

Ever since Solomon had shown me his shack full of hanging deer and elk I had been bugging my dad almost every day to borrow Brother Boni's rifle so that we could go hunting for rabbits. But with everything that had happened last week and most of my free thinking time preoccupied with my green-eyed Bonnie and how in the world would I ever get to see her again, I had forgotten all about it.

My dad let go of my mom and walked into the cabin. When he came back out to the porch he had a rifle in one hand and a box of bullets in the other. Sarai followed him and stood by the door with her arms crossed, frowning at me.

"Alright, Dad!" I said. "You remembered!"

"Well, you've been doing pretty good lately, *mi 'jito. And* Brother Chavez said you helped him out a lot this summer. So," he said, smiling, "I thought it might be nice to give you a reward."

"Don't let him carry it. Promise me," my mom said. She walked over to me and laid her hands on my head. I knew she was praying for me.

"Dad! Mario's crazy!" Sarai said. "How can you even let him get *close* to a gun? He's going to kill everybody!"

"Sarai! *Callate*! Why do you talk like that? Your brother's not crazy, and he's not going to kill anybody. We're just going to see if we can get some rabbits to eat with that red chili your mother's making."

So that's what that other delicious smell was. Uhmmmm! Red chili and fresh toasty rabbit! And maybe some toasty trout too! Wow! We were going to have a feast tonight!

My dad walked out the door and down the steps, but I stood still until my mother finished praying for me. When she was done, she kissed the top of my head and let out a deep sigh. She was getting ready to say something to me, but I rushed out the door and stood next to my dad.

"Can I at least hold the bullets, Dad?"

He handed me the box.

"Don't spill 'em," he said.

He waved at my mother and Sarai. "Don't worry," he said. "He'll be all right. We'll stop and tell Max to come home."

I turned and waved too. Then we started walking down the trail towards the Tabernacle.

"Dad, I saw a bunch of rabbits by the Elk Horn yesterday," I said. I couldn't believe it. I was actually going hunting with my dad with a real rifle. A *real* one! I had shot my BB gun that Max had bought me a few years ago for Christmas, but not a real live gunpowder-and-bullet gun. Man, wait till I told Puggy and Chato! They were *not* going to believe me!

We walked past Max's trailer and Chato and Beanie's empty cabin. The camp was almost completely empty now and it was hushed except for the quiet sounds of the soft breeze rustling through the cottonwood leaves and the river gushing towards El Vado Dam. The birds were flying around with their musical conversations, but these beautiful Chama sounds, the ones I daydreamed about and heard in my head when I was back in school in Albuquerque, had replaced the noisy, busy, people sounds of the camp meeting.

We walked in silence until we got to the camp well. This was the well where everybody in the camp got their drinking water. We stopped and my dad asked for the box of bullets.

"Did you say you saw some by the Elk Horn?" he asked.

"Yeah," I said, pointing toward the fence on the other side of the camp. "Right over there by the fence."

I opened the box and handed him a fistful of bullets. I couldn't believe I was actually touching real bullets. One time in Albuquerque my mom had made me put my right hand on the Bible and promise I would never touch a gun or anything that had to do with a gun. She had been nice enough not to mention that today.

"Hey, we're not going after an army," my dad said, laughing. "Here, just give me three of those and put the rest back in the box."

I did as he asked and stacked the rest of them back in the box.

"Is this Brother Boni's twenty-two?" I asked.

My dad nodded. "Yup. This is Brother Boni's famous twenty-two."

He loaded the shells, then clicked a little switch on the side.

"What's that?" I asked.

"That's the safety," he said. He put the rifle in my hands so that I could see what he was talking about, but he didn't let go.

"In the future, if you ever handle a rifle, always put this little switch on when you're not shooting, OK?"

I nodded and rubbed my hand on the rifle. The wood was dark and almost the color of the barrel. It felt dangerous, and that made my heart beat even faster.

"Are you going to let me shoot it?" I asked.

"Sure," he said, taking the rifle back.

"When?"

"I'll let you know," he said. He put the rifle under his arm and we started walking up the trail to the other side of the camp.

"Your mom said you talked to an angel last week, is that true?"

I was wondering when he was going to ask.

"Yes, sir."

"This isn't one of your stories, is it?"

"No, sir."

"You're not lying?"

"No, sir."

We walked past Brother Savage's cabin and slowed down when we got to the middle of the campgrounds. This was where the Bible School students had their yearly bonfire. It was always a big deal. Brother Chavez would have me help him put pails of water on the outside just in case a spark would shoot out and start another fire, he would have something to put it out with. This year's bonfire had been extra special for me because there hadn't been anyone around to bully me or chase me.

I walked closer to the black, burnt circle. The charred logs hadn't completely been removed yet and you could still smell the smoke in the ground.

"So, what did he look like?" my dad asked. He had found a big log to lean on and he motioned for me to join him.

I climbed up the log and straddled it facing him. He was still holding the rifle under his arm and had the barrel pointing to the ground. He turned around to face me, still leaning on the log, because he couldn't turn his neck.

"Well," I said, "he was real big, he wore pretty jackets, and he was a Navajo."

"A Navajo?"

"Yup. That's what he looked like. 'Member those guys we saw dancing in Gallup?"

"Yeah."

"Well, he looked just like those guys. Only real, real tall." I put my hands as high as I could over my head. "And with a lot of muscles."

"Humph," my dad said. He took the rifle from under his arm, then turned and leaned it against the log in back of him. He looked back at me.

"A Navajo, huh?"

"Yeah, Dad. He didn't look English like all the books say, or have wings or anything."

"Yeah?"

"Yeah. And he smelled like apples, Dad. Just like my *Mamou's* kitchen."

"So, what did he say, this Navajo angel?"

"He said that Jesus was brown and that He had black eyes just like me."

"Really? He's brown?"

"Yeah, that's what he said. And he said he's always taking care of me and that he's the one who never lets me drown. Do you 'member when I fell off my high chair when I was a baby?"

My dad looked surprised. My mom had been surprised at this part too.

"Yeah. I do."

"Well, he said he was the one who caught me just in time so that I didn't break my neck."

"Really," he said, looking off to the side like he was remembering. He smiled and looked back to me. "Well, do you think I could talk to him and maybe thank him for always saving your life?"

I shook my head. "I don't know, Dad. It seems like he only appears when I'm in trouble. But he said even when I don't see him, he's always with me. He said God sent him." Maybe this was a good time to tell him. "Dad, did you know that God isn't Assembly of God?"

"Yeah, I kinda' thought so."

"Really, Dad! You knew that?"

"Yes I did, *mi 'jito*. There's nowhere in the Bible that says God is *any kind* of religion. He's just Almighty, All Powerful, All Loving and All Forgiving God."

"Wow! That's what *he* said, Dad! He said God is just God!"

"Well, that's right. He's just God and that's all there is to it."

Wow! How come I never knew my dad knew all this?

"How come you know all this stuff, Dad?"

"You just have to open the Book and read, *mi 'jito*'"

"Dad, how come nobody tells these Assembly of God people that God isn't Assembly of God?"

"Because most of them think heaven is reserved only for the Assembly of God, and Catholics think it's reserved only for Catholics and Baptists think it's reserved only for Baptists, and Methodists, and Presbyterians, and so on and so on. Each religion thinks heaven is reserved only for their group and nobody else. But they're in for a big shock. There's nothing religious about heaven."

"Hey! That's what my angel said too! He said God wasn't religious!"

"Well, he's right, son. As a matter of fact, when He was on the earth, Jesus called all the religious guys "Sons of the Devil" and "snakes." He wasn't real happy with them. But I guess we didn't learn much from them, because here we are again, everybody in their own religion thinking they're the only ones going to heaven."

"But does that mean the Assembly of God is bad?"

"Not at all, *mi 'jito*. It's a very solid doctrine."

"What does that mean? Doctrine?"

"Well, that just means that everything they believe in, they have Scripture to back it up."

"Are they going to heaven?"

"Well, hopefully, a lot of them will."

"But not all of them?"

"No, unfortunately, probably not. Remember, just because a person goes to a certain church does not necessarily mean they're going to heaven. Only those who have accepted Jesus Christ as their personal Lord and Savior and live according to what He says to do in the Bible are going to make it to heaven."

"Are Catholics going to make it into heaven?"

"Sure. If they have Jesus in their heart."

"Really? Catholics are going to make it too?"

"Yup. If they repent, confess Jesus Christ with their mouths and believe in their hearts that God raised Him from the dead in three days, they'll be there."

Wow! I couldn't believe it! Some Catholics were actually going to make it to heaven! And it sounded like some Assembly of God guys weren't! Wow! I was going to have to tell Sister Velma. This news was definitely going to shock her!

"But don't they pray to Mary and all those statues?"

"Not all of them. Some are actually beginning to open their Bibles and read that there's only one person to go to, and that's Jesus."

"Are the Baptists going to go too, even though they're afraid of the Holy Spirit?"

"Oh, sure. Hopefully, there'll be plenty of Baptists too. Who told you they were afraid of the Holy Spirit?"

"Sister Velma. She said that one time in Sunday School."

He laughed. "Well, I don't know if they're afraid of Him; they just get a little nervous when He shows up in ways they're not used to, or don't approve of."

Boy, they sure would have been nervous the night the Ortega Brothers sang. They would have probably run out of the Tabernacle, especially when the message in tongues had started.

"Well, if there are some Catholics going to heaven, how come you switched?"

I had forgotten all about hunting rabbits. My dad had never talked to me about these things. Maybe he just thought I was ready now. Maybe God had decided that the days of me causing my dad extreme embarrassment were over, and I was actually growing up a little.

I remembered the time just four years ago when I had climbed the back steps of the Tabernacle after a morning service, and I had seen my dad talking to three sisters from the *Concilio Misionero Femenil*. I don't really know why, but I got on my hands and knees, crawled over to where they were standing, put my head between the legs of one of the ladies, and just looked up her dress. I guess I just wanted to see what was up there. She screamed when she realized I was down there looking up her dress, then the rest of the ladies screamed, then my dad screamed, then the lady tripped over me trying to get away, then I got up and ran out the back door as fast as I could. I got beat pretty good for that one.

But this summer, I hadn't humiliated him once. But whatever the reason, he seemed like he wanted to talk, and I was going to take advantage of his wanting to talk. He wasn't even talking to me like a kid, but like he knew I was going to understand him. Like it was important for him, right now, to tell me these things.

"Because I had never had an experience with the Holy Ghost before, *mi 'jito*," he said. He turned away from me and looked down at the burnt logs. "I know your mother told you I was getting ready to become a priest. I loved the Catholic Church, son, the rituals, the traditions, all the ceremony. I never felt anything inside when I recited all those memorized prayers, but I just thought that's what God was all about. I thought as long as I followed those traditions, I was going to be all right. I didn't think I had to feel anything." He turned back to look at me. "Then I met your mom. And she started telling me about *experiencing* God, and talking directly to *Him*. Which, of course, was a very different thing for a Catholic. I mean, we would never *think* of talking directly to God! That's why we had priests, and Mary and all them saints; I thought only *those* guys could talk to God. And I was getting ready to *become* one of those guys!"

He paused and looked away again, like he almost couldn't believe it himself.

"But I'll tell you what," he said, looking back. "The night I went with your mother to that prayer meeting in your *Mamou's* living room was the night that would change my life forever. After Brother Giron spoke that night..."

"You mean, Uncle Joe preached that night?"

"Yeah, he sure did."

"Did he sing 'Jericho Road'?"

"Nah, there wasn't any piano around. Anyway, after he preached and said would anyone like to come forward and make Jesus Lord of your life, I went up because I knew that if I didn't, your *Mamou* wouldn't let your mom go out with me."

"You mean you only went up because you wanted to go out with my mom?"

"That's right, son. Hey, she's a beautiful woman. And boy, was I in love."

"Alright, Dad!"

We both started laughing. I guess love would make even a real smart guy like my dad do crazy things. In the middle of my laugh I thought of Bonnie. I think I was in love too. Was ten years old too young to be in love? I didn't think so.

My dad stopped laughing and continued, "So, anyway, I went up, not expecting anything, thinking I would just get this over with for your *Mamou's* sake, so she would see that I was doing what she wanted so I could go out with your mom. But when I got to the front, where Brother Giron was, something incredible happened to me. To this day I can't explain exactly what or how it was, but Brother Giron told me to lift my hands, and when I did, the exact instant I did, it felt like a massive amount of electricity hit my body. Kaboom! Just like that! Your mom told me later that I flew back about six or seven feet and landed on my back with my hands still raised and I was speaking in tongues. And when I came out of it, whatever it was, still on my back, that's what I was still doing, speaking in tongues. Me. Mr. Macedonio Santos. The devoted Catholic from Ensenada, New Mexico, soon to be Father Santos of Chama--slain in the Spirit, flat on my back, filled to overflowing with the Holy Ghost, and speaking in tongues just like all the *Aleluyas* I used to make fun of."

I just stared at my dad with my mouth open. Wow. Wow! No wonder my dad could never be a Catholic again! How could *anybody* have an experience like that and be the same? Maybe it was kinda' like me thinking Virgie was the most beautiful girl in the universe until I saw Bonnie, and now Virgie looked liked an ol' rag doll.

"Is that when your family got mad at you?"

"Yeah, they sure did. Your "G" couldn't believe I would embarrass the family like that. 'How could you do this?' she said, 'You're getting ready to become a priest.' She said Catholics are supposed to be Catholics until they die, and no *Aleluya* was going to be a son of hers, and that's when she and the rest of the family disowned me."

"Were you sad?" I asked. I could feel the tears starting to gather in my eyes. I couldn't believe a mother and a family could do that.

"Sure, I was sad, but there was no turning back after what had happened to me. The Holy Ghost had gotten ahold of me, and I had gotten ahold of Him, and I was not about to let go. Jesus was absolutely real to me. He was no longer on the cross, and as much as I loved, respected and greatly admired Jesus' mother, I began to feel extremely happy that I didn't have to go through her or anyone else when I wanted to talk to Him!"

He reached up to my face and wiped the tears that had come down my cheeks.

"But my "G" says you're her son now, doesn't she?"

"That's right *'jito*. She got over it when she saw that no matter what, I was never going back. Plus, she's a mom, and I'm her baby son, Just like you, I'm the baby of my family."

"Really, Dad? You're the baby too?"

"I sure am. And anyway, your "G" believes like we do now."

"Does she still smoke Bull Durhams and drink whiskey?"

He laughed and helped me off the log. "No, I don't believe she does those things anymore. C'mon. We gotta get some rabbits to go with that red chili."

We walked around the black, smoky ground and back on to the trail. The sun was almost at the top of the trees. It would be completely down in about three hours. We still had plenty of time.

"I've still got some questions," he said.

"OK," I said. It felt so good to tell my dad the truth. Maybe I should try it with everybody. Nah. I'll just take it slow for now. See how the truth works first.

"Not everybody gets to see angels, you know."

"I know."

"That's a special gift. We'll have to see what God wants you to do with it."

"You mean God's gonna want me to do something?"

"Sure. Why not?"

"Because it's me, Dad. I'm usually doing something really stupid to embarrass you, why would God want to use me?"

"That's exactly why, *mi 'jito,*" he said.

"Huh?"

He stopped and turned me to face him. "Because you're the unlikeliest person in the world for something like this to happen to. Who would ever believe it: Mario Santos, the preacher's kid who's always getting into trouble, being visited by angels. Navajo angels to boot! Always remember this, *'jito.* God will use whoever or whatever He feels like using. No matter if it's somebody or something that nobody else would ever think of. As a matter of fact, He *prefers* doing it that way. Your mom's pretty excited, you know. She's always told me that God was saving you for a purpose."

"Really?" Me? God was saving *me* for a purpose?

"That's right," he said. We started walking back up the trail. "And I believe she's right."

We walked in silence for a while. Wow! This was a bunch of stuff to think about! Maybe I really *was* growing up!

"Did you remember to put your left shoe and left sock on first today?" he asked, putting his arm around my shoulder.

"Yup," I said, "and I put the *trapo* tag on the inside. The one by the stove."

"They're playing a double-header today," he said.

"I know. I saw it in the Journal."

My dad would buy the Albuquerque Journal every day and we would check the box scores to see how the Yanks had done the day before and who they were playing today. But it was impossible to get good radio reception in the mountains.

"Do you think they'll go to the Series this year, Dad?"

"Hope so," my dad said, "It'll sure be boring if they don't."

I looked up the trail toward the fence and saw something moving in front of one of the empty cabins.

"Dad! Look! Right over there!"

We stopped and I pointed to where I had seen the movement, and sure enough, right in front of the steps of the cabin, four long ears moved back and forth.

"Shhh!" my dad said. He knelt down on his good leg and put his hand on my shoulder to get down also.

"Can I shoot 'em?" I whispered excitedly, getting down on both knees.

"Just wait," he whispered back.

He put the rifle up to his shoulder. "I need one of them to get out of the grass so that I can see it clearly."

I looked to where the rabbits were and saw one of them hop to the back of the cabin, by the fence, but the other one moved out of the grass to the trail.

"There he is, Dad!" I whispered, pointing.

"Shhhh! Not so loud. I see him. I see him."

This was it! I was getting ready to help kill an animal. I felt very excited. I had never killed an animal or even seen a real animal killed before. But here I was. Hunting! Real hunting!

I was looking at the rabbit when I heard the gun go off. The sound made me jump and when I did, I saw the rabbit go up in the air a few feet then land on its side.

"You got it, Dad! You got it!"

I grabbed his hand and helped him up.

"Yeah, I think you're right, *'jito*, I think we got 'im. Let's go see."

I grabbed his hand and practically dragged him, I was in so much of a hurry to get to the rabbit. We had killed a rabbit! My dad had actually killed a rabbit! I was a real hunter!

When we got up close to the rabbit, about three feet from it, we could see that his legs were still kicking.

"He's suffering," my dad said. "Let's make sure he doesn't suffer anymore."

He brought the rifle up to his shoulder and took aim, but I stopped him.

"Let me kill him, Dad! Let me kill him!"

My dad put the rifle down and carefully handed it to me.

"OK," he said. "Get real close to it, and be careful."

I walked up to the still-kicking rabbit, almost right on top of it, and pointed the rifle. This was the first time I had ever shot a real gun and I didn't want to mess it up. I looked through what I thought was the gun sight, saw the rabbit's furry body, and squeezed the trigger. I put the rifle down and looked at the rabbit. It was still kicking. I had missed! I had been almost right on top of it, and I had missed! I couldn't believe it!

"Oh, man!" I said, "I missed, Dad!"

"Yeah, I can see that. Here, give me the rifle. We can't let that rabbit suffer anymore."

"Dad! Let me just try it one more time! Please! I won't miss this time, Dad! I promise! I promise, Dad! Please!"

He didn't say anything. He just nodded and backed away a few steps.

I stepped up to the rabbit again, this time with the rifle about a foot from it. It was still kicking its little paws but it wasn't making any sound. I looked at it, and thought that it looked kinda' pretty and soft, and I wasn't real excited about killing it anymore. As a matter of fact, I was feeling pretty sad. But I knew I had to do it. My dad said we had to make it quit suffering. I looked through the sight again and squeezed the trigger one more time. I put the rifle down and looked. It was still kicking. I had missed again! I couldn't believe it! The barrel had almost been touching it, and I had *missed*! Unbelievable! In all the history of hunting, I was going to go down as the worst hunter ever! Inches away from the target, and I *missed*!

My dad reached down and slowly took the rifle from my hands.

"I'm sorry, Dad," I mumbled. "I can't believe I missed."

"I need another bullet," he said quietly.

I put my hand into the pocket where I had jammed the box of bullets and silently took one out and handed it to my dad. He took it and put it into the empty chamber.

He put the rifle to his shoulder and took aim, then pulled the trigger. The rabbit jumped a few inches off the ground and quit kicking. This time it was dead.

We both looked at it and didn't say anything. We didn't go towards it or anything. We just stood still for a few minutes and stared at it. I didn't feel like I thought I was going to feel. I didn't feel excited anymore. I felt terrible. I felt like I had killed my dog. It looked so beautiful just lying there. After wanting so much to shoot a real gun and kill something, now, I didn't even want to look at one.

I looked at my dad and I could tell by the look on his face that he was feeling the same way I was feeling. He didn't look like he had enjoyed killing either.

I had eaten rabbit before, and it had tasted great. But I knew that I would not be able to eat this rabbit. There was blood on its soft fur by the neck, and it was dripping down to the ground. I was glad I had missed. I felt like crying.

My dad walked over to the rabbit, reached down and picked it up by the ears.

"C'mon," he said, "Let's take the rifle back to Brother Boni. He'll probably want the rabbit too."

We walked silently up the dirt road to the top of the hill by the entrance of the campground where Brother Boni had his small cabin. He was outside chopping wood. When he saw us he buried his ax into the stump he was using as his chopping block and came towards us.

"'*Ora si!*" He said, smiling real big. "'*El Mario mato su primer conejito!*'"

"I didn't kill it, Brother Boni; my dad did."

Brother Boni looked at us and shook his head. "*Que paso?*" he said. "You were supposed to have a good time hunting. You both look like you killed your dog!"

Oh, man! Why did he have to say that?

"Well," my dad said, handing the rifle and the rabbit to Brother Boni, "I guess we didn't enjoy killing as much as we thought we would."

Brother Boni took the rifle and then held up the rabbit. "*Bueno,*" he said, "*Pues,* I guess I'll just have to fry it up myself. I shot a porcupine yesterday! It was a little greasy, but it tasted pretty good!" He saw the look on my face and laughed, then looked past us and pointed to a light green official looking truck going down to the Elk Horn Lodge. Oh, oh! I knew *that* truck!

"They've been checking the river by the Blue Spruce and the Little Creel and now they're going to check the fishermen down by the Elk Horn," he said.

He started to say something else, but I didn't wait to hear what it was. I turned and started running back down the hill on the dirt trail towards the river as fast as I could. I needed to get to Max and Rudy quick or they were going to be in some big trouble! That light green truck belonged to the game warden!

I ran past some empty cabins off the trail and through the tall brush. I could see Brother Finkenbinder's cabin just ahead. I wonder how many more fish Max had caught? And now that Rudy had discovered that little gold Mepp, he had probably caught a bunch too!

I got to the clearing by the bend and stopped. There they were. Still fishing, with their backs to me. I started yelling and waving my arms, but either they didn't hear me or they just didn't want to stop. They were both in the water. Max was out further, of course, and Rudy by the shore about shin deep.

The steep bank gave me a little bit more speed and I got to the rocky shore just as Max's rod bent over double again with another trout. I heard him laugh as he started back to the shore with his fish. When he turned, he saw me and smiled real big.

"Hey, Mari! Check out those two sacks over there. We're gonna be able to feed Albuquerque!"

I turned around saw two gunnysacks by the tackle box. The tops were closed and tied by wire. I went to one of them and opened it.

"Oh, my God!" I said. Inside the sack were about ten to fifteen beautiful trout. And they didn't look like stockers.

"Whaddaya think, Mar? Huh? Not bad for a guy who's usually fishing for babes, huh!" Max said, laughing. I turned to look at him just as he stepped on to the rocks, carefully reeling in his latest catch.

"And that's not even my sack; that one's Rudy's," he said. With his free hand he pointed to the other gunnysack. "Check that one out. That's mine!"

I turned back and opened the other sack. Oh, no! Oh, my God! It looked like there was almost double what was in the other sack!

"Max!" I said turning back to him, "Max, you guys need to get outta' here. The game warden just went down to the Elk Horn checking licenses! I think he's gonna come here next!"

"What?" Max said. He walked over to me without bothering to take the fish out of the water. "What about the game warden? He's where?"

"I just saw him go down to the Elk Horn to check on the people who are fishing! Brother Boni said he's been going to all the places, checking!"

Max looked quickly up the river to where the bend started. I knew he was thinking the same thing I was. The Elk Horn's fishing area was only about one hundred yards past the bend. If he wanted to, the game warden didn't even have to go back up the road to come into the campground; he could just come right around that bend.

He turned and yelled to Rudy.

"Hey, Rood! C'mon, let's get outta' here!"

"Hey, man," Rudy said, "I'm having a good time. Whaddaya mean, let's get outta' here?"

Rudy, not the quickest guy in the world, had apparently not heard a single word we had been saying.

"Get your pole, get your fish, and let's get outta' here! Unless you wanna have a good time in the Tierra Amarilla jail!" Max shouted.

Max quickly got his fish out of the river and on to the rocks, then reached down and took the hook out. He threw the trout into his sack, handed me his fishing pole, picked up his gunnysack with both hands, and started running across the rocks towards the trail.

"Meet me at the cabin, Mar!" he yelled, not even turning around.

Rudy, who was still in the water, seemed confused and started looking around. "What did he say about Tierra Amarilla?" he said, watching Max run up the bank and on to the trail.

"He said you better get outta' here with your fish or you're gonna be in a lot of trouble, Rood! I just saw the game warden go down to the Elk Horn to check on people fishing!"

Rudy finally heard what I was saying and he started running out of the water to where his gunnysack was.

"Here!" he said, handing me his pole, "Can you take care of this?"

Before I could answer him, he had thrown his sack over his shoulder and started running in the same direction as Max.

I watched as he disappeared into the tall brush and into the cabins, and then I realized I was holding two fishing rods, there was a tackle box at my feet, I didn't have a fishing license, and I was sure that a game warden was going to come around that bend at any minute.

That was so nice of Max and Rudy. Just give the fishing poles to Mario. He's always in trouble anyway. Maybe they'll just handcuff him to scare him. Well, thank you, Max, but I didn't feel like getting handcuffed today. Of course, I didn't think the game warden would actually handcuff me. I mean, I didn't even have a fish, but I didn't want to take any chances. I hoped he didn't talk to my dad. If he did, he might handcuff me for missing that rabbit.

I bent down and closed the tackle box, picked it up and started running, but not towards the trail. Instead, I ran along the steep bank and headed toward the logs that were right below the trail. If I could get to those logs, then maybe I could hide the poles and the tackle box in all those dry branches, where nobody could see them, then come back later when the coast was clear to pick them up.

I climbed the bottom log and was thankful that I didn't have to step into any mud. My new Keds were still looking pretty good, and I wanted to keep them that way.

I shoved the poles and tackle box into the branches between two logs. Everything looked good from what I could see, but I needed to get higher to make sure. I was climbing up the bottom log to see if the equipment was hidden good enough when I heard a vehicle behind me. I turned and my heart stopped for a second when I spotted the game warden's truck coming around the bend.

Man, oh man, oh man, oh man! There he was! Just like me and Max thought! I hope Max was hiding those fish!

The truck drove right across the rocks where Max and Rudy had been happily breaking the law just a few minutes earlier, and right up the bank. Just like that. Man, those trucks could go anywhere.

I sat down on the middle log and watched as the truck drove slowly to where I was sitting and stopped. I looked up and saw the driver get out. I still couldn't tell who it was, and I couldn't see if there was anyone else with him. Most of the time if it was one of the Spanish guys, then he would probably just say hello and how's it goin', and then take off. But if it was an English guy, then forget it. They *never* just stopped and said hello and then take off; they always wanted to know *everything*!

Whoever it was, walked in front of his truck and right up to the logs and squatted down. I shielded my eyes so I could see him. Maybe it was one of the guys my dad knew. Oh, oh. It was one of the English guys. Here we go!

"Hey thar, young mayen, what'cha doin?" he said. I wonder if it's a law or something that says that an English game warden always has to sound like he's from Texas. Even some of the Spanish guys tried to sound like that. I hope I *never* sounded like that!

"Oh, just standin,'" I said.

"Whaddaya mean, you're just standin'?"

See what I mean? Even when I *wasn't* hiding anything, they couldn't settle for a simple answer. Of course, today, I *was* hiding something. But still, I guess they just thought that all brown people, including little boys, looked naturally suspicious.

"Well, you know. I'm just standin'. Uh..lemme see," I said, obviously not knowing when to shut up. "I got two legs, and, uh, yeah, there's two feet down there, and I'm standin' on both of 'em at the same time. So, uh, I guess I'm standin'."

I couldn't believe I was talking to the game warden this way! But ever since I had finally stood up to that Colorado bully in front of green-eyed Bonnie, I had begun to feel a little braver. Or maybe a little stupider. I know it sounds crazy, but I thought I was getting like this because of my new underwear. Honest! For some reason, wearing real boys' underwear, instead of my sister's panties, made me feel braver! It really did!

"So you're a little smart alec, huh?"

"Well, not really, sir," I said. "It just sounded to me like you didn't know what standin' meant."

He turned and looked at the truck.

"Hey, Migayle," he said, "I guess we got a smart one here."

The passenger door opened and a man got out and walked over to where the first guy was. It was Miguel Ancira. He was from Chama and he had known my dad for years.

"Hey, Mario," he said, tipping his cowboy hat back.

"Hey, Miguel."

"What's goin' on?"

"Oh, nuttin'. Just standin' here checking out the river."

He looked over to his partner. "What's the problem, Bob? It's just Superintendent Santos' little kid lookin' at the river."

Bob the English guy laughed, "Well, hayell," he said, "that explains it. Idn't he that crazy keyid who tipped over the outhouse? Idn't he the one who's always almost drownin'? Huh? Idn't he?"

Wow. News traveled fast in Chama.

He laughed again, but this time, I didn't say anything. And the reason I didn't say anything is because while Bob was talking his nonsense, I had looked down to make sure everything was hidden, and my heart stopped again when I saw Max's shiny reel sticking out from underneath the bottom log! Oh, no! It must have fallen down when I had shoved everything through the branches!

I climbed up quickly over the top log, right between the two game wardens, walked past them over to the truck's front bumper, and sat down.

"Hey," Bob said, "what're yew doin', keyid?"

"Well, lemme see, sir," I said, looking up at him. "This time I'm sittin'. Do you need me to explain to you what sittin' is?" Wow! Just like with the Colorado bully, I couldn't stop saying crazy things now either! At least, so far, I hadn't cussed. Not yet, anyway.

"See whut ah mean," Bob said, looking at Miguel. "He's jest a smart alec little keyid."

"Just ask him what you gotta ask him, and let's get outta' here," Miguel said. "We still gotta go to El Vado and check the people fishin' there! Hurry up, man!"

When Miguel stopped talking, Bob walked over to the truck and leaned on the hood. "Somebody at the Elk Horn said they saw two young guys catchin' a ton of fish rat thar by that bayend." He pointed to the bend, then leaned closer to me. "Di'djew see anybody, keyid?"

So somebody from the Elk Horn, who probably was from Texas and had paid a bunch of money for an out-of-state fishing license and probably had some real fancy fishing clothes and equipment, and wasn't catching any fish and couldn't stand to see anybody else catch fish, had seen Max and Rudy catching one right after another, and had told on them. Fishing jealousy was a very terrible thing.

"Nah," I lied. There I go again. Maybe God would understand if it was for a good cause. "Just a couple of old people with

195

their walking sticks. Looked to me like they were going toward the Elk Horn."

As long as they were both looking at me, they wouldn't be looking down at the logs, and they wouldn't see Max's reel.

"Are yew shore?" Bob asked, his face about six inches from my face. His breath smelled like tobacco and onions and *pedos*. Whew! Talk about a horrible combination! How did *pedos* get in there? Man, what had this guy eaten?

"Pretty sure," I said, backing my head away from his face. I knew my mom was making something good for dinner, but if my face stayed there any longer, not only would I lose my appetite, but I would also lose the tortilla I had eaten earlier this afternoon. Whew! Poor Miguel! He had to drive around with this guy. Just thinking about that gave me *asco*!

"But if anybody's catching more than they should," I said, "and you guys catch 'em, then bring the extras over here and I'll ask my mom to fry 'em up for ya'. I love trout!"

Miguel laughed. "We'll do that, Mario," he said. "Tell your mom and dad I said hello, OK? C'mon, Bob. Let's go. There ain't nothin' here."

He walked over to the passenger door and got in, and I got up from the bumper and away from Bob's face. I walked past the front of the truck and over to the tall grass by the driver's side. I turned around, put my hands into my pockets and looked at Bob.

"Anything else, sir?" I asked, smiling.

Bob slowly got up from the hood and looked at me. "Yew're jest a smart ayess little keyid, ain'tcha?"

"Well," I said, "I'm not sure what an 'ayess' is, sir, but sometimes I think I'm kinda smart and other times I actually think I'm pretty dumb. How 'bout you, sir? You ever think you're kinda dumb? Do game wardens ever think they're kinda dumb, or do they always think they're smart?"

Bob walked over to his door and put his hand on the chrome handle. "I have a feelin' we're gonna see each other again, keyid," he said, looking back at me. "And by the way," he said, "I think yew *dew* know who was fishin'."

When he said that, I raised my eyebrows and just shrugged my shoulders.

He looked like he wanted to say something else, but he didn't. He opened the door and got in, shut the door, put the truck in gear, and drove off down the trail.

I watched as they drove past the outhouse, around the turn by Puggy's cabin and up the road toward the Tabernacle.

I held my breath as they passed our cabin, then I waited a few minutes right where I had been standing and when I was sure that they were safely gone, I crossed the trail, climbed back down the logs and shoved Max's reel back underneath the branches, this time making sure it was out of sight.

I looked around to make sure no one had seen me, then I climbed back up to the trail and started walking to the cabin. I wonder what my mom did when she saw Max's fish? It was usually me that was in trouble. As a matter of fact, I could never remember Max even *being* in trouble. So this was going to be interesting.

When I got to the cabin, I saw my dad and Sarai sitting outside in the porch, facing the road.

"Hey, Dad," I said, walking up the steps, "When'ja get here?"

"He got here right when Max brought all those fish in, making mom almost cry!" Sarai said, before my dad could say anything.

"What? What are you talking about, Sara?" I said. I wasn't sure how much she knew and I didn't want to say anything.

Sarai got up from the table and stood right in front of me.

"You know good and well what I'm talking about!" she said, almost yelling. "You and Max were..."

"Sarai! *Callate*! Be quiet and sit down!"

"But Dad, you know Mar..."

"I said, sit down!"

My dad motioned with his finger for Sarai to get back to the table, and by the sound of his voice and the look on his face she knew better than to disobey.

She gave me that look that sometimes made the little hairs on my neck stand up, and then she sat down. Was there ever going to be a time when my sister was going to like me or almost like me? She had actually hugged me last week when she found out that I might have had something to do with Finky and JoJo falling headfirst into all that *caca*, so there *was* hope.

I sat down across the table from my dad.

"Are you OK?" he asked.

"Yeah. Sure," I said.

"I saw those game wardens talking to you. I almost went down there, but it looked like, from what I could tell, from here, that you were handling things all right."

"Yeah, it was OK, Dad. Miguel was there."

"Yeah, I saw that. That made me feel better."

"Why are you talking to him like this, Dad?" Sarai asked, apparently upset that my dad wasn't yelling at me. "He broke the law! Mario's *always* breaking the law!"

"Mario wasn't even *fishing*, Sara!" my dad said, looking over to my sister. "So how can you say he was breaking the law?"

"Because he probably *made* Max catch all those fish! Max *never* gets in trouble, Dad, and one day around Mario and he's going to jail!"

"What? What do you mean, Max is going to jail? Nobody's going to jail, and how could Mario *make* Max catch all those fish? Mario didn't make Max *or* Rudy catch all those fish! Max caught those fifty-three trout because he *wanted* to, not because anybody made him!"

Wow! Max had caught fifty-three trout! Wow!

"What you should be doing," my dad continued, "is *thanking* your little brother for keeping Max and Rudy *out* of jail by *warning* them!"

Well, thanking me would have been a little bit too much for Sarai, so she just crossed her arms and turned her back to us.

"Wow! Max caught fifty-three?!" I said.

"That's right. But I wouldn't get too excited; right now he's catching something else from Cidelia Santos. You might want to wait a little bit before you go inside."

I nodded. Poor Max. He must be catching it good from my mom. Still, it was hard to feel sorry for him. Fifty-three beautiful trout! I bet he couldn't wait to tell the Chama guys.

"Where are the fish?" I asked.

"Your mom stuffed most of 'em in the stove, and the rest are in your pillowcase.

What? In my pillowcase?

"Sorry, son, but when your mom saw that game warden truck coming up the trail, she put those fish anywhere she could, and your pillow was the first thing she could grab."

"It's OK, Dad," I said, "I like the smell of fresh trout."

"Well, that's good, *'jito*, because you're gonna smell 'em tonight."

I stayed out on the porch with my dad and sister until Max and my mom came out. I didn't want to interfere with anything that was going on inside. But whatever his punishment was, it couldn't have been very bad because he came out smiling and holding a pillowcase full of fish with one hand and a gunnysack full of fish with the other.

"Hey, Mari," he said, smiling even more when he saw me. "You wanna go help me clean these fish?"

"Sure," I said, getting up from the table.

My mom came and stood at the door with her hands on her hips. She looked at us both and shook her head. She didn't look mad or anything. I think she was just relieved that none of us were going to jail today.

"Try not to get too dirty--and hurry up," she said. "It's getting late and I want to eat in a half hour. Youd better change your shoes, *'jito*. You don't want to get blood on those new Keds."

She was right. I looked down at my pretty new shoes and smiled. They were still nice and white.

I went inside the cabin and put on my old shoes. I hadn't put them on since the day me and Chato had floated down the river. They still had the new cardboard I had put in that day. Wow! That day seemed so long ago, and it was only last week! Wow!

Max was waiting for me at the bottom of the steps, and when I came out, we both started walking to the river.

"You OK?" I asked.

"Yeah, I'm al right," He handed me the pillowcase. "Here, help me carry these, OK?"

"D'jou get hit?" I asked, taking the pillowcase from him. It was heavy.

"Yeah. She hit me a couple of times with the fly swatter, but it wasn't bad."

We walked in silence for a while. The fly swatter wasn't bad; it was when she used the cord with the plug at the end that really hurt.

"Those game warden guys give you any trouble?" Max asked.

"Nah," I said. "It was Miguel and some new English guy from Texas or something. He smelled like *pedos*."

"What?" Max said, laughing. "*Pedos?*"

"Yeah, just like *pedos*. It was weird."

"He wasn't related to Beanie, was he?" Max thought that was pretty funny and laughed some more.

"Well, anyway," he said, when he finished laughing, "Thanks, man. It was better to get hit with a fly swatter than go to jail."

"Do you think they would've really thrown you in jail?"

"I dunno, man. Fifty-three big trout. That many fish might've even made Miguel mad."

"Yeah, I guess," I said.

We could hear the river getting closer.

"Did Rudy get away OK?" Max asked.

"Yeah, I'm pretty sure he did. I hid your fishing rods in the logs."

"Wait till I tell the Chama guys!" Max said. I looked over at him and saw a big smile on his face. He was already a legend with the girls; this was definitely going to make him one with the Chama guys.

"Anyway," he said, putting his arm around me, "you saved me and Rudy today. And you saved him *twice*! As a matter of fact, you even saved my skin with the Baca twins and Chinche during the camp meeting! Whew! *That* was a close one! I already thanked you for that one, but, thanks again, OK?"

"Yup," I said. I was glad that we were at the river. I wasn't used to having all this thanks, and I was getting a little embarrassed.

Max and I climbed down the little steps someone had carved into the bank a long time ago and found a spot where we could squat and rinse the fish after we had gutted them. Max used my shiny, new knife to cut them open, and when he had taken the guts out, he threw them on the logs. We knew that by morning the logs would be clean because the birds and little animals would come and eat whatever we threw. Then he handed me the fish and I ran my thumb along the spine to make sure all the blood was gone. It was a good thing I had changed shoes. Splotches of blood, fish guts and black Chama River mud began to collect on the tops of my old shoes, and I could feel the cold water seep into the cardboard covering the holes on the bottom.

Max gutted the big Brown that he had caught and handed it to me. I brought it up to my lips and kissed that big, beautiful hooked jaw again. This was one incredible German Brown! I had never seen one this big! All of these fish were big and beautiful. Wow! We probably *could* feed Chama!

By the time we finished, the sun had almost gone down, and the air was beginning to cool. Pretty soon the birds would stop singing and the only sounds would be the very soothing rumble of the river and the breeze shooting through the trees. I just loved this place.

When we climbed back up to the trail with the clean fish, we saw a car parked in front of the cabin. There was a man and a woman standing on the steps talking to my dad, who was standing holding the door open with my mom standing right behind him.

We waited because we didn't know who it was, and Max probably didn't want to advertise that he had just caught fifty-three trout. But my dad saw us and motioned for us to come up.

By the time we got to the cabin, the two people were sitting at the table with my dad, and my mom had gone inside to get dinner ready.

I didn't recognize them, but they recognized us. Or should I say, they recognized Max.

"*Este es el Max?*" The man said, smiling at Max. "*Mira, que grande!*"

Then he looked real surprised when he looked at me. Like he couldn't believe his eyes.

"*Y este es el baby?*" He asked, with his eyes real wide.

"*Si,*" my dad said, looking over at me. "*Este es el baby. El Mario.*"

"*Ay, mira nomas!*" The man said, putting his hands to his face. "*Que grande! Crecieron pronto!*"

"That's right," my dad said, "They grew fast. They're getting big."

My mom came out and talked to the lady.

"*Quieren comer algo?*" she asked. She *always* asked company to stay and eat.

"*No, gracias,.*" the lady said. She looked like she had been crying. "We better go. We still have to get things ready at the house."

She looked from my mom to my dad. "*Lo apreciamos mucho, Reverendo,*" she said, getting up from the table. The man got up with her and they both went to the door. My mom hugged the lady and shook the man's hand. And my dad came over and did the same thing.

"*Bueno,*" my dad said, "I'll be there in about an hour."

The lady walked over to the car and looked back. "I don't know what we would do without you, Macedonio. You've always been the one we could count on."

My dad waved and smiled, and the couple got in their car and drove off down the dusty trail.

"Who's that, Dad?" I asked. I handed my pillowcase of cleaned fish to Max and he took them into the cabin. Dinner smelled like it was ready except for the fish, and a big stack of fresh tortillas under a clean *trapo* was already on the table.

"That was your cousin Antonio's brother, Canuto, and his wife Dulcinea."

I sat down across from my dad and stared at the stack of tortillas. The butter was next to the stack and my mouth began to water. The red chili would soon be on the table and I could hear the first of the fish that we had just brought in sizzling in the hot grease. That was quick. My mother must have had the pan on the stove and ready to go as soon as we got back. She must be as hungry as the rest of us.

"What'd he want?" I asked. I wonder if my mom would mind me eating a tort without washing my hands? I lifted the *trapo*, took one out and reached for the butter knife.

"Don't touch the food until you've washed your hands!" She shouted from inside the cabin.

I put the tortilla down and shook my head. Man! How in the world did she know?

"Moms just know," my dad said, reading my mind. He reached over and took the tortilla and put it in front of him.

"Hurry up," he said, smiling. "I'll save it for you."

Yeah, right. I knew that tortilla would be long gone by the time I got back. But that was OK, because there was plenty.

I got up from the table and went inside the cabin. Maybe it was because I was starving, but the different aromas coming from the fresh tortillas, steam from the red chili and smoke from the frying trout, hit me smack in the face and made me kind of dizzy. Washing my hands was a small price to pay for the coming feast.

My mom was at the stove stirring the chili and expertly turning the trout, and Max was right next to her covering the fish with my mom's special flour mixture. I could see that a few of them had already been cut in half because they were too big for the pan. When she would take one of the trout out of the pan, he would hand her another one. Maybe he felt he should help because he was the one who had caught so many. There was no way we were going to eat fifty-three trout. We might eat two or three each at the most, but that was it. We'd put the rest on ice tonight and tomorrow my mom would have me delivering them to the different families that were still here.

"Where's Sarai?" I asked, heading to the wash basin by the rollaway bed. I hadn't noticed until now that my sister was gone.

"Nina came by for her when you were cleaning the fish," my mom said. Nina was Rudy's sister. They must be having a fish feast, too. I wonder if Rudy had gotten into trouble.

"Why?" Max asked, laughing. "Do you miss her?"

"Uh, no, not really," I said. Actually, it was kind of nice not being nagged at. I wondered again if my sister would *ever* like me. Probably not.

I washed and dried my hands, then went and stood between Max and my mom.

"Almost ready?" I asked.

"Almost," my mom said. "Did you wash good?"

"Yup."

"Then go back out and wait with your dad. The food'll be out pretty soon."

"And don't eat too many tortillas," she said, as I walked back out to the porch.

When I got back to the table, my dad was just finishing the tortilla he had taken from me. He smiled at me and reached under the trapo and took out another fresh one.

"Here you go," he said, handing me the tortilla. "I told you I'd save it for you."

I took it from him and sat down. Uhmm, it was still hot. After a while I would get another one and take it inside to make it toasty. But for right now, this soft and fluffy one would have to do. I put a big slice of butter on the tortilla and watched it melt.

"How come our cousins came to see you, Dad?" I asked.

I spread the melted butter and folded the tortilla and took a bite. Oh man. I had heard my dad preach one time about people who were addicted to different things. I wonder if being a ten-year-old kid addicted to Cidelia Santos' tortillas counted?

"Because Dulcinea's brother, Bennie, died today. And they want to have the funeral tonight, and asked if I could officiate," my dad said.

Max came out carrying a big plate full of fried fish.

"You mean Big Bennie, Dad?" Max asked, putting the plate on the table.

"Yeah. Do you remember him?"

My mom came out holding the pot of red chili with both hands. She set it on the table next to the fish and went back inside the cabin.

"Yeah, I do," Max said, sliding on to the bench next to me. "He was at the parade a couple of years ago."

"You mean the church parade?" I asked, taking another bite. About the middle of every camp meeting, my dad would get all the musicians and singers together and they would ride through Chama on the back of pick-up trucks and flatbeds singing and playing, and my dad would be in back of one of the trucks preaching. That was our big parade; it was a pretty big event and it seemed like everybody in the village would come out.

"Oh ,yeah," my dad said, "that's right. That's right. That's the time they lifted him up and put him in the back of one of their trucks."

My mom came out with plates and silverware and set them out in front of us. My dad moved over so she could sit down.

"Is everybody ready?" She asked, sitting down. "OK. Max, you caught the fish, so you pray for the food."

We all bowed our heads and Max prayed. I had heard him pray a few times back home, but I never remembered it being so short. It was basically, "Thanks, God, for not letting me get caught. Bless it. Amen." And that was it. I thought maybe my mom would make him pray longer, but she didn't say anything. I mean, what more could a guy say to God, especially after today, but "Thanks?"

When Max finished praying, the stack of tortillas was the first thing everybody reached for. When we all had out torts my dad put a couple of fish on his plate and served his chili on the side. Just like I liked it. I reached for the chili and fish and did the same thing. Eat the chili by itself, using the tortilla as the spoon, and leave the fish alone. Each one was delicious on its own, and that's how it should be enjoyed. Some people just liked to mix everything up. Like Max. He would just throw everything on his plate and mix it up. He said it didn't matter because it was all going to get mixed up when it hit the stomach anyway. But to me it was how the food hit the *tongue*, not the stomach, that mattered. Even when my mom would be cooking four or five different things, and I would walk into the kitchen, I would enjoy each scent on its own. Anyway, food was pretty important to me.

There was no talking for awhile, just chewing, drinking and swallowing sounds. We were all pretty hungry. Max handed me half of the big German Brown. It was delicious. Native-born trout always tasted better. And I must say, I didn't see one trout, out of all of them that we cleaned, that looked like a stocker. I don't know what happened in the river today, maybe something happened in the water that only fish know about. But whatever it was, I hoped it happened again when I got out there!

I saved the crispy tail for last, rolled it in a piece of buttered tortilla, put it in my mouth, closed my eyes and chewed very slowly. Wow! These were the moments that I would daydream about when I was back in school in Albuquerque. I wonder of

Jesus likes German Browns fried just right with the tail fin crispy? The Bible says He ate fish. He even ate fish *after* He rose from the dead! He was even *cooking* those fish! Wow! He probably *did* like German Browns, otherwise He wouldn't have made 'em! Maybe, if my angel ever appeared again, I would ask him.

Max cleaned his plate with the last of his tortilla, then he sat back and patted his stomach.

"Thanks, Mom," he said, "that was excellent."

My mom had her elbows on the table and her hands under her chin. She looked like she was enjoying watching us devour her food.

"Well, thank you, Max," she said, smiling. "and if you ever break the law like that again, I'll use some firewood on you instead of that little fly swatter. I might even turn you in to the game warden."

Me and Max looked at each other with raised eyebrows. We knew she would never turn him in, but she just might use the firewood. When she was *real* mad, she would use whatever was handy. Thank God it was usually the fly swatter.

"How come they want you to do the funeral, Dad?" Max asked, looking back to my dad, and changing the subject. "I thought they were Catholic and didn't like *Aleluyas*? And if he just died today, how come they have to have the funeral tonight? That's kinda' quick, isn't it?"

"Well, they are Catholic, son. But they need some help, and they asked me. I'm a relative and a minister, so I'm gonna help them."

"How come they don't get their priest?" Max asked.

"Because they can't find him. And the one in Parkview said it wasn't his territory."

"What? It isn't his territory? It's only ten miles away!" Max said.

"Well, I know, but apparently, that's what he said. So I'm gonna go down there and help them tonight. And because he was so big, I guess they couldn't find a funeral home to put him in because he couldn't fit into any of their caskets. You know he was pretty big, right?"

"Yeah, I remember," Max said, nodding.

"Dulcinea just told me now that he was weighing something like six-hundred-and-fifty pounds."

"Whoa!" Me and Max said, at the same time. "Six-hundred-and-fifty pounds!"

"Yeah, he was a big guy. So, anyway, she says they have him laid out on the kitchen table right now and they wanna' bury him pretty quick before he starts stinking. Canuto said they've already dug a big hole for him up at his ranch in Monero."

"Monero? Isn't that where those two witches live that threatened to kill you if you went up there to preach?" Max asked.

My dad and mom looked at each other.

"Hey, wait a minute," Max said. "Didn't I hear you guys say one time that they were Big Bennie's aunts?"

"Well, actually," my dad said, "They're his aunts' aunts. Or something like that."

"But didn't they say they were going to kill you because you were an *Aleluya* and you better not bring that *Aleluya* stuff up there?" Max asked.

My heart began to beat a little faster. I knew this story. I had heard my sister Rachel telling my mom of the thing that had happened before I was even born. My dad had started a church in the little town of Monero and he and my Uncle Alvaro were getting ready to go up there one night to preach when he got word from the two witches that if he went they would kill him. But of course, he went anyway. I guess that's what you did if you were a preacher. Didn't matter what anybody said; if *God* said to go, then you went.

"Yes, they did threaten me," my dad said.

"But you still went."

"Of course I still went, son. But I didn't go by myself. Your Uncle Alvaro, your sister Rachel and your Aunt Esther went too. And three other very important people went with us also." My dad smiled and pointed to the roof. "The Father, The Son, and The Holy Ghost. I *never* go anywhere by myself!"

"But they said they were going to kill you, Dad; how come you still went? And how come you took Rachel and my aunt Esther? Aren't witches pretty powerful?" Max asked.

"I went because God told me to go. We had already started a church there. We couldn't abandon the people just because some witches threatened us. Remember I told you guys about the time the Catholics in Gallina threatened to kill Brother Giron if he went up there to preach? Well, you know he went anyway and sure enough, after the service, he was walking out with another Brother and a bunch of 'em who were hidden by the trees opened fire. One of the bullets hit Brother Giron in the neck and another hit Brother Miguel Sanchez in the leg. As you know, Brother Sanchez died from the wound, but Brother Giron just tied a hanky around his neck and went ahead and preached another service. That Brother Giron, now there's an incredible man. Anyway, I felt I had to go; that's what I've been called to do, and I took your sister and your Aunt because they provided the piano-playing and the singing and because I knew them witches couldn't do anything to us because we were covered by the Blood of Jesus Christ. And nothing, absolutely *nothing*, or *nobody* is more powerful than the Blood of Jesus!"

"Well, did they do anything to you?" Max asked.

"Yeah, they tried to scare us a little bit, but we're still here '*jito*," my dad said. He looked over at my mom and smiled. She just smiled back. She must've known about those witches too, and she still let my sister go. And according to my sister and Aunt Esther, things did get a little crazy.

They said it was real dark when they got to where the mountains on each side come right down to the road. Rachel said my dad was driving, my uncle was in the passenger side, and she was in the back seat behind my dad and my aunt was sitting next to her.

She said that they were going real slow because the road wasn't very good and it was dark, but she could tell by the lights that they were coming up to the big turn. Well, she looked out her window and saw six big balls of fire, like big beachballs, coming down the mountain toward the car. She turned to my aunt and told her to look out the window, but my aunt, who already *had* looked out the window, said not to look at them or talk about them because my "G" said not to talk about witches on Friday, and to keep staring straight ahead. Rachel said my dad also told her not to look at them or pay attention to them because he said that was just the witches trying to scare them. But my sister looked anyway, and she said the big fireballs came next to the car and started bouncing up and down. She said they kept bouncing up and down by her window until the car made the turn, and then, she said, they just bounced right back up the side of the mountain.

My dad looked back to Max. "Nothing happened to us then, son, and nothing's going to happen to us now. Because, like I told you, when you're covered by the Blood of Jesus, the only thing they can do is try to scare you. We're still here, *'jito*, your sister, your Aunt and your Uncle. We're still here. We're still in one piece. And we're even a little chubby." He laughed, and we all laughed with him.

"Always remember this." He looked over at me. "You too, Mario, listen. There shall be no weapon formed against you that will ever prosper. That's what the Bible says. That means the weapon has not been made, or will ever be made, that will harm you or hurt you. You guys understand that? Nothing. No witch, no thousand witches, no spells, no curses, *nothing*, can harm you when you're covered by the Blood of Jesus Christ! There is nothing more powerful in this *universe* than the Blood of the Lamb of God, Jesus Christ!"

Wow! I felt like shouting "Amen!" or "Halleluiah!" or something.

"Halleluiah! Amen! Preach it, brother!" My mom said.

Alright, mom! Reading my mind again!

"But what if they go to the funeral tonight? They're still Catholic and you're still an *Aleluya*; won't they still try to do something to you? How can they be witches and still go to church?"

"You'd be surprised at who goes into churches! You think the Devil just goes to bars? He's already got those guys. Believe me, he shows up to church every Sunday wearing a nice skirt or a nice suit."

"Really, Dad?" I asked. "The devil? Even in Assembly of God churches? He wears a skirt?"

"That's right, '*jito*. Sometimes he does. Even in Assembly of God churches."

Wow! The devil shows up wearing a suit! He even dresses in skirts! And even in Assembly of God churches! Does his tail show when he wears a skirt? What about his horns, how does he cover his horns? Oh, man! This was crazy! Did I have a lot to tell Sister Velma!

"So, what if they go tonight? What will you do?" Max asked.

"I'll just do what God wants me to do. I'll try to provide comfort. Preach a short sermon on what's waiting for us on the other side, pray for them and whatever else the family wants me to do."

"But, what if..." Max started to ask something else.

"Don't worry, son. I'm covered by the Blood Of Jesus Christ, remember? And besides," he said, looking at me, "if what's been happening with your little brother lately is any indication, we've got some pretty big warriors traveling with us at all times. Or at least, *he* does!"

When my dad said that, he smiled and pointed at me.

Max looked at me.

"Yeah, I heard something about that. Something about a big Navajo, right?" He said, putting his hand on my head. "You're gonna have to tell me about it someday, buddy."

He got up from the table and stretched. "That was great, Mom. I'm sorry I put you through all that trouble, OK? Thanks for only hitting me with a fly swatter. I told Rudy I'd go over, is that alright? I'll be back in a while."

He walked over to my dad and put his hand on his shoulder.

"Be careful, Dad," he said. "I don't care if those witches *can't* do anything to you. Be careful anyway, OK?"

"You don't ever have to worry about me, son. God always takes care of me."

Max walked out the door and started up the trail by *Hermana* Frita's cabin.

"Tell Sarai if she's going to sleep over there tonight, she needs to come and get her stuff!" my mom shouted after him.

"OK!" He yelled back. He waved his hand without turning around.

"Hey, Dad," I said, "This is Friday, right?"

"Yeah. That's right."

"Are we supposed to be talking about witches? I mean, didn't my "G" say not to talk about *brujas* on Fridays?"

My dad laughed. "You're not nervous, are you, *'jito?*"

I shook my head. "Nah, you said not to worry. So I'm not." And I really *didn't* feel scared. I don't know why, but I didn't.

"From what you've told me about that big Navajo, I don't think you're ever going to have to be afraid of anything."

Both my parents stared at me, and that *did* make me nervous. I know they wanted to ask me a lot of questions, which I didn't mind, especially if I could answer them. This was a very different feeling. My parents actually wanted to know something from me, besides why did I put my head between an *hermana's* legs and look up her dress. Or why did I throw a cherry bomb in the Tabernacle while Brother Savage was preaching. This was a *nice* feeling! But it made me nervous when they just sat and stared at me.

"You have any plans for tonight?" my dad asked me.

What? Do I have any plans for tonight? No way! My friends were gone, my dog was in Santa Fe, I was thinking of sneaking into Max's trailer to think about Bonnie. But that was it.

"Nah," I said.

My mom lifted the *trapo* covering the tortillas and took three of them from the still big pile. She got up and walked inside the cabin.

"You wanna go with me tonight?" my dad asked, still staring at me. It wasn't a bad stare, or a mean stare or anything. It was almost like he had just discovered me or something. "I think it would be interesting for you. And besides, I'd like the company. What do you say?"

Wow! I couldn't believe it! My dad seemed like he really wanted my company! I know he loved me and everything, but now he actually wanted my company for something important! I mean, this wasn't like going to the store to get some milk, or ordering egg foo yong from his favorite Chinese place on West Central Avenue in Albuquerque. This was a funeral! A real *different* funeral! And from the sounds of it, there were going to be people there that didn't like *Aleluyas*! Maybe even the two *brujas* from Monero! Wow! It almost felt like he wanted me to go with him to a battle! What an honor! *He* was the one who was used to fighting demons and witches, and now he was asking *me* to go with him! Whew!

"Really, Dad? You'd let me go with you?"

"Yeah, I really want you to go with me. I think it would be good for you."

Just then my mom walked in and sat down. She had the three tortillas on a paper plate and she put it down in front of us.

"I think this is the way you like them, right, *'jito*?"

She handed me one and put the butter dish by me. Man, oh, man! She had gone and made each of us a toasty tortilla! And she made them just right. Just crispy enough on one side, but not like a cracker, and still a little soft on the other. I put a big slice of butter on the soft side and watched it melt. I was still very full from dinner, but that didn't stop my mouth from watering as I saw the butter trickle over the edge of the tortilla on to the table.

"Thanks, Mom," I said, picking it up and taking a bite. "Absolutely delicious!"

My dad buttered his after my mom did hers and the three of us chewed in silence.

"I'd like to take Mario with me tonight." my dad said, finishing off his tortilla. "What do you think?"

My mom was slower with her food and took her time chewing.

"I think it's a good idea," she said, when she was finished chewing. She looked at me with the same look my dad had been giving me, but she didn't take another bite. Like she still had something to say.

"Did you see your angel today?" she asked.

"Nope. But he was around." With all the commotion of trying to hide Max's fish, I hadn't told them about Rudy falling in the river and almost drowning.

"Really?" she asked. "How did you know? Did he talk, did he say something, what?"

"No, he didn't talk. I just know he was there."

She looked over to my dad.

"You won't leave him alone, will you?" she asked.

"Of course not," he said. "He'll be with me the whole time."

"Most of those people aren't fond of us, you know."

"Yes, dear, I know."

My mom nodded. "OK," she said, "Go put on some clean clothes and your new shoes." She picked up her tortilla and took another bite.

I quickly got up from the table and went into the cabin. I needed to get ready fast because I didn't want her to change her mind. I could hear them talking on the porch while I changed and I wondered what had brought on all these changes in my parents. My mom didn't seem quite so afraid for me anymore. Not even today when I went to the river. She usually hated when I even *walked* by the rushing water. It must've been hard on her all these years hearing about me almost drowning practically every day, and probably thinking every time I walked out the door that she might be seeing me for the last time. But I didn't see that look in her eyes anymore.

There was still concern there, but not that horrible, pained, what-in-the-world-did-you-get-into-now-that-almost-took-your life look. She also seemed relieved last week when my dad told her Brother Chinche would no longer be bothering me.

I made sure to put my left shoe on first, tied my last shoelace and walked over to the water basin. I rinsed my hands and wet my hair. I looked in the little mirror hanging on a nail over the basin. Maybe one of these days hair sticking straight up and looking like you just got out of bed would be the latest hairdo. I decided to leave my hair just like it was. If anybody said anything, then I would just say I stuck a bobby pin in the wall socket when I woke up, and I hadn't had a chance to fix my hair.

When I got back to the porch, my dad was already out the door and was waiting for me on the front step. He usually shaved twice a day, because he had such a heavy beard, but it didn't look like he was going to do that tonight. He was just a regular *Chamero* tonight. He had a coat on, but no tie, and he had his Bible in one hand and the car keys in the other.

"You ready?" he asked.

"Yup," I said.

My mom grabbed my arm before I could walk out.

"You stay close to your dad, OK?"

"OK, Mom."

"And don't go with anybody, even if they ask you to go. You just tell them you can't leave your dad, OK?"

"OK, Mom."

She put both of her hands on my head and started praying. I could hear some of it. She said something about the Blood of Jesus and then she started praying in tongues. I got goosebumps a little bit when she started praying that way. I always got goosebumps when she prayed in tongues. It was a beautiful sound.

She opened her eyes and looked at me.

"The Holy Ghost is with you, *'jito*. I just know He is."

She reached up and tried to put my hair down, but it didn't work.

"One of these days, your hair's going to go down," she said, smiling. She kissed the top of my head and gave me a gentle push out the door.

I jumped off the step and started walking to our big white Plymouth with my dad.

"Hey!" my mom yelled out from the porch. "I heard from Vangie at Kelly's; you know they got that big radio. She said the Yanks won the first game of the doubleheader today. And she said Mickey hit a dinger from the left side *and* the right side!"

Was there another mom in the world that knew that Mickey Mantle was a switch hitter? Was there another mom in the world that even *cared* that Mickey Mantle was a switch hitter? Was there a mom in the *universe* that knew that a home run was a "dinger"? I didn't think so.

Vangie was my mom's cousin and she worked at Kelly's grocery and dry goods store in town. She knew we loved the Yanks, so every time she would hear something about them on that big radio, she would tell us.

My dad and I stopped and looked at my mom and the three of us waved our arms in the air and cheered. The Mick had hit a couple more! When we were finished yelling, we got into the Plymouth.

My dad couldn't turn his neck, so I had to look behind to make sure he didn't hit anything. I liked doing that, though, because it seemed like I was helping him drive, even though I was just turning my head.

"Did you make sure the tag was on the inside when you finished drying your hands?" he asked. "They still have one more game to go."

"I sure did," I said, looking out the back window as he put the car in reverse. "You're clear, Dad, go ahead."

We backed out and turned on to the small dirt trail. My mom was standing on the step and waved as we drove in front of our cabin. She was smiling, so I guess she really *did* think I would be all right.

The moon was full and very bright and the stars shimmered so pretty and looked so close it seemed like I could just reach out the window and touch them. As if appreciating the beauty of the night, my dad drove more slowly than usual through the camp. He also didn't want to raise too much dust. During the camp meeting he would ask Brother Chavez to drive the water truck on all the trails to wet them down, but nobody had done it since almost everybody had left on Sunday.

We drove up the little hill past Brother Boni's cabin, past the ditch by the Elk Horn and on to the little highway. I opened my window and took a deep breath. It was a little cool outside, but I loved the smells going in to town, and I figured that since we would probably be leaving back to Albuquerque sometime tomorrow, I'd better get all I could.

The little neon signs in front of the Elk Horn and Little Creel lodges said "No Vacancy" because it was Friday and people from all over New Mexico and Colorado and other states were in town to do some camping and fishing. Maybe one of the lucky ones would discover Max and Rudy's spot. Maybe if we had time before we left, *I* would be the lucky one and go down there and run that little gold Mepp across that pool. If I caught any, I would probably let the fish go because we already had enough. Just the thrill of having a trout slam into that spinner would be enough for me.

We crossed the bridge and drove by the "Y" Motel. Even *they* had a "No Vacancy" sign up. It looked like there was going to be a lot of people in town this weekend. I guess I wasn't the only one who loved to come here.

My dad reached for the radio and turned it on, but all we got was a bunch of static. It would have been fun to see if the Yanks were on.

"I had to try," he said. "You never know. Maybe a signal could have gotten through."

"Yeah," I said. We *always* tried, but it never worked.

I stuck my head out the window and took in another deep breath. Uhmm. We were getting close to the sawmills and I loved the smell of cut lumber. I looked up the road and saw the turn by the railroad tracks. The train had stopped running for the day, but the smell of the engine smoke and the railroad ties was still in the air and was mixing in with the sawmill smell. I closed my eyes and just enjoyed it. God, I loved this place! Pretty soon we would cross the tracks, pass Brother Nickerson's house, and be right in the village.

I put my head back in and reached over to try the radio again. Right when I touched the dial, my dad slammed on the brakes. I heard the screech of the tires and I flew forward and hit the side of my head on the dashboard.

"You OK?" my dad asked. I sat back in the seat and rubbed the spot that had hit the dashboard. It didn't hurt a lot, but I could feel a bump already starting to form.

"Yeah, I'm OK," I said. "What happened? Was there a train coming? I didn't even hear the whistle, did you?""

My dad pointed to the front of the car. Standing right in front of the car like they owned the road were two of the biggest dogs I had ever seen. They looked kind of like different German Shepherds, but not that brown. They were more grey than brown. One of them was skinny, but as tall as the hood of the car and the other one was real wide, almost fat, and it was about a head shorter than the other one. The headlights of the car made their eyes look crazy. Like they were glowing a bright yellow.

My dad honked the horn, but they didn't move.

"Those things are huge!" I said. I scooted up in my seat to get a better look.

My dad honked again, and this time both dogs showed their fangs and growled.

The taller one looked like it had some front teeth missing.

"Wow, Dad! I've never seen dogs like that!"

"They're not dogs," my dad said, quietly.

"Huh? What do mean?"

"I told you, *'jito*, they're not dogs."

"Are they wolves?" I asked. I knew there were wolves in these mountains, but I had never seen any. I had seen all the other wildlife out here: the elk, the deer, a few bears, and I had even seen a mountain lion running across Cumbres Pass one time, but I had never seen a wolf.

He honked again and started moving forward but they didn't move; even though he was getting real close, they just showed their fangs and growled louder. When the car was almost on them, they moved and started coming to my side of the car.

"Roll your window up quick!" my dad said.

I reached for the window knob and started rolling it up as fast as I could. Before I could get it up all the way, the wolves or whatever they were jumped on my window like they were trying to get to me! They wanted to get in so bad, they looked like they were trying to bite the window!

My dad grabbed me and brought me closer to him, and that's when I saw these two, big, beautiful and familiar hands grab the heads of those two things like they were baseballs, and then smash their noses right into each other. Boom! Just like that! Then the heads came together hard a second time! Then those two big hands smashed the wolves faces hard against the window and I saw blood coming from both of their noses.

The wolves yelped like they had been hit by a car and took off running like crazy down the tracks.

My dad let me loose, and I went back to the window. I put my face close to the glass and saw the blood dripping down. Then a familiar face came close to the window and smiled at me.

"Don't worry, kid," my angel said. "I was in the back seat all the time."

Then he stood up, walked to the back of the car and disappeared.

"Wow!" My dad said. "That was weird! You all right, *'jito*?"

I guess my dad hadn't seen my angel.

"Whew!" I said. I moved my head from the window and sat back in my seat.

"There's blood on the window, Dad." He turned his whole body in his seat and took a closer look at the window.

"There sure is," he said. He turned back in his seat and put the car back in gear. "I wonder what in the world made those things go away? And not just go away, but go away *crying*! Did you see them smash their heads together? Man, I wonder why they did that! That was very strange."

"I don't know, Dad, but *something* sure scared 'em."

The car crossed the tracks, went around the bend and headed into town.

I turned and got on my knees and looked in the back seat. There he was, all scrunched up, like he could barely fit. This time he was wearing a shiny, purple jacket and a black, kind of glittery shirt.

He smiled real big at me.

"One thing I gotta' say for you, kid; it's never boring around you."

I turned my head and looked at my dad.

"Don't worry, he can't hear or see me, and if you say anything, he'll just think you're talking to yourself."

When he said that he laughed and slapped his knees.

"What're you looking at, '*jito*?" My dad asked.

"Oh, nothin'. I just thought I'd look out the back window to see if those wolves are following us."

"Those weren't wolves," my dad said.

"Well, what were they?"

"Well," my dad said, "I think we're gonna find out soon enough."

"He's right, you know," my angel said. I turned back and looked at him. "Those things weren't wolves. But don't worry; I ain't ever gonna let anything touch you."

He looked real uncomfortable all bent over like that. Even though the car was a pretty good-sized ol' Plymouth, it was still too small for him.

"You mind?" he asked. I shook my head but didn't say anything. I didn't want my dad to think I was talking to myself.

"Thanks," he said. Then he sat up straight. His head and shoulders went through the roof! "That's more like it."

I couldn't believe it! My angel was sitting through the roof! And he had a big smile on his face and his arms all stretched out with the wind blowing in his hair like he was cruising in a convertible on Central Avenue! He was crazy! I loved him!

My angel looked at me and put his head back and laughed that big laugh.

"You know," he said, still chuckling, "Most of the time when you're in the car I ride on the hood, but tonight I decided to ride in the back seat just to see how smooth this big ol' Plymouth was. I had gotten word earlier that Teresita and Patrecina were on the prowl tonight and were gonna try to scare you."

Huh? Teresita and Patrecina? Who in the heck were Teresita and Patrecina?

He brought his head back into the car and put his big face close to mine.

"Better known as Terry and Patsy," he said, smiling. "But that's not important right now; you'll meet them in person soon enough. The word's out on you, kid."

His eyes were incredible. They glowed. But not like those wolves. That was a scary glow. His were like a quiet glow. I don't know how else to explain it. I remembered the first time I had seen him when he pulled me and Chato out of the river. I remember how his eyes glowed behind his sunglasses.

He sat back up and spread his arms wide.

"Everybody in my world has heard that there's something special about you, kid. But that means that not only good spirits know, but also the bad spirits. So me and your other, uh, your other angels, have to be a little more alert. Of course with you, we've had to be alert even when you were inside your mother! You didn't even let us relax then!"

When he said that he put his head back and laughed again.

"But don't worry," he said, when he stopped laughing. "When The Holy One has chosen someone, nothing or no one can change it."

When he said 'The Holy One', he bowed his head for a few seconds, then he looked up and smiled and reached down his hand and patted my head.

The Holy One? Terry and Patsy? The word's out? What in the world was he talking about? This was kind of a lot of information to not be able to ask any questions. But if I started talking to the empty back seat, my dad would *really* think I was crazy! But maybe not. I mean, he knew I had an angel, right?

"Hey, Dad," I said, turning to him, but still kneeling on the seat, "Do we know a Teresita and a Patrecina?"

"What?" he asked, very surprised. Like he couldn't believe I had asked him. "Teresita and Patrecina? Who told you about them? How did you know about them?"

"I, uh, uh, I uh, I don't know, I just heard their names somewhere." I said, kind of semi-lying. Was there such a thing as a semi-lie?

"Well, 'jito, you might've just met them."

"Huh?"

"I told you you'd meet them," my angel said from over the roof.

Hey, I just thought of something. How come if there's a roof, I can still see my angel, and hear him too? Wow! Was something crazy happening to me?

"Those are the names of Big Bennie's aunts," my dad said.

"Huh? The ones in Monero?"

"Yup."

"You mean the ones who said they were going to kill you?"

"Yeah. The same ones."

"The witches?"

223

"That's right *'jito*."

"Wow!"

"Did your mom tell you? It was your mom, wasn't it?"

"Do people call them Terry and Patsy?"

I know my dad wanted to look at me after I said *that*, but he couldn't turn his neck.

"That's right, *'jito,*" he said. "But how did you know that?"

I sat back down and put my head back on the seat. I had to do it. I was tired of always hiding things from my dad. This was my dad, the guy I loved and respected more than anybody in the world. This was the summer I had started telling him the truth. I might as well go all the way.

I turned and looked up at my angel. He was still enjoying the ride. He looked like one of those advertisements in Life Magazine of people riding around in their brand new convertible. I was going to have to ask him how come I could see through the roof.

"Go ahead and tell him," my angel said, looking down at me. "It's time."

He put his head back up and shook his long hair in the breeze.

"Dad," I said.

"Yes, *'jito.*"

"Dad, I'm gonna tell you the truth."

"Good, son. The truth is always good."

"You might think I'm crazy, Dad, and I might be; everybody else thinks so. But what I'm gonna tell you is the truth, OK?"

"Sure *'jito,* go ahead."

He had said earlier before we left the cabin, that the funeral would be close to my *Mamou's* on Eighth Street. It looked like we were getting close to the turn-off.

"Dad, I told you I have an angel, right?"

"That's right *'jito.* You told me that."

"Well, uh, he's the, uh, he's the one who told me about those ladies."

"Really?"

224

"Really."

"When?"

"Right now," I said.

"Right now? You mean, right now, right now?"

"Yes, Dad. Right now, right now. He's in the back seat."

"Your angel's in the back seat?"

"He's in the back seat, Dad. But you can't see him. Only I can see him. And his head is through the roof, Dad."

"Your angel's head is through the roof."

"Yes, sir. Actually, his shoulders and chest are too, Dad."

"And you can see that?"

"Yes, sir."

"You can see his body through the roof."

"Yes, Dad. I don't know how, but I can see him through the roof. And he's been talking to me, Dad. That's how I knew about those two, uh, those two...were those two things in the road, were they Terry and Patsy?"

"So he's the one who told you they're called 'Terry and Patsy'?"

"Yup."

"Well, he's right. And yes, those two things were probably the aunts from Monero."

"Wow! You mean they can turn themselves into animals too?"

"Yeah, some of them can. Ask your angel if I can talk to him."

"Tell your dad he can talk to me through you," my angel said. "And if I have permission to answer him, I will. But he won't be able to see me. I'm telling you, kid, for some reason you've been chosen. You know how rare it is for someone to get to see and talk to one of their angels? Daniel did, Mary did, they got to talk to Gabe, and so did the Apostle Paul. He just never wrote about it. He thought it might sound like he was bragging. Besides, people back then really had a problem with worshipping angels instead of the One they needed to be worshipping. That's why we can't appear to just anyone. Tell your dad he has some pretty big angels too. But they're not Navajo."

When he said that last part, he laughed again. This angel, *my* angel, loved to laugh.

"He said you can ask him things through me, and if he has permission, he'll answer you. He says you got some pretty big angels too, Dad."

"Really? Well, praise God. That's good news. Tell him thanks. And tell him thanks from me and your mom for always taking care of you. We appreciate it very, very much." my dad said.

"Tell your dad he's welcome," my angel said, bringing his head back in to the car. "But as much as I love you, kid, it's my extreme privilege, pleasure *and* duty, to obey my Creator, The Holy One."

When he said that, he bowed his head again. I waited until his head was back up before I said anything.

"He said you're welcome, Dad, but he's just obeying God."

The car slowed down as we got to Eighth Street and my dad turned the car and drove toward a house that had a bunch of cars parked in front of it. My *Mamou's* house was about a block up the street.

"Get ready, kid," my angel said, "It's gonna be an interesting night. Just remember two things: Number one, I'm always there even if you can't see me. And number two, whenever you feel even a little bit afraid just say, "the Blood of Jesus." Can you remember that?"

"Just when I'm afraid?" I asked.

"What?" My dad said. "Afraid? Afraid of what?"

"Actually," my angel said, "you can say it anytime you feel like you need to."

"Nothin', Dad." I said, "just talkin' to myself."

"You got that?" my angel asked. "Anytime you need to."

I nodded as the car stopped and my dad turned off the headlights and then the engine. The man that had been at the cabin earlier came up to the car and opened the door for my dad.

"Macedonio," he said, grabbing my dad by the hand and helping him up. *"Gracias por venir; 'ora si podemos comenzar."*

"Todo esta listo, Canuto?" my dad asked.

"Si, it's all ready," Canuto answered.

My dad got out and looked around, then motioned for me to go ahead and get out.

"It's OK," he said. "Just remember to stay close to me, all right?"

"OK, Dad." I said, closing the door. The blood on the window had dried but it wasn't red anymore, or even dark red. It looked like it was black. Almost like mud instead of blood. The night was very cool and crisp and there was no breeze at all; the air felt like it had weight, making it seem like I was walking into something that was standing still.

My dad and Canuto waited for me in front of the car, and when I got there the three of us walked toward the crowd of men and women gathered around the front door that had a bare little yellow lightbulb on top of it. The cloud of cigarette smoke was very thick, and because there was no breeze to move it, and very little light to penetrate it, the faces were`partially hidden behind the tobacco fog, making it almost impossible to clearly distinguish who the people were. The glow from the tips of the cigarettes made it appear like there was a flock of fireflies buzzing around the group. They all turned to look at us and I could hear the words *"Aleluya,"* *"Sacerdote"* and *"Santos"* sprinkled in conversation around the group.

When we got closer I could see that some of them were drinking beer and others were taking a drink from a bigger bottle that was being passed around. I was in the middle, with Canuto and my dad on either side of me, and when we were almost at the door, the group parted to let us through. The conversations with the same words continued, but this time in whispers.

The cloud of smoke swirled around our heads, and right as we got to the door a hand came out of the murky air and grabbed my dad's arm.

"Macedonio," a voice said, through the thick haze. I recognized the voice, even though I couldn't quite see the face. It was our cousin, Antonio.

"*Gracias, primo,*" he said. "Thanks for being here, *bueno?*"

My dad stopped at the door, turned, and the two men hugged.

"I'm just glad to do it, Antonio. *Y la familia,* is everybody taking it OK?"

"Yah, as good as can be expected, no?" Antonio said. "We told him this was going to happen if he didn't take better care of himself, no? *Pero el era muy cabezudo,* no? He never listened to anybody, no?"

"*Yo creo que* being *cabezudo* is a Chama disease."

When my dad said that, the people laughed. That made me feel better. As long as they were laughing, that meant they probably wouldn't shoot at us like they did with Brother Giron. But it's pretty hard to keep people laughing at a funeral.

Antonio and my dad shook hands and then we walked through the door and into the house.

The cloud of smoke that had surrounded us outside followed us inside, and seemed more stifling in the small house. I hoped my lungs weren't going to get black like those pictures I saw in the National Geographic of coal miners who had died because of what they were breathing. How in the world could people enjoy putting smoke in their lungs? Whew! I don't know, but it didn't seem like anybody in this place even *cared* what their lungs looked like!

The room looked like it was a combination living room and kitchen and it was packed with people gathered around a real big table set up in the middle. And on that table was the biggest, most gigantic human being I had ever seen. So this was Big Bennie! Wow! He was so big, that even though the table was very big, several *bigger* boards had to be set on top of the table so that the man's body wouldn't spill over! Wow! How in the world did they get him in here? No wonder they couldn't find a casket big enough! Maybe if they put three or four caskets together! Whew! This guy was huge! Maybe he was a world record!

My dad put his hand on my shoulder and moved me to where some older people, and the lady, Dulcinea, who had been at the cabin earlier, were sitting.

We stopped in front of them and my dad started talking to them in Spanish. The older couple were probably Bennie's parents. They looked sad, and the old woman and Dulcinea looked like they had been crying. The older guy just puffed his cigarette and nodded his head and didn't say anything.

"When are you going to bury him?" my dad asked Dulcinea.

"We gotta get him outta' here tonight as soon as you're done," she said. "Canuto borrowed the sawmill's forklift and he also borrowed Andres Blea's big logging truck to take the body tonight. We've already got the hole dug; we just have to bury him. *Pobrecito, mi hermanito.*"

"How in the world did you get him in here?" my dad asked. He must have been reading my mind.

"We had to take the whole window out," she said, pointing to a space on the opposite wall that was covered with a big blanket. "Canuto and Antonio even had to take the frame out."

"*Mira no mas! Bueno,*" my dad said, "where do you want me to stand?"

"*Donde quieras,*" Dulcinea said, "maybe with your back to the door, because most of the people are already on the other side of the room."

"You know I'm going to do it the way God wants me to," my dad said.

"*Seguro que si,*" Dulcinea said. "Don't worry about it. The priest had his chance. Anyway, I know you're a true man of God, and I know your words will be what God wants."

"*Bueno,*" my dad said, "let's get started."

My dad walked around the table to where Big Bennie's head was laying, and I followed right behind him. Bennie's head was combed real nice but it looked way too small for his massive body, almost like it didn't belong to him. And his face looked real young too. It was as if someone in heaven had said, "Hey, let's put a tiny kid's head on this big guy," and God had said "OK." Poor Bennie. He was beginning to smell a little sour, but laying there, real peaceful-like, not bothering anybody, he seemed like he had been a nice guy when he was alive. Maybe he had talked to Jesus before he died and he was in heaven right now. If he did make it, God had probably already given him a smaller body that went with his head.

As I was looking at his head, I realized I had never stood this close to a dead person that wasn't in a casket, but for some reason I wasn't afraid. I probably would have been if my dad wasn't standing right next to me. And also, I knew that even if I couldn't see him, my angel was right here with me.

There were people crying and blowing their noses all around the room, some quietly and a few others a little louder. It looked like they were all standing except for Dulcinea and her parents. There were so many of them that some were leaning on the table, and every once in a while a hand would reach out from the crowded room and pat Big Bennie's arm or his leg and even his stomach.

I felt bad that this huge man had died, but I couldn't feel sad because I didn't know him. And plus, I couldn't stop thinking about how *big* he was! I was standing up right next to him and I could barely *see* over that stomach! As a matter of fact, it was a sad thing to say, but I felt worse for the rabbit my dad killed today than I did for Big Bennie! Whew! Maybe something was wrong with *me*! At least Bennie had a chance to get into heaven, and the rabbit didn't. Unless, of course, animals went to heaven too. Was that possible? Do animals go to heaven when they die? Is it possible for animals to sin? And do animals that sin go to hell? That was definitely something I would ask my angel.

My dad opened the small Bible that he had brought and cleared his throat.

"*Vamos a comenzar,*" he said. "Let's all bow our heads."

When he said that, the people bowed their heads and did the sign of the cross. I used to practice doing the sign of the cross in front of the mirror at home when no one was around, but it never felt right. I never knew whether I should go to the right side of my chest first, or my left side after I had touched my forehead. And did left- handed people have to do it the same way as right-handed people? Oh well. I guess it was OK. I mean, the cross was a *good* thing.

My dad started praying and the room got quiet. The only sounds were his voice and a few people sniffling. They seemed to respect him, even though he wasn't a priest. I think some of them knew him when he *was* going to be a priest, and decided not to be mad at him anymore.

During my dad's prayer, Dulcinea's mom started crying real loud and saying, "*Mi 'jito! Mi 'jito! Ay, mi 'jito!*" and that made all the ladies and some of the men start crying too. Actually, when she said that, I looked at her and *I* almost started crying! Poor old lady. So what if Big Bennie had been real big. This was her son! And moms don't care what you look like. They just love you anyway. I was beginning to feel sad for Big Bennie, and I felt bad for feeling worse about the rabbit than for him.

Right as my dad was finishing the prayer, there was a commotion at the door. I turned to see what was going on and saw two old ladies pushing their way through the crowd. One was tall and kind of thin, and the other one was short and chunky. They were dressed in black like most of the other ladies, and they had black scarves on their heads.

They got to where my dad and I were standing and stood right behind us. I noticed that their noses looked very bruised, real dark blue and purple, and both of them had *tapones* in their nostrils, like maybe their noses had been bleeding. The short one even had a black eye. They glared at me and gave me the chills, like maybe *I* was the one responsible for their bruises. Why did they look like they hated me so much? They looked like they hated me so much their *faces* were even twisted! But those eyes. I had seen those eyes somewhere, but I just couldn't remember where.

The people behind me started whispering, and I heard the word *"brujas"* several times. When I heard that I felt my hands go cold and I got the chills even more.

So here they were! I had been waiting. Finally, the famous sisters from Monero: Teresita and Patrecina. Terry and Patsy. *"Las brujas."* The ones who had threatened to kill my dad. The balls of fire rolling down the mountain. The wolves blocking the road. Standing right in front of me, looking like they had gotten jumped by a bunch of *pachucos* on their way to the funeral. They didn't look like what I thought a *bruja* was supposed to look like. They looked kind of like normal, wrinkled up old ladies, only beat up. And I noticed they didn't have any brooms with them either.

I took a deep breath but didn't take my eyes off of them. There was something in the air around them that made my chest ache. Like a horrible smell that I could taste somewhere inside of me. My mom had told me one time that real evil things even have a smell. This must be the smell she was talking about.

They took a step towards me and I could feel the little hairs on the back of my neck stand up. Then I remembered what my angel had told me.

"The Blood of Jesus Christ," I said, looking right up at them.

When I said that they made a growling sound, and jumped back. And an "Oooh!" went up from the people around us. The *brujas* had shown their teeth when they had growled and I saw that the tall one was missing her front ones.

When I said "the Blood of Jesus Christ" and they had growled, and the crowd had "Ooohed," my dad turned and faced them. They glared at him the same way they had glared at me, but it didn't seem to faze him. He just put his hand on my head.

"You OK?" he asked, rubbing my head.

"Yup," I said. I took my eyes off the sisters and looked up at him and smiled.

"You sure?" He asked.

"I'm sure, Dad," I said.

My dad smiled at me and nodded, then he turned back around and opened his Bible again. The people who were crowded around the table moved and mumbled to each other as the sisters slowly made their way to where Big Bennie's feet were, glaring at me and my dad the entire time.

I was so excited about what had happened when I had said "the Blood of Jesus Christ" that I was tempted to say it again just to see what would happen. But I had a feeling that Jesus' name was a powerful weapon to be used, and not a toy to be played with. Wow! How had I come up with *that*? Maybe all my mother's prayers were finally working! Wait till I told her about this!

My dad cleared his throat again to speak, and the sisters reached into their pockets at the same time and took out some rosary beads. A few of the other ladies in the room had theirs out also.

"There is no more powerful force in the whole universe," my dad said, "than the Blood of Jesus Christ."

I couldn't believe it! My dad was thinking the same thing *I* was! This was crazy!

I was looking at the sisters when he said that, and they growled and jumped back *again*! I promise! I am not lying! They growled and jumped back! It was true! Demons tremble at the sound of Jesus' name! Wow! No wonder those witches hated my dad! He knew the secret! That's why he wasn't afraid of them! And it wasn't even a secret! *They* were the ones that were afraid of *him*! Oh, my God! The witches were the ones that were afraid! If my dad kept talking about the Blood of Jesus, those *brujas* would probably run out of the room! Or maybe they would melt just like that ugly *bruja* did in "The Wizard of Oz"! Alright, Dad! Alright, *Jesus*!

"And it's because of the Blood that Jesus Christ shed on the cross two thousand years ago," my dad said, "that we can look forward to spending eternity with him."

When he mentioned the Blood of Jesus Christ again the sisters turned at the same time and faced the wall where the window had been taken out. They couldn't even face us! Any fear that I had, left me. My hands were warm again and I didn't even mind the smoke. There was nothing to be afraid of in here. As a matter of fact, there was nothing to be afraid of anymore. I realized that the only weapon those *brujas* had was fear, and when they couldn't scare you, then they were completely powerless. I had a protection on me that was incredible. How come I had never known about this before? Was it OK for a ten-year-old kid to know this stuff?

My dad kept talking about how Jesus had made it possible for everybody to be saved and how we couldn't do it on our own and how much He loved us and was just there waiting with His arms wide open, and I looked around, and everybody seemed to be listening to him.

"Big Bennie made his choices in this life," my dad said. "If he made the right ones, and we all hope that he did, then he's with the Father right now; but if he didn't, well, then he's in a very uncomfortable place."

When he said that, the room got very quiet.

"But I, like everybody else in this room," he continued, "knew Bennie. And he was a good guy, so I'm believing he made the right choices."

When he said that I saw Dulcinea smile and nod her head. I could tell she was liking what my dad was saying. I looked around and other people were nodding also.

I loved it when I saw people like my dad's preaching. Plus, he was pretty good anyway. He had gotten their attention by letting them know there was a hell, and then he had made them feel good by saying that Bennie was a good guy and just might've made it to heaven. Way to go, Dad!

"And let me also say this," My dad said, "I know a lot of you won't like me saying this."

Uh,oh. I got a little nervous. He had been on a roll, as Max would say. Things were going pretty good. What was he going to say? I didn't think this was a good time to make these people mad.

"But when we all stand before God one day," he went on, "and don't worry, we're all gonna stand before Him. He's not going to care what religion you are; He's not gonna ask what church you went to. Believe it or not, that's not going to count one bit on that day. It don't matter if you're an *Aleluya*, a Baptist, a Catholic, or whatever. Uh, uh. When you stand before God, He's only going to ask you one question. And that's "What did you do about my Son Jesus?" That's all He's gonna ask you. And then He'll ask, "Did you accept Him for who He said He was? Or did you reject Him?" That's it, *mis hermanos y hermanas*. What did you do about my Son? That's it. That's what He's gonna ask you then, and that's my question for you tonight. What have each of you done about Jesus? Is He the Lord of your life? Or is He just some kind of religious thing that you take out of the box whenever you need something?"

I looked around the room. It was very quiet. Even the guys standing by the door had quit shuffling.

"God is asking Big Bennie that question right now, and one day He's going to ask each of us. What is your answer going to be?"

The room stayed quiet. A few people cleared their throats, and someone standing by the door blew their nose. But besides that, it was pretty quiet. Some people were looking at the floor, some stayed looking at Bennie, but most of them looked right at my dad, waiting to hear what he was going to say next. Even the *brujas* had turned back from the wall and were glaring at him.

"Get ahold of somebody's hand, and let's pray." my dad said. He took my hand in his and I turned around to see if anybody wanted to get my other hand. But before I could turn around completely, I felt a huge hand grab my other one. It felt familiar. I looked up and saw my angel standing next to me holding my hand! My angel was smiling at me and holding my hand! And because he was so tall, my arm was straight up in the air like I was trying to reach the ceiling! Oh, my God! I know the other people couldn't see him, so to them I'm sure it looked like I was some nutty kid acting very odd! Like I wanted to ask a question! This was crazy! How strange did this look to the people? Instead of holding someone's hand, like his dad had asked, the preacher's ten-year-old kid had decided to hold his hand straight up in the air and smile at the ceiling!

"Now this is what I call a funeral!" my angel said. "You probably shouldn't be looking up at me and smiling, or these people are *really* gonna think you're strange!"

And I would've looked away, but his head and shoulders were outside the house! I could see him through the roof! Was I Superman or something? Did I all of a sudden have x-ray vision? This was too crazy! Man, oh, man! Was I going to be able to tell *anybody* about this? Would they believe me? Would Puggy even believe me? Was I going to be able to see through the roof when we got back to Albuquerque? Whew!

Oh well, my arm was being held straight up in the air, and I couldn't do anything about it.

I looked up at my dad and he was looking at me like, "Ok, son, I'm trying to get serious here. This is not the time for you to do one of your crazy things."

"Did you have a question, *'jito'*?" My dad asked. My poor dad. Here he was, finally trusting me to act normal at a very important gathering, and here I was with my arm straight up in the air for no apparent good reason and with everybody looking at me. Even Big Bennie, if he could've, probably wanted to turn and look at the strange little boy the preacher had brought.

"No, sir, I don't," I said.

"Uh..OK..well, uh, your hand.."

"I know, Dad, let's just pray."

"Is there a reason your hand is...?"

I pulled on his hand, and he leaned his head down.

"My angel is holding my hand up, Dad," I whispered in his ear, "and he's real big."

"Oh," he said. He stood up and looked at the same spot on the ceiling I had been looking at. When he did that, the people looked up too. Boy, they must've thought we were completely crazy! Or maybe that we were real spiritual, and we were seeing God or something! The only ones who weren't looking up were the *brujas*. They were fidgeting around and looking at the floor. They knew! Oh my God! They knew! And they were afraid! Alright!

My dad smiled at the ceiling, then looked back at the people and said, "Let's pray."

The people looked around at each other, like, "Is this part of the *Aleluya* ritual before they pray? Do they look at the ceiling and smile?" But they bowed their heads to pray anyway.

"Father, I come to You in the name of Your beautiful Son Jesus Christ," my dad began. "We love You and praise You. And we want to tell You thanks for letting Bennie live as long as he did, and for allowing him to bless our lives. He was a good man, Father, and I pray that he is now enjoying being in Your presence. Please give his family peace during this very difficult time. And please let us know, Father, that one day we will all stand before You, whether we want to believe it or not. *Everybody* is going to stand before Your judgment seat and answer that big question, What have we done about Jesus Christ?' I pray, Father, that we will be able to answer that He was the Lord of our lives, and that we did our best to live for Him."

"Halleluiah!" my angel said. He still had my arm straight up in the air.

My dad stopped talking and opened his little Bible.

"This Book," he said, holding the Bible up, "This Book that we all believe in, says that we have all sinned and come short of the Glory of God."

My angel started waving my hand back and forth.

"Preach it, Pastor! You preach it!" he said.

The people looked at my hand going back and forth and whispered among themselves. My dad glanced over at me, but kept going on.

"That means that everybody in here has sinned and needs salvation."

When he said that, my dad paused and looked around the room.

"And, no," he said, "There isn't a church on earth that can save you. There's no church that died for you. There was no church that died for Bennie."

He walked around the table and placed his hand on Bennie's chest.

"It was Jesus," he said, softly patting Bennie's chest. "Jesus is the only one that died for Bennie's sins and your sins. And tonight, He's going to give you a chance to spend eternity with Him. And if you want Him, just say this prayer with me. You don't have to say it out loud; you can say it in your heart."

He walked back to where Bennie's head was and placed his hands on Bennie's shoulders.

"Father," he said, with his head bowed, "I recognize that I'm a sinner."

He paused to give whoever wanted to pray with him, time to repeat what he said. I looked at the people, and saw that some of them were actually moving their lips. Of course, I guess they could have been saying a Hail Mary or something. But I believed that in spite of the distraction of his crazy son waving his hand in the air, the people had been touched by what God had my dad say, and they were praying with him.

"I repent, and I want to ask you to forgive me of my sins, and please come into my heart."

He paused again, and more people started moving their lips.

"Thank You, Father, in Jesus Christ's name, amen."

When my dad finished my angel shouted, "Halleluiah, kid! Seven more souls into the Kingdom! Praise God for your dad's obedience, and just Praise the Living God of all creation!"

And he got so excited about the new people getting saved and about praising the Living God, that he bowed his head and lifted his hand with my hand still in it! He must've forgotten that he was still holding my hand! And so, all of a sudden, there I was, not only with my arm still straight up in the air, but now I was also dangling about three feet off the ground, with my feet almost touching Big Bennie's head! Oh, my God! Oh, my *God*!!

When the people saw me floating in the air, there were gasps and someone shouted, *"Ay, mi Jesus!"* and someone else shouted *"'Dios, perdoname'!"* and *"Es una senia!"* And then someone said, "Yes, it's a sign, it's a sign!" And then, *"Es La Virgen,"* it's The Virgin!" And then someone else answered, "What do you mean, it's *La Virgen*? Can't you see it's a little boy and not 'The *Virgin*?" And then another voice shouted, "Maybe it's Bennie trying to tell us something!" And then a woman's voice cried out, "We all know what it is! It's a sign from God! What the preacher said tonight is the truth! We need to repent! Repent!"

And with that everybody in the room fell on their knees, even the *brujas*, who looked absolutely *terrified*!

My dad looked up at me with his mouth and his eyes wide open, and a look on his face of total amazement. I just knew he couldn't believe what he was seeing, and he looked like he was holding his breath just waiting for me to fall on Big Bennie's small head.

I smiled at him and shrugged my shoulder. What could I do? I pointed to where my angel was, even though I knew he couldn't see him. The truth was, it felt pretty neat just standing on the air. Or at least, *looking* like I was standing on the air.

My angel lifted his head and laughed when he saw the people kneeling down.

"Sorry, kid," he said, "I guess I got a little carried away. You want me to float you upside down all around the room, and *really* shake these people up?"

He laughed again, then slowly let me down.

"Nah, I'd better not," he said. "Knowing these guys, they'd probably make a statue that looked like you and start praying to it. And it's a good thing you're not a girl, or they'd start calling you *"La Virgen de Chama."*

He laughed and softly put my feet on the ground, then let go of my hand.

"Reverendo!" the same woman said, "Please pray for us again! We need to pray again! God used your little boy to give us a sign!"

My dad, who had not taken his eyes off of me during my slow descent to the ground, now turned back to the crowd that were now on their knees, and repeated the same prayer that he had just prayed. And *this* time instead of just moving their lips, the people were now saying the prayer out loud.

"Great news, kid!" my angel said. "Fourteen more! That's a total of twenty one into the Kingdom! Maybe we oughta' float you around people's heads *everytime* your dad preaches!"

"If you said this prayer tonight," my dad said, "that means that your sins have been forgiven and you're on your way to heaven. It's that simple."

He stopped talking and looked around the room. Everybody was still on their knees and were all looking at me with wide eyes.

"It's OK," he said, reaching over to help a few of them up. "You can get up now."

He turned and looked at his cousin.

"Dulcinea?" he said, "You want to tell them about the burial?"

I looked over at Dulcinea and she was helping her mother and father to their feet. Even *they* had knelt down! Maybe we *should* do this more often!

"Look out, kid!" my angel said, "Two powerless old *brujas* on the way out!"

I quickly turned from Dulcinea to the other side of the table just as Teresita and Patrecina ran past us, not even looking at us, pushing people out of their way, and out the door.

"Phew!" I said, making a face. "What was that?"

"Yeah, they did kinda' stink, didn't they?" my dad said.

"And that wasn't just evil stink either," my angel said, laughing, "them ladies are gonna have to change their skivvies as soon as they get home."

I looked up at him with a big question on my face.

"That means underwear, kid," he said, and laughed again.

Dulcinea walked up to my dad and put her hand on his arm.

"I'm sorry, Macedonio," she said, "I didn't know they were coming. Canuto had told them not to, but they did anyway."

"That's OK," my dad said, smiling, "I think they're sorry they did."

They both laughed, then Dulcinea turned to the crowd and told them that Bennie was going to be buried right now at the ranch and they were welcome to go and would everybody move from in front of the window because the forklift was waiting outside to load Bennie onto the logging truck.

The people moved away from the window and someone took the blanket down and then a bunch of men gathered around the table and began pushing it toward the window. It looked like they were having a hard time until I saw a big arm in a purple coat reach down to give them some help.

"Hey, I couldn't let them do it alone," my angel said. He gave the table a push and made it go so fast to the window that the guys who were pushing it had to run to keep up.

"*Orale,*" Antonio said, patting a couple of the guys on the back. "I guess we're stronger than we thought."

The other men laughed and agreed with him, and I heard my angel say, "Oh yeah, you're strong alright."

As soon as the table was next to the window, the people began to hurry out so they could see Bennie loaded on to the truck.

When they passed by me and my dad a lot of them stopped and shook his hand and said stuff like, "*Gracias, Reverendo,*" and "That was great, Macedonio," and one lady even said, "You can still come and be our priest, Macedonio. It's never too late." Of course, I don't blame her for trying. My dad was a great man. And the Catholics really *did* miss out when he became an *Aleluya*.

And they even shook my hand too. I got a little embarrassed because some of the ladies took my hand and kissed it! They actually kissed my hand! That was crazy! The only one who had ever kissed my hand before was my dog Tippy. And then two of the older ladies knelt down before me and did the sign of the cross! They knelt *down*! And did the sign of the cross! Oh, man! Was this crazy or what!?!?

I thought of doing the sign of the cross back to them, but I still didn't know what side to go to first, and I didn't want to get embarrassed, so instead, I just reached out my hand and patted their heads! I patted their heads! Man, oh, man! Talk about crazy! I don't *even* know why I did it, but they seemed like real nice old ladies, so I just patted their heads.

After they all left, we watched as the forklift driver carefully put the two blades between the boards and the table, and lifted Bennie. He backed up slowly, then turned the forklift around and drove it to the big flatbed truck that was close by, and put Bennie up toward the front, by the cab. When the driver had set the body down, some men threw a few ropes over Bennie's body to tie him down so he wouldn't be lost somewhere along the way to the ranch. Then the same men who had tied Bennie down put two thick boards down from the back of the truck, and the forklift drove up them and stopped close to Bennie's body. Then the men tied the forklift down.

How incredible was this? Would I ever see a six-hundred-and-fifty-pound dead man get loaded out of his front window by a forklift onto a logging truck, to be buried in a big hole on a ranch? Heck, would I ever be dangling three feet in the air over the small head of a six-hundred-and-fifty-pound dead man? Nope, I don't think so. This had been a one-of-a-kind funeral in what had turned out to be a one-of-a-kind two weeks in Chama, New Mexico. Whew! I didn't even want to ask what else could happen!

Dulcinea and her parents stood next to my dad by the window, and we all watched silently as the big truck belched smoke out of its two big pipes, and then pulled slowly on to the road.

Bennie's mom began to cry as the truck drove up the road.

"*Mi 'jito, mi 'jito, pobrecito, mi 'jito!*" she cried.

I had started to feel pretty bad for Big Bennie too. How hard had it been for that poor guy to get around? And did he even get around? And how in the world does someone get to be six-hundred-and-fifty pounds? Whew!

"*Bueno,* Mace," Dulcinea said, "We'd better get up there. My parents want to be there when they put him in the ground."

"Yah, we better be getting back *tambien*." my dad said. "It's getting late. I've got to get this boy back before his mother worries too much."

Dulcinea put her hand on my cheek and squeezed it. But not hard.

"You're a very different boy," she said. She looked like she wanted to smile, but she was too sad. "But I like it. Thank you for coming with your dad, OK?"

I nodded. "OK," I said.

She put her head down and kissed me on my forehead.

"And anytime your dad comes to visit us, please come with him, OK? I would really like to talk to you."

I nodded again.

We walked out the door and into the cool Chama night. The scent of tobacco was still in the air, but at least there wasn't any smoke.

My dad hugged Dulcinea and her parents, and we walked to our big Plymouth; and they walked over to a car that had the motor running, and it looked like there were people in it waiting for them.

I opened my door and saw the black blood that was still on the window. I smiled. The Blood of Jesus Christ. Wow! Just the Blood of Jesus Christ! Nothing more powerful in the whole universe! Yeah! I guess those were two *brujas* I wasn't going to have to worry about. At least, not tonight anyway.

I got in and shut the door and my dad started the engine. He hadn't said much to me since the crazy events during the funeral. Maybe he was still thinking about me dangling in the air over Big Bennie's body. It *was* pretty crazy.

We backed out and got back on the main road. Our clothes smelled like cigarette smoke and I knew that my mom would make us leave them out on the porch tonight.

We crossed the railroad tracks and the Nickerson house and headed back to the campground. Suddenly I was very tired, and I just wanted to fall asleep. Sarai was going to sleep at her friend's place tonight, so that meant I was going to have the whole rollaway to myself.

"Everything OK, *'jito*?" my dad asked.

"Yup," I said.

"You have a pretty interesting angel."

"Yes, sir. He is that."

"I think some of those people want to make you a saint."

"I ain't that, Dad."

He laughed.

"Maybe not," he said, "but they think you can walk on air. You're gonna have to tell me about that, OK? Not tonight, *'jito*. But sometime soon, OK?"

"OK, Dad. My angel said twenty-one new people put Jesus in their heart tonight."

"Twenty-one? Really? At that place?"

"Yup. That's what he said."

"Well, praise God!" he said. I looked over at him, and he was smiling real big.

"He said maybe he outta have me dangling over peoples head's *every* time you preach."

My dad laughed out loudly.

"Well, maybe we will," he said, "maybe we will."

"Did I embarrass you, Dad?"

"Nah. It was actually kinda' neat, you know? I mean, those people will never be the same. Who am I kidding? *I'll* never be the same! But it's a good thing you're not a girl; otherwise they would have christened you *"La Virgen de Chama"* tonight."

I turned quickly in my seat and looked with surprise at my dad.

"Hey! That's what he said, Dad!"

"Really? Your angel said *that*? He said the same thing?"

"Yup! He sure did!"

"No! Really?"

"Yup! Really!"

My dad laughed again and I heard a big laugh come from the back seat, but when I turned to see if my great Navajo was there, all I saw was an empty seat.

I turned back around in my seat and shook my head. Wow! How great was that? My angel and my dad kinda' thought the same! Alright!

"You 'member that lady in Taos, don't you?" my dad asked.

"I don't know, Dad. Which one?"

"You 'member, doncha? The one who made that tortilla?"

"Oh, yeah! The one who made that tortilla, and when she took it off the stove, the cooked part looked like Jesus. Yeah, I 'member! And then people started coming from all over to pray to it, huh?"

"Yeah. It seems crazy, *'jito*, praying to a tortilla. But I guess people just need things like that."

We both shook our heads at the same time, and drove in silence for a while. I wondered if somebody finally ate that thing, or were people still praying to it.

"Well, son, I don't know if I'll ever have as interesting a night as I did tonight. I knew God wanted me to take you for some reason."

Then he got quiet and reached over and put his hand on my head.

"He's chosen you for something special, son. That is an absolute fact."

We rode in silence as we both thought about what he had just said.

Before this summer, the only thing I or anybody else thought I could be chosen for was to always be in trouble, embarrass my parents, lie to everybody, and finally drown so they wouldn't have to worry about me so much.

But here I was, with an angel who actually talked to me, a beautiful green-eyed girl who liked me, and not only that, I had found out more about God in this one week than I had in my entire ten years, I had brand-new U.S. Keds, and I would never, *ever* have to wear my sister's panties anymore! Wow!

"Dad?"

"Yes, *'jito.*"

"Dad, I'm so sorry I'm always embarrassing you."

"Don't worry about it, son."

"I don't *know* why I do some of the things I do, Dad. I just *do* 'em! Like that time I looked up that lady's dress while she was talking to you--I don't know why I did it. Or that time that..."

"I said, don't worry about it, mi *'jito.* And besides, you didn't embarrass me this summer. In fact, you kind of helped me solve a few problems. Brother Chinche and his posse, God bless 'em, were driving me crazy too. And now, I probably won't ever have to worry about him always trying to get someone in trouble for nothing. And he'll probably *never* want go close to another outhouse!"

We both laughed on that one.

"I love you, Dad."

"I love you too, *'jito'.*"

"Should I try the radio, Dad?"

"Sure, you never know."

I turned the radio on and the same static came on.

"Turn the dial," he said. "Maybe you can get KOB in Albuquerque. I've gotten it sometimes at night."

I turned the dial slowly and then we heard a voice advertising the 'Dick Bills Show' on KOB.

"Hey, Dad! It's the Dick Bills' song! It's KOB!"

"Alright! Wha'd I tell you?"

We listened as the song finished:

Saddlebags all filled with beans and jerky,
Headin' for K circle B,
TV land for you and me,
K circle B in Albuquerque.

And then the guy came on and yodeled. I tried doing that, but I never could. And after he finished yodeling, the announcer came on and said to stay tuned for the news, weather and sports.

"Alright, Dad! Maybe we'll get to hear the Yanks' score!"

The news came on and I laid down across the seat. Whew! Too many unbelievable things! And I was only ten years old! Wow!

Was my angel always going to be with me? Would he go to school with me? Would he dangle me in front of my teachers? Would the Yankees win if I didn't put my left sock on first? Would I have to do that for the rest of my life? Would the green-eyed girl understand, when we were married, that I had to put my left sock on first and that the tags on the towels had to be on the inside so that my Yanks could win? Would she understand my love for a team on the other side of the country? Was the Rapture going to happen before I could get married? Would I ever be tempted to put my head under another outhouse?

Oh, man, way too many things to think about.

Tomorrow I would be leaving my favorite place on earth for another whole year. Maybe God would actually let me live here one day. Yeah! Then I would *never* have to leave!

And that's how I fell asleep: listening to the radio, thinking about being chosen, thinking about that gorgeous river, thinking about trout, and thinking about coming back to Chama one day and doing something special.

****

LaVergne, TN USA
16 November 2010
205068LV00002B/87/P